Feel Secure in Yourself

A Guidebook for LGBTQIA+ People and Those with a Different Label or No Label

Edited by

A. Lee Beckstead

Jacks Cheng

Sulaimon Giwa

Mark A. Yarhouse

Iva Žegura

Part of the LGBTQIA+ Peacemaking Book Project

ROWMAN & LITTLEFIELD
Lanham • Boulder • New York • London

Published by Rowman & Littlefield
An imprint of The Rowman & Littlefield Publishing Group, Inc.
4501 Forbes Boulevard, Suite 200, Lanham, Maryland 20706
www.rowman.com

86-90 Paul Street, London EC2A 4NE

British Library Cataloguing in Publication Information available

Library of Congress Cataloging-in-Publication Data
Names: Beckstead, A. Lee, 1966– editor. | Cheng, Jacky Li-Yang, editor. | Giwa, Sulaimon, editor. | Yarhouse, Mark A., 1968– editor. | Žegura, Iva, editor.
Title: Feel secure in yourself : a guidebook for LGBTQIA+ people and those with a different label or no label / edited by A. Lee Beckstead, Jacks Cheng, Sulaimon Giwa, Mark A. Yarhouse, Iva Žegura.
Description: Lanham : Rowman & Littlefield, [2024] | Series: Diverse sexualities, genders, and relationships | Includes bibliographical references and index.
Identifiers: LCCN 2024005334 (print) | LCCN 2024005335 (ebook) | ISBN 9781538190401 (cloth) | ISBN 9781538190418 (paperback) | ISBN 9781538190425 (epub)
Subjects: LCSH: Sexual minorities. | Gender identity. | Self-acceptance.
Classification: LCC HQ73 .F44 2024 (print) | LCC HQ73 (ebook) | DDC 306.76—dc23/eng/20240320
LC record available at https://lccn.loc.gov/2024005334
LC ebook record available at https://lccn.loc.gov/2024005335

Contents

Praise for
Feel Secure in Yourself: A Guidebook for LGBTQIA+ People and Those with a Different Label or No Label

"This is an exceptionally thorough and detailed book aimed at supporting people across the LGBTQ community and even those who feel they sit outside it. The text particularly embraces the challenges of holding different attitudes towards faith, religion, and sexuality and so will be helpful for those who feel unable or unwilling to come out."

—Dominic Davies, founder of Pink Therapy;
fellow of the National Council of Psychotherapists, UK

"I applaud the clinicians, researchers, and community leaders who held divergent viewpoints but came together to produce *Feel Secure in Yourself: A Guidebook for LGBTQIA+ People and Those with a Different Label or No Label.* Their contribution to common-ground ideas about sexuality, gender, race, ethnicity, faith and purpose of life, emotional health, resilience, and relationships will benefit readers who are also committed to collaboration, heterodoxy, and truth-seeking."

—Zander Keig, author of *A Third Space: A Nonconformist's Guide to the Universe*; host of *The Umbrella Hour* podcast

"This is a book for those interested in making peace across different views. It is, in itself, an effort at peacemaking across differences in values and ideas about LGBTQIA+. Grounded in research and including over a hundred contributors, this book will make a contribution to scholarly literature, clinical practice, and individual readers."

—Jenell Paris, professor of anthropology and sociology, Messiah University

Diverse Sexualities, Genders, and Relationships

Series Editors
Richard Sprott, California State University,
East Bay and President of APA Division 44
Elisabeth Sheff, Sheff Consulting

The Diverse Sexualities, Genders, and Relationships Series highlights evidence-based approaches to understanding and serving diverse individuals and families whose relational or sexual practices or identities have been marginalized and understudied; reports of emerging empirical research on these topics; and analyses of the latest trends in cultural and societal developments on the status and place of diverse sexualities, genders, and relationships. Books in the series emphasize the intersections of race, culture, age, social class, (dis)ability, and other factors that shape the social locations of relational, sexual, and gender minorities as they intersect with institutions in fields such as education, law, medicine, religion, and public policy.

The books in this series serve as sound and critical resources for the training and continuing education of professionals directly serving diverse communities in professions such as counseling, marriage and family therapy, social work, healthcare, criminology, human services, and education. They are also useful for educators teaching undergraduate and graduate level university courses in anthropology, cultural studies, gerontology, psychology, sexuality studies, sociology, and women's and gender studies. Finally, these books interest educated laypeople who wish to better understand diversity among relational, sexual and gender minorities.

Titles in Series:

Love and Freedom: Transcending Monogamy and Polyamory by Jorge N. Ferrer
Please Scream Quietly: A Story of Kink by Julie L. Fennell
The Handbook of Consensual Non-Monogamy: Affirming Mental Health Practice edited by Michelle D. Vaughan and Theodore R. Burnes
Mental Health Practice with LGBTQ+ Children, Adolescents, and Emerging Adults in Multiple Systems of Care edited by Cristina L. Magalhães, Richard A. Sprott, and G. Nic Rider
Polyamorous Elders: Aging in Open Relationships by Kathy Labriola
177 Lovers and Counting: My Life as a Sex Researcher by Leanna Wolfe
What Is Compersion? Understanding Positive Empathy in Consensually Non-Monogamous Relationships by Marie Thouin
Feel Secure in Yourself: A Guidebook for LGBTQIA+ People and Those with a Different Label or No Label, edited by A. Lee Beckstead, Jacks Cheng, Sulaimon Giwa, Mark A. Yarhouse, and Iva Žegura
Relate to Others with Confidence: A Guidebook for LGBTQIA+ People and Those with a Different Label or No Label, edited by A. Lee Beckstead, Jacks Cheng, Sulaimon Giwa, Mark A. Yarhouse, and Iva Žegura

Acknowledgments

A. Lee Beckstead, Jacks Cheng, Sulaimon Giwa, Mark A. Yarhouse, and Iva Žegura

Thank you for reading this guidebook. We hope the ideas, experiences, and skills shared here will empower you in some meaningful way. The 110+[1] contributors to this book project attempted to find agreement about their chapter topic(s) to help a wide range of people. This has been a group effort, and we know we have not covered everything. We will disappoint, but hopefully not offend or invalidate. We hope you are inspired to learn more about these issues, including through our companion chapter e-resources and online resource lists.[2]

The LGBTQIA+ Peacemaking Book Project was designed to be inclusive, research based, affirming, and comprehensive. Each guidebook was overseen by five coeditors chosen for their distinct and diverse areas of expertise. Each chapter was coauthored by three to 15 clinicians, researchers, or community leaders who also hold divergent viewpoints, sometimes politically opposing. We hope these diverse perspectives and checks and balances against prejudice will help you and other readers appreciate the commonalities and differences between and within cultures, communities, and nations. We want to explicitly recognize that the issues addressed in these chapters are not limited to specific age-groups. Older adults, with their unique experiences and challenges, are an integral part of the diverse communities we aim to serve.

To promote collaboration between communities, we have brought together coauthors and coeditors who have been at odds in the clinical literature, professional debates, and legal disputes. We have conservatives and progressives who feel differently about same-sex marriage and parenting, and we have proponents and opponents of LGBTQIA+-affirmative approaches and "conversion

---

[1] It is difficult to say how many contributed to this guidebook and book project. Some might have contributed to the development of a chapter topic or provided feedback on a draft, or their contribution may be in the companion e-resource, given how the final content was divided. We also included content from coauthors who ended the collaboration for various reasons but allowed their contribution to remain in the chapter.

[2] www.FindingCongruence.com

therapy." Rather than take sides, contributors agreed to pool their resources for a collective inquiry to clarify what works and doesn't and for whom. The reason for this respectful adversarial collaboration is to promote individual and community health and flourishing.

Those with differing viewpoints often meet to debate each other's ideas. These experts are rarely in the same room without this opposition. Academics and researchers rarely collaborate with mental health counselors, and researchers rarely translate their findings into self-help resources for the general public. This book project and these chapters serve as *that room* where experts along many spectra have come together to improve the common good and help a wide range of readers regarding sexual/gender diversity.

One safety guideline proposed by contributors to engage in this process is acknowledging that all coauthors and coeditors participated in this book project independently of their various affiliations. All ideas and skills in this book project do not necessarily represent all the contributors' viewpoints or reflect the viewpoints of their various affiliations. Collaboration in this book project does not necessarily mean coauthors and coeditors agree with or promote the work or views of the other contributors or the ideas or strategies presented in the other chapters.

With these diverse ideas and skills, we want a broad readership that includes (a) readers who feel resolved about being LGBTQIA+ but want more self-love and confidence in relationships and when responding to stress, rejection, and prejudice; (b) readers who are questioning or distressed about their sexual orientation or gender identity and are coming out or considering it; and (c) academics, clinicians, researchers, religious leaders, parents, and other providers and individuals who want to learn updated and common-ground ideas and skills about sexuality, gender, race/ethnicity, faith/purpose of life, emotional health, resilience, and relationships.

We should address how we arrived at using the LGBTQIA+ acronym. It was popular in the 1990s to say "GLB" to indicate everyone who is not exclusively heterosexual. It then became popular to say "LGB" to center lesbian women's experiences and then add "TQIA" to recognize more aspects of sexual/gender diversity. Lesbian, gay, bisexual, transgender, queer, intersex, and asexual/aromantic can be considered overarching categories that represent multiple sexual and gender identity subcategories. Each identity label, however, can also be perceived as a distinct and binary label (for example, you are transgender or you are not transgender), which does not speak to everyone's experience. Some individuals prefer more specific sexual and gender identity labels (for example, androsexual, heteroflexible, transmasculine, agenderflux). Some prefer the term *queer* because it is inclusive of queerness in the sense of both gender identity and sexual orientation. The terms *sexual/gender diversity* and *sexual/gender minorities* remove labels to reflect intersecting continuums and identities. A plus sign was added to the LGBTQIA acronym as an attempt to acknowledge this spectrum of diversity. Coauthor Dr. Candice Metzler noted the following about using LGBTQIA+ to describe a population:

> This approach largely emerged as a way to consolidate political power to gain visibility, inclusion, and protection. This categorization has created conflict for people who (a) do not want to be associated with other experiences/subgroups within the framework, (b) do not feel included within this group, or (c) feel like their experiences are overshadowed by more dominant and visible experiences within the group.

In this book project, we use "LGBTQIA+" because many use these labels to self-identify and experience community. They also highlight a broad range of sexual and gender diversity. Yet we recognize that some individuals have different sexual/gender minority identities not represented by this term. We ask readers who do not identify with "LGBTQIA" to respond to "LGBTQIA+" as if it includes your identity. This request applies also to those who do not identify according to their sexual attractions or gender experiences. We will also use "sexual/gender diversity" and "sexual/gender minorities" throughout because we consider all these terms as similar and representing people who are sexually, gender, and relationally different and diverse and stigmatized, marginalized, and disadvantaged because of it. This acknowledgment is crucial as it reflects the reality that individuals of all ages can face challenges related to autonomy, agency, and informed decision-making.

To recognize our collective responsibility, the lead coeditor, Dr. Lee Beckstead, acknowledges working on this book project in Utah, a gathering place for Indigenous peoples. This land, named for the Ute tribe, is the ancestral homelands of the Shoshone, Paiute, Goshute, Navajo Nation, and Ute tribes. Dr. Beckstead acknowledges their painful history of genocide and forced removal from this land. He hopes to honor and respect the Indigenous people still connected to this land. Coauthor Jim Struve expressed the importance of this acknowledgment in this way:

> Every community owes its existence and vitality to generations and ancestors who contributed to their hopes, dreams, and energy that led to this moment in our history. Some were brought here against their will, some were drawn here from distant homes pursuing hopes or fleeing violence and poverty, and some have lived on these lands from time immemorial. This guidebook offers guidance for healing harms inflicted on people because of their gender or sexual orientation or both. As you read this guidebook, we invite you to acknowledge that we are not the first generation to confront toxic harm and violence.
>
> Take a moment to reflect on ancestors who preceded us and the legacy of historical harm and violence inflicted on many generations of individuals who also wanted to express their authentic identity. Also, consider harms and

violence that have similarly been perpetrated against the authentic identities of Mother Earth and our environment.

We encourage you to go beyond the words in this book and take concrete steps for personal investment in the *congruence of words AND actions*. Beyond digesting the words that fill the pages of this book, "we must be the change we wish to see."

We hope the following helps you with what you need regarding sexual/gender diversity.

Chapter 1

Strengthen Resilience: Live True to Yourself

Debra Harley,[1] Sara Mishly, R.A.,[2] Stephen P. Stratton, Maksim,[3] Neo Samas, Jeannie DiClementi, Nate Cannon, Weston V. Donaldson, Jenna Brownfield, Alejandro Gepp-Torres, Alex Toft, Katina Sawyer, A. Lee Beckstead, and S. Candice Metzler

This guidebook aims to educate and help readers live truer to themselves—in whatever way feels authentic and healthy to them. This chapter first provides an overview of the concerns and strengths of living with a stigmatized sexual/gender identity. Then, we highlight how these issues impact Russian and Arab/Middle Eastern LGBTQIA+ individuals, including sexual/gender minorities who do not identify as LGBTQIA+. We center these marginalized, oppressed, and resilient communities so that they become part of the public discourse and add to how people with socially shamed identities adapt and feel empowered to live their lives. We hope readers find common ground and connect with our global challenges and strengths. We also hope we do not reinforce incomplete and default stereotypes by presenting single-person stories and generalizations of cultural experiences (Adichie, 2009; Louis & Browne, 2023). LGBTQIA+ individuals must often balance managing their own self-identity and personhood and their universal experiences as sexual/gender minorities.

- As you read the following, how do your experiences overlap and differ?

---

[1] The order of authorship does not reflect the amount of content each author contributed to the chapter but rather coauthors' combined content and labor put into both the book chapter and e-resource.

[2] This coauthor chose to use their initials for safety reasons.

[3] This coauthor chose to use a pseudonym for safety reasons.

- Which ideas and strategies would help your empowerment and resilience?
- What are your hopes for reading this guidebook?

Adapting to Sexual/Gender Minority Stress

About 3 to 20% of the U.S. population, depending on the generation they were born, self-identifies as not exclusively heterosexual or aligned with their birth sex (Jones, 2023). Many grow up experiencing or fearing discrimination for being different regarding their sexuality or gender (Simon et al., 2020). Pachankis and Bränström (2019) estimated that 83% of sexual minorities around the globe may be currently "in the closet" and hiding their sexual orientation from all or almost everyone they know. Although LGBTQIA+ and other sexually/gender-diverse individuals have experiences that are unique to them, they likely all cope with their own form of social stigma and stress. We call this unique and additional chronic stress and cumulative negative effects on the mind-body *sexual/gender minority stress*.

LGBTQIA+ individuals, in general, can experience adverse childhood effects due to encountering and internalizing false and negating information and little or no positive information about themselves (Schnarrs et al., 2022). This invalidation and lack of support are a backdrop to experiencing or fearing punishment, ostracization, harassment, rejection, or violence in reaction to their gender-diverse expression and nonheterosexual desires and experiences. Prejudice and oppression and lack of acknowledgment, inclusion, positive options, and social safety occur structurally through laws, religion, education, work, media, families, and peer groups. Minority stress can result in developmental disadvantages and fewer social benefits for LGBTQIA+ individuals, on average, compared to their exclusively heterosexual cisgender[4] peers (van der Star et al., 2021).

LGBTQIA+ individuals, in general, can suffer more physical/emotional health problems and economic disadvantages depending on their country's level of structural stigma (Zentner & Von Aufsess, 2022). In the United States, research has found that youth who are same-sex attracted[5] suffer higher levels of depression and anxiety than their peers between the ages of 12 and 15 (Pachankis et al., 2021). Sexual/gender minorities living in rural locations tend to fare worse than their peers in urban areas (MacDougall et al., 2022).

Social stigma against LGBTQIA+ individuals can also negatively affect exclusively heterosexual, cisgender individuals. Countries with higher levels of social and

---

[4] Cisgender individuals are those whose gender matches their sex assigned at birth. Transgender/nonbinary individuals are those whose gender does not match their sex assigned at birth.

[5] Some studies that follow investigated only experiences of LGB or LGBT-identified individuals instead of the range of LGBTQIA+ individuals. As such, we will note any specifics while also noting when such findings may apply to the broader LGBTQIA+ communities.

institutional homophobia, for example, tend to have decreased economic stability and life satisfaction for their general public, including decreased life span for males overall and especially men with HIV (Lamontagne et al., 2018). This research did not investigate other reasons for these findings besides homophobia. Structural and institutional stigma are only a few considerations among many, including genetics and intergenerational trauma, that may contribute to physical/emotional health problems. Protective and resilient factors can also vary considerably.

It is so easy to fall into simplistic categorization of people, yet lived experiences are more complex than demographic checkboxes. Some who identify as straight, for example, are also sexually attracted to individuals of their same gender, while some who identify as gay or lesbian are also sexually attracted to individuals of other genders. There may be twice as many people who are sexually attracted to men *and* women than there are people exclusively attracted to their same gender (Savin-Williams, 2016). Bisexual, mostly straight/gay, fluid, pansexual, heteroflexible, queer, and other *plurisexual/polysexual* individuals represent the majority of sexual/gender minority individuals. However, they may not know this and could suffer their own form of sexual/gender minority stress (*monosexism*, *bi-negativity*) (Dyar et al., 2020). Not identifying as LGBQ+, despite feeling same-gender attractions, can be due to *bisexual erasure/invisibility*, not knowing positive expressions of an LGBQ+ identity, or wanting to avoid the punishment, shame, and stereotypes of being LGBQ+. Asexual/aromantic individuals similarly experience their own social erasure, invisibility, and stigma (Asexuals.net, 2022).

Primary transgender and cisgender social narratives and norms also do not reflect everyone (Anonymous, 2015). Misunderstanding, violence, lack of resources, and health disparities can occur between cisgender, transgender, and genderqueer individuals (Lefevor et al., 2019), especially when "only-one-valid-way" and hierarchical narratives within queer/straight communities become negative toward diversity.

The social disregard for LGBTQIA+ individuals is further complicated for those with other disadvantaged social statuses, such as race/ethnicity, skin color, language, age, class/financial security, disability, health, mental health, education, employment, faith, immigration/refugee status, geographic location, body size, or appearance. These individuals may experience *multiple minority stress* (Ramirez & Galupo, 2019) for being a marginalized social minority within another marginalized group (a minority of the minority). This *intraminority excess stress* may reduce these individuals' health, resilience, and sense of coherence by increasing their chance of social rejection and anxiety from expecting rejection or attack (Mahon et al., 2021).

- If you experience an increased likelihood and incidence of rejection or attack, and are aware and perceive that the reason is unjust and social safety is not guaranteed, what effect does it have on your emotional state and actions?

* What helps you recover from rejection and discrimination?

From an early age, racialized[6] sexual/gender minorities must manage *intersectional minority aggressions* (Mallory & Russell, 2021) and face unique and compounding barriers. Internalized racism alone is associated with significantly poorer mental health for racialized sexual/gender minorities and is exacerbated when experiencing high levels of heterosexist and racist discrimination (Velez et al., 2019). Individuals within multiple marginalized groups can suffer cumulative stress and have higher levels of wear and tear on the body due to restrictions from resources to cope with discrimination, including from within the LGBTQIA+ community (Felipe et al., 2022).

LGBTQIA+ individuals who are part of intersecting social groups that are disempowered due to lack of inclusion and representation may feel invisible, incomplete, inferior, and not whole. Some are questioning their identities and are in the process of "coming out" to their multiple social networks. They may feel like there's nowhere for them to belong. This is due to external factors (spaces excluding them and not being built with them in mind) instead of internal causes (they struggle to belong). For many, there are no simple answers. Conflicts and resolutions differ depending on ethnic/cultural groups, and identity development varies with each generation (Hammack et al., 2018).

As LGBTQIA+ individuals navigate oppression throughout life, they also build resilience, both personally and socially (Etengoff & Rodriguez, 2021). Some research suggests that racialized LGB adolescents experience better health compared to White LGB peers, which may be due to racialized communities providing more support and life skills to buffer and develop strengths in response to social stigma (Kiekens et al., 2021).

Affirming social changes are occurring for LGBTQIA+ individuals. LGBTQIA+ individuals can find language, stories, and information about sexuality and gender more than ever before. Yet online media can present misleading information, wrong advice, and one-sided biases that "box" people into stereotypes and limited options that fail to affirm all intersecting identities (Campbell et al., 2022). Media often fail to include LGBTQIA+ voices and visibility when speaking about issues that are about or will impact such individuals.

---

[6] Racialization is the process by which individuals and groups are inevitably assigned color. People are not colored. The assignment of race to people became a means to a goal, a mechanism to legitimize dispossession, destruction, and exploitation of resources from people whom White colonizers judged to be inferior and underdeveloped. The use of the phrase *people of color* avoids an examination of this colonial history, which continues to this day, whereas the use of *racialized* allows for such examination.

LGBTQIA+ individuals remain vulnerable across political climates. Policies, communities, and families continue to neglect, reject, and oppose them. In 65 countries, homosexuality is a crime; in 12 countries, the penalty can be death; and in 14 countries, gender-diverse expression is criminalized (Human Dignity Trust, 2024). Violence globally against transgender/nonbinary individuals continues to rise, especially against young, Black, Latine, transfeminine women (Sherman et al., 2020).

Some Good Things About Being Sexually and Gender Diverse

A study conducted in the United States on young gay and bisexual cisgender males (Harper et al., 2012) revealed some views that might help us understand some benefits of being sexually diverse and how we can build and maintain a positive sense of self in the context of discrimination. They found two major views connected to a positive personal conceptualization of being gay or bisexual: *flexibility* and *connectedness*.

Participants talked about flexibility in terms of sexuality, environment, and gender. Participants who identified as bisexual felt less restrained about categories and saw the possibility of being with more than one gender as an upside. Some declared having access to spaces tailored explicitly to sexually diverse youth a privilege that heterosexual people didn't have. Some said their sexually diverse identities allowed them to explore gender roles more freely and display masculine and feminine traits. This last view is also found in a study of adults living in Spain (Strizzi et al., 2016) about the positive aspects of being LGB. Participants found that their identities made them less obliged to follow traditional gender scripts.

Besides flexibility, connectedness was also part of participants' positive personal conceptualization. They felt they could make more meaningful connections with women in comparison to heterosexual men and also within the LGBTQ+ community. This social connection helped them obtain support from others who had gone through similar experiences.

Regarding relationships and connectedness, a U.S. study (Solomon et al., 2005) that compared same-gender couples in and not in civil unions and married heterosexual couples found that same-gender couples had a more egalitarian distribution of household tasks, expenses, and relationship maintenance behaviors than heterosexual couples. Couples satisfaction studies report similar results when comparing same-gender and heterosexual couples (Roisman et al., 2008).

A study conducted in Great Britain with young people who identified as heterosexual or LGBT (Scourfield et al., 2008) explored how they responded to distress and found some common views about resilience. The first was thinking of sexual diversity as being as natural and unchangeable as heterosexuality, in contrast to the idea that it's a choice. Knowing that sexual orientation emerges and is discovered helped some participants accept it more easily.

A second view was that you somehow become stronger when you face adversity. Fighting back when being bullied or surviving experiences like homelessness helped participants assert their identity. This study also highlighted that other LGBTQ+ youths had ambivalent or even self-destructive behaviors in response to stress, so it's essential to understand that resilience is not the only possible response to adversity and that the hardships one can go through as LGBTQIA+ should not be minimized.

Surrounding yourself with supportive people in supportive environments was the third and most common view that this study found linked to resiliency. Participants talked about moving to cities perceived as more accepting of diverse identities and connecting to LGBTQIA+ organizations as strategies that helped them.

It's important to highlight and expand on this last finding since ideas around community and social support are some of the most commonly found in studies regarding resilience. A study of LGBTQ-identified youths from Washington State (Higa et al., 2014) found that having LGBTQ peers, heterosexual allies, and accepting family members were considered positive life factors. Involvement in their local LGBTQ community was also commonly cited as a positive factor in this study, highlighting the importance of connection and belonging.

Positive media representation can also build resilience and social safety. An online survey of bisexual cisgender and transgender individuals (Johnson, 2016) found that 39% of those diagnosed with mental disorders thought that negative media representation somewhat affected their mental health and that "seeing realistic, positive portrayals of people like them in media would help with self-identification and acceptance" (p. 13).

The U.S. study mentioned earlier on gay and bisexual male youth (Harper et al., 2012) also found four major views linked to resilience. The first was *acceptance*, be it self-acceptance or feeling the acceptance of others. Self-acceptance and social acceptance allowed them to be authentic and self-determined, which led to feelings of happiness. Being accepted by others who didn't judge them for being bisexual or gay and making meaningful connections helped them during adversity. A second view was *self-care*. Emotional self-care was in response to the negative emotional impact that resulted from living in a heterosexist society and included being mindful of when and to whom to disclose your sexual orientation and gender diversity, in the interest of staying safe. Physical self-care was also mentioned in terms of protecting yourself from possible STIs. The third view was *rejecting stereotypes* that don't fit you. Participants expressed the importance of developing a positive sense of self that is not constrained by stereotypes of how LGBTQIA+ people are depicted. The fourth view was *activism*. Participants talked about the importance of knowing the story of the LGBTQIA+ community to act in an informed manner toward the future. Activism was seen as a way to educate and support younger LGBTQIA+ people to promote their well-being.

Next, the following sections on sexual/gender minorities living in Russia and Arab/Middle Eastern societies illustrate the arguments made so far about the relational harms from prejudice and discrimination and the benefits of family and community support and personal resilience. Coauthor Maksim (a pseudonym for safety reasons) first outlines the Russian sociopolitical landscape and psychological research devoted to the LGBTQ+[7] community, with a focus on those with a stigmatized sexual orientation. While many studies on this topic in foreign languages are available to most researchers and those interested, the Russian-language segment of the research is largely uncovered. The following outlines this research and aims to show that sociopsychological research in Russia on the needs of the LGBTQ+ community is becoming one of the topical scientific directions.

- As you read the following, consider what might be fear-based negative attitudes, what those fears may involve, and how understanding those fears can identify areas for education and intervention.

Supporting Russian LGBTQ+ Individuals

One gets the impression that Russia is a country with a prevailing negative attitude toward people who are LGBTQ+. However, modern research carried out in Russia shows a slightly different picture. Many of the new generation, born in the early 2000s, have a more positive attitude toward people with non-cis-heteronormative experiences, despite prevailing negative attitudes.

Russia has a history of reinforcing widespread negative attitudes against the LGBTQ+ community. In the USSR in 1934, there was article 154 of the USSR Criminal Code, and since 1960, article 121 of the USSR Criminal Code on sodomy. After the abolition of the article on sodomy in 1993, activism in the LGBTQ+ community became more visible until a federal law appeared in 2013 prohibiting the "propaganda of non-traditional sexual relations among minors." Human Rights Watch (HRW) reported in 2014 that Russia's 2013 federal law coincided with an increase in homophobic rhetoric in state media and homophobic violence around the country. In 2018, HRW reported that prohibiting LGBTQ+ Russian youth from accessing accurate information about

---

[7] This section does not cover research on intersex, asexual, or aromantic Russian individuals. See Intersex Russia (https://www.intersexrussia.org) for more information.

themselves, their relationships, and their health leaves them vulnerable to anti-LGBTQ+ slurs, hostility, and marginalization from teachers, peers, and family members. Consequently, in March 2017 and between December 2018 and February 2019, leaders in Chechnya detained, tortured, and killed gay, bisexual, and queer men, influenced by false ideas about gender and nature (Scicchitano, 2021). Since then, ongoing Russian policy changes against the LGBTQ+ community continue to increase prejudice, fear, harm, and lack of support for LGBTQ+ civil rights in the Russian population.

Russian Social Opinion Toward the LGBTQ+ Community

In recent years, more scientific studies have been devoted to this topic. At the same time, there are specific difficulties in using the results of these studies to educate a broad audience. This is primarily difficult because of a contradictory attitude toward the LGBTQ+ community in the political arena: Some speakers argue that same-gender sexuality is unnatural and caused by social influences. Others point to loyalty toward the LGBTQ+ community. This sociopolitical contradiction actualizes the problem of uncertainty for LGBTQ+ Russian individuals. The persisting negative attitude toward the LGBTQ+ community heightens attacks and fears of rejection and reduces the possibility of safe and productive interactions between them and society in various social spheres (Gevlenko, 2018).

As an example of heightened attacks and fears, Ilyin (2020) believed that the attitudes broadcasted by the West regarding tolerance toward the LGBTQ+ community and changing school curricula on gender and sexuality are dehumanizing in nature, as they infringe on the rights of the majority. The spread of Western tolerance in Russia, according to Ilyin, can destroy Russian values and the stability of Russian society. Similarly, the Levada Center in 2020 showed that one in five Russians wants a society where LGBTQ people do not exist and 39% want to isolate them from society (Kuhr, 2020). Leaders in the LGBTQ+ community saw this research as damaging and triggering of more hatred where the level of violence is already very high.

Since the early 2000s, Russian Public Opinion Research Centers have conducted a sociological study of how the LGBT community is treated in Russian society. In July 2021, the results showed that the surveyed women (38%) and young people (from 18 to 24 years old—68%) believe that sexual orientation is a personal choice of each person. Yet 12% of the respondents indicated that LGBT people are dangerous for society, 13% viewed same-gender sexuality as a social disease, and 23% (typically people over 60 and men) believed that people who are same-gender attracted need medical correction (Russian Public Opinion Research Center, 2021). Articles also appear in Russian science sources that condemn non-cis-heteronormative behavior, considering it through the prism of mental illness and immorality (Abdurasuli, 2020). Research in October 2021

(Statista, 2023) found that most Russians were either disgusted by or scared of LGBTQ individuals, although nearly one-third felt calm about gay and lesbian individuals.

Russian science magazines have been actively publishing special issues devoted to the social, psychological, and political aspects of the LGBTQ+ community.[8] A study conducted in the Tomsk region showed that some are ready to accept an LGBTQ+ individual if they are a close relative (Temnikova & Averina, 2016). You can also find studies indicating that 65% of respondents belonging to the generation of the 1990–2000s have a low level of homophobia and are tolerant of the LGBTQ+ community (Chudinova, 2018; Balenko & Kondrashikhina, 2021). However, a study among respondents aged 18 to 65 found that same-gender/queer relationships are often viewed as based only on sexual interest, and heterosexual cisgender relationships are considered to be more romantic (Rikel, 2020).

In August 2023, the *Kommersant* newspaper published a sociological survey conducted by Russian Field that found that 62% of Russians say it is necessary to limit the rights of homosexuals, and 55% of respondents say it is necessary to limit the rights of transgender people (Gabdullina, 2023). Eleven percent of respondents expressed complete rejection of people with a nontraditional sexual orientation and advocated restrictions on their residence in the country. Lawyers believe that this attitude was influenced by laws adopted in Russia against positive information about LGBTQ+ people. Fear and negative attitudes toward representatives of the LGBTQ+ community in Russia can be associated with the negative attitude of authoritative political figures, reference groups, and prevailing social stereotypes. The broadcast of normalizing and humanizing images of the LGBTQIA+ community is needed to balance out unjustified and harmful ideas and stereotypes.

Experiences of Russian LGBTQ+ Youth

Next, we describe the results of studies conducted among adolescents with LGBTQ+ identities. For Russia, these studies are difficult to conduct. Many may not disclose their sexual orientation and may try to hide their gender expression due to negative attitudes from adults. Scientists may also be wary of conducting research for fear of being accused of "promoting non-traditional relationships among minors." Despite this, research has been carried out to identify the experiences and adaptations of Russian LGBTQ+ youth.

For example, it was found that Russian adolescents with non-cis-heteronormative experiences face difficulties in socialization, which harms

---

[8] For example, special issues can be found of the magazines *Psychology in Russia, Psychology Magazine* (HSE), and *Sociology of Power* (RANEPA) under the president of the Russian Federation.

their mental health. These difficulties are associated with stressful situations during the developmental period of becoming aware of their sexuality and gender diversity and when more meaningful feelings arise about another person (Kon, 1989). In Russian psychology, analyzing the works of Vygotsky and Stern, Sergei Melkov (2017b) concluded that sexuality is a biological instinct, while erotica is a cultural phenomenon that implies love for the personality of another. Melkov believes that cultural development directs sexual impulses to the spiritual experience of intimacy with another person. He considers these processes as a "fusion" of the biological and the social in each personality.

Regarding the influence of cultural attitudes on the development of LGBTQ+ youth, Dozortseva et al. (2011) compared 26 men with a same-gender sexual orientation with 29 men with a heterosexual orientation. Results indicated that the semantic perception of men (father, man, boy) by same-gender-attracted men was associated with negative emotional characteristics (indifference, hatred, anger). The researchers drew the following conclusion:

> In general, the image of a man among [this sample's same-gender-attracted cisgender men] probably indicates emotional deprivation and traumatization at an early age: they associate boys with hatred and anger, the image of a father with hatred, resentment, indifference, loneliness, sadness. Heterosexuals, on the contrary, include these images in the system of positive semantic connections. (p. 10)

Zueva and Kazaryan (2020) found that difficulties in childhood and parental attachment prevented Russian same-gender-attracted men from identifying with their father. We can conclude that attachment to the father has a meaningful impact on forming a positive identity in gay/bisexual men. These studies suggest that it can be difficult for gay/bisexual men to have a secure relationship with their father, others, and themselves because of homophobic attitudes. The assumption that same-gender attractions are caused by attachment wounds by the father or masculine figures has been disproved in other studies (for example, Freund & Blanchard, 1983). Findings from these Russian studies emphasize the need to educate caregivers about the harmful impact of their homophobic attitudes on their child's secure attachment.

Based on the above, we can conclude that sexual/gender minorities can face difficulties in self-disclosure in front of another person, especially caregivers, when cultural norms impose a ban on their experiences. Awareness of one's inconsistency with cultural norms and biological needs, with negative attitudes from caregivers and culture, can lead to difficulties with emotional well-being and adjustment.

In modern Russian psychology, the psycho-emotional properties of adolescents with non-cis-heteronormative experiences have been studied. One study (Erzin, Semenov & Antokhin, 2017) involved 100 adolescents between the ages of 14 and 21 and found a high level of social pessimism and affectivity and a low level of self-control and attachment. Another study (Semenova et al., 2019) found that exclusively same-gender-attracted and bisexual adolescents had high levels of feeling emotionally unstable and being open to new experiences. Attachment concerns characterized them, along with a predominance of introversion and impulsivity.

One factor that negatively affects the emotional health of the Russian LGBTQIA+ community is the process of stigmatization and discrimination from adults and peers. A sociopsychological study (Erzin & Semenova, 2017) among adolescents aged 12 to 16 concluded that 96% were stigmatized because of their sexual orientation. The process of stigmatization and discrimination acts as a trigger for the onset of depression and plays a crucial role in the decline in mental health. This study once again confirmed that it is necessary to carry out preventive and educational work among the population to reduce sexual stigma. This education would increase positive attitudes and prevent the emergence of psychogenic disorders in adolescents with a non-cis-heteronormative identity.

Empirical studies (Zayka & Lebedeva, 2020) conducted among Russian same-gender-attracted and bisexual cisgender adolescents show a low level of acceptance from others, a high level of emotional discomfort, a low level of satisfaction with their activities in various fields, and a higher level of escapism and social isolation than adolescents with a heterosexual identity. The level of adaptation and self-acceptance is lower among bisexual adolescents than adolescents with a same-gender-attracted and heterosexual identity. Thus, the perception of stigma and experiences of discrimination decrease sociopsychological adaptation in adolescents and increase problems in building trusting and emotionally positive relationships with the social environment, leading to isolation from society.

Promoting Eudaemonic Well-Being

Eudaemonic well-being (living a purposeful and fulfilling life, pursuing one's potential, contributing to society, feeling happy and in good spirits) is becoming a topical research focus in Russia. Adolescents with non-cis-heteronormative experiences manifest a low level of psychological well-being. Personal homophobia negatively affects psychological well-being, including autonomy, self-acceptance, and self-determination. There is also a relationship between the level of neuroticism and self-assessment of health (Zayka & Lebedeva, 2020).

Studies conducted in Russia have established that the defense mechanisms among adolescents with a nonheterosexual identity are denial, rationalization, and repression. Erzin, Antokhin, and Semenova (2017) found that sexual minority adolescents use the following coping strategies: "strategic planning," "preventive overcoming," "proactive overcoming," "reflexive overcoming," "seeking instrumental support," and "seeking emotional support." The authors of this study explained that these results come from the fact that adolescents in Russia with a same-gender sexual orientation expect an unfavorable outcome from life situations; therefore, they often make plans for retreat or protection from aggressive behavior on the part of society. Avoidance coping is based on survival and safety and does not allow a person to seek emotional and instrumental support, a lesser-used strategy, to enhance positive feelings (Giwa, 2022). The authors explained the results by the fact that the respondents do not have a trusting relationship with the social environment: estrangement prevails.

Building Positive Romantic/Sexual and Community Relationships

One essential aspect of socialization is building positive relationships that affect a person's emotional state. Rejection and ignorance on the part of a romantic/sexual partner can lead to adverse emotional effects: distress, internalized homophobia, and self-aggressive behavior (suicide, unsafe sexual contacts) if the rejected individual does not have personal and social resources to buffer the rejection. One study (Ozerina & Rodionov, 2020) found that difficulties in assessing and understanding a partner's emotional state and managing one's psycho-emotional state are more pronounced in bisexual cisgender individuals than same-gender-attracted cisgender individuals. The researchers explained this as the result of the reduced ability of bisexual individuals to express their emotions in a negating and unsafe society. The ability to use emotions for productive cognitive processes may be lower in sexual minorities living in oppressive cultures.

Melkov (2017a), in his work devoted to the psychology of stigmatized men in Russia, found that stigmatization based on sexual orientation leads to the internalization of homophobia. Melkov identified three types of self-awareness in men with a stigmatized sexual orientation: (1) having a negative attitude toward oneself, others, and the world as a whole; (2) striving to live according to traditional social normativity; and (3) experiencing an asocial orientation. A positive self-attitude is fundamental for achieving a high level of self-actualization and mental health. Shaekhov and Malysheva (2021) found that internalized homophobia among men who identified as homosexual is low. The researchers explained this result by pointing to the fact that the study involved respondents who were in social networks dedicated to supporting individuals with an LGBTQ+ identity.

A positive self-attitude and an individual's emotional state are the basis for positive and trusting societal relationships. In this context, it is necessary to consider eudaemonic well-being among sexual/gender minorities. Comparative analysis among same-gender-attracted, bisexual, and heterosexual individuals found differences (Shaekhov, 2021). Bisexual individuals suffer more stigma and have greater difficulties in interpersonal relationships than exclusively heterosexual and same-gender-attracted individuals. Traditional gender norms can also negatively affect eudaemonistic well-being. In the comparative analysis, the "autonomy'" scale was negatively interconnected with "achievement orientation" and "acceptance of impersonal sexuality"; the scale for "personal growth" was negatively interconnected with the scale of male norms adopted in society (Repko & Aleksandrova, 2020). Another study (Shaekhov & Malysheva, 2021) found that belief in a competitive world and rejection of one's sexual identity are predictors of low psychological well-being.

The literature review by this section's author makes it possible to assert that in modern Russian sociopsychological studies, individuals with non-cis-heteronormative experiences tend to be viewed and treated negatively. Consequently, adolescents with a stigmatized sexual/gender identity in Russia have low connectedness with the social world, which can lead to depressive symptoms, low self-control, and self-aggressive behaviors. The problem is not in the adolescents but in their society. Positive family relationships are essential in developing a positive understanding of oneself, including one's gender identity and sexuality. Positive relationships with caregivers and with others with non-cis-heteronormative experiences can lead to lower anxiety and depression and prompt the building of trusting relationships with the social world, which enhances psychological well-being in adulthood. Thus, a positive self-perception and sense of connectedness within the political, social, and family environment will favorably influence relationships and eudaemonic well-being.

Living With Dangerous Uncertainty: This Is Not Research, This Is Reality

As there are changes in Russian society in an affirming direction toward the LGBTQ+ community, the legal status of the Russian LGBTQ+ community is becoming more hostile. Russia's 2021 National Security Strategy designated those who do not conform to heterosexual, cisgender "family norms" as perverse and a national security threat. Russian president Vladimir Putin, in a speech about the Ukraine war on September 30, 2022, conflated education that affirms transgender/nonbinary youth and adults with propaganda that falsely reports that children are being coerced to believe they are "some other genders [sic] and [should] be offered sex-change surgeries" (Mackinnon, 2022). In October 2022, the Russian government fined TikTok for not removing what it considered "LGBTQ propaganda" from their online content. Putin's executive order in November 2022 enacted "The Fundamentals of State for the Strengthening of Traditional Russian Spiritual and Moral Values," which expanded the prohibition of sharing information about "nontraditional" sexual relations to all age-groups, not just minors.

Putin has used the idea of Russia as a defender of traditional Christian values to justify the invasion of Ukraine and to restrict access to affirming LGBTQ information (Luxmoore, 2022). Tougher laws are one way the Ukraine war has made life more difficult for LGBTQ+ people in Russia. For example, LGBTQ+ advocates have been identified as "foreign agents" and forced out of Russia (Ilyushina & Gelman, 2023). Conversely, Ukrainian president Volodymyr Zelenskyy has promoted the rights and protections of gay soldiers and their partners, including the possibility of legalizing same-sex civil unions after the war. Many young Russians also believe there is no need to restrict the rights of members of the Russian LGBTQ+ community.

In contrast, in July 2023, Putin banned all gender-affirming surgeries and hormone therapy, prohibited changing gender on official documents, annulled any marriage with a spouse who changed their gender identification, and banned adoptions by such couples. In November 2023, Putin passed another law that banned the "international LGBT social movement," equating it to an extremist organization. The ban prohibits public displays of "the movement," including any symbols of "the movement" and posting information about "the movement" on social networks and conducting any conferences on the topic. However, in Russia, there are no leaders, ideologists, or official followers of this "movement," making it unclear who will be held accountable. There are also no clear legislative criteria on which an individual can be held accountable. They may simply impose a fine or send you away for up to 10 years. Legal practitioners are waiting to see who will be taken first and for the commencement of prosecutions against those who promote LGBTQ+ "propaganda."

At the time of finishing writing this section in December 2023, many Russian people with an LGBTQ+ identity were not advertising it. We hoped that researchers would not fall under this law. We would like to note that on November 17, 2023, Putin said that people with an LGBT identity are also part of society and have the right to win cultural competitions. Yet at the time of finishing this section, no legislative framework protected the rights of sexual/gender minorities in Russia, which makes it easier for them to be stigmatized, attacked, harassed, and discriminated against.

Navigating the Queer Arab/Middle Eastern Identity[9]

Little is known about the lives and experiences of LGBTQIA+ individuals in Arab and Middle Eastern countries, as reflected in limited research, publications, media presence, public figures, and artistic representations. Same-gender attraction is still a taboo in most conservative Arab and Middle Eastern cultures. It is also considered a major sin in most of the predominant religions in this region. It is our observation that the sensitivity of this topic has been worsening over the past few years, making discussions not only unacceptable and heavily censored but also dangerous and life-threatening. Trouble can occur in many areas, including but not restricted to the law, family relationships, community attitudes, and individual psychology. It is honestly not clear to us why attitudes toward the LGBTQIA+ community in few Arab countries that were mild or positive have suddenly worsened in a short time.

One clear example can be found in Lebanon: There was strong visibility of the LGBTQIA+ community in Beirut, depicted in the presence of public queer spaces and nongovernmental organizations. This was holistically supported by the Lebanese Psychological Association and the Lebanese Psychiatric Association announcing in 2013 that homosexuality is not a disorder and as such should not be treated as a disorder. Although decades behind the West, Lebanon was the first Arab country to make such an announcement. During the same time, there were several court rulings by the Lebanese civil and military courts that did not criminalize individuals engaged in same-sex sexual behaviors (it is relevant to note that homosexuality is still criminalized in Lebanese law under the vague Code 534). Beirut became widely recognized as a refuge for Arab LGBTQIA+ individuals (Michli & El Jamil, 2022). However, this positive momentum did not last long. It was followed by the emergence of extremist groups publicly threatening, attacking, and closing down safe spaces for LGBTQIA+ people in Beirut. At the same time, there were hate speeches by religious and political leaders who also tried to introduce bills that explicitly criminalize same-sex relationships (MENA Rights Group, 2023).

Unsurprisingly, many LGBTQIA+ individuals residing in this part of the world choose to be reserved and hidden. Sometimes, there is a layer of safety in invisibility. Others seek safety and freedom in tolerant Western countries, hoping to actualize the life they dream of. Some become unofficial ambassadors who shed light on the serious and limiting challenges faced by LGBTQIA+ individuals back home. This bravery comes at a high cost, though, of leaving their

---

[9] Coauthors Mishly and R.A. are only responsible for this section and not the content in the other sections.

homes and loved ones; of being haunted by societal shame, hate, ostracism, and treason; and of the risk of never being able to return home safely.

Nevertheless, there are many LGBTQIA+ individuals residing in Arab and Middle Eastern countries who are not considering seeking asylum. Some cannot afford to leave for various reasons, such as tenuous financial health, family responsibilities, and weak passports and visas that are frequently denied. Youth and women are also less likely to be able to seek asylum or emigrate because they are usually under a firmer societal and familial grip compared to adult men. For example, in many Arab/Middle Eastern cultures, women and youth are not allowed to travel without a legal guardian, and they are not allowed access to their passports or legal papers.

On the other hand, many LGBTQIA+ individuals in this part of the world do not wish to emigrate, not because they are stuck but because they have a solid attachment to their homelands, families, careers, and culture. They refuse to relinquish those rights and see themselves as essential agents in their homelands. Therefore, sexual/gender minorities in the Arab world are usually represented under two narratives: victims in a region portrayed as a black hole for LGBTQIA+ people, or people destined to live incomplete lives as half-selves. Both narratives are disempowering and do not capture the real complexity of the situation or the resilience and agency of these individuals in building their own lives and identities right where they are.

We hope in this section to highlight some of the important themes that emerged in our clinical and civil work with LGBTQIA+ individuals residing in Arab and Middle Eastern countries. We will specifically focus on themes that are less spoken about and documented in the literature on Arab and Middle Eastern sexual/gender minorities and that can only be deeply felt while listening to individual narratives. Though some themes are not unique to Arab and Middle Eastern cultures, we will explore them from the perspective of our culture, which can place different weight and significance on the individual.

By the end of this section, we hope readers will appreciate the struggles, uniqueness, depth, and beauty of the Arab/Middle Eastern queer blend while steering away from stereotypes and oversimplifications. We also hope that mental health providers will find a perspective that enhances their understanding and approach to this population. It is imperative to emphasize that the vast cultural, racial, ethnic, and religious diversity of this region makes it impossible and naïve to draw any unified conclusions or generalizations. We also do not claim to provide any answers or solutions in this section. We only hope to echo the voices and narratives that deserve to be heard.

Family and Religion in Collective Societies

Navigating Risks to and by Families

Fear of family rejection is a common and well-documented stressor for LGBTQIA+ people across different cultures. However, things can be more complicated in collectivist societies like Arab and Middle Eastern ones, where many individuals identify themselves through their families and religious affiliations. Without proper public sectors and social security in many of these countries, kinship becomes a major source of community, social support, tribal protection, and financial security. In Arab societies, a person represents their nuclear and extended family. Thus, their actions and personal lives can bring honor or shame to all the family tree's roots, branches, and leaves.

While some LGBTQIA+ individuals fear for their lives and safety, especially in the absence of laws that protect people who are sexual/gender minorities, others dread the anticipated grief and loss of their loved ones. We have seen families using physical violence, locking up their child, or forcing them into "conversion" and "hormonal" interventions or heterosexual marriage as a "corrective method." In contrast, we have also seen parents who were surprisingly accepting despite being religious, conservative, and less educated. While negative reactions were expected from families with authoritarian, oppressive, and aggressive dynamics, they also came from supposedly loving, "open-minded," well-educated, and less religious parents. From our experience, it is extremely difficult to predict what reaction will come from what parent in this part of the world, and following any stereotype can be dangerous.

Furthermore, it is common for family and religious struggles to emerge as the first topics and sometimes the primary reason to seek psychotherapy. Unfortunately, we observed they are also one of the main reasons some seek "conversion therapy," which is still legal and practiced in many countries in this region. In countries where homosexuality is criminalized, "conversion therapies"' are aligned with the law, whereas affirmative care can cause trouble. For professionals working with LGBTQIA+ individuals in Arab and Middle Eastern countries, it is important not to immediately shut down or ever shame individuals asking for help to change their sexual orientation or gender identity. Rather, take time to compassionately and curiously understand and assess the distress behind such a request. Although the right answer is to deny this service and explain that it is neither effective nor ethical, we observed that in practice, a knee-jerk reaction could increase hopelessness, helplessness, and the risk of dropout in search of someone who will offer it. Spend time helping these individuals understand their sexual orientation and gender identity objectively and factually, and slowly help them build a realistically positive and hopeful projection of themselves and their future. It also helps to provide information on internalized homonegativity/biphobia/transphobia and the role of societal stigmas in it. These steps may help individuals accept their sexual orientation and gender identity without a sense of defeat.

We observed that despite these steps, some might repetitively ask or insist that there must be something they can do to change, stop, or reduce their sexual/romantic desires if they try hard enough. For this reason, therapists need to be patient and empathic and not rush the individual. After all, affirmative therapy is about affirming the person's experience and reducing the effects of minority stress on the person rather than encouraging a specific way to self-identify.

Furthermore, it is common for LGBTQIA+ people in this part of the world, especially those from tribal backgrounds, to worry that their sexual orientation and gender identity will not only put them at risk but also endanger their whole family. Some risks to family that an individual might worry about include having their sisters divorced due to "shame"; their cousins dropped from the marriage selection or employment pools; their parents accused of failure, immorality, or even infidelity; and exposing their family to shame and exclusion from social surrounding and privileges unless they "clean their honor," which can range from killing to complete disownment. Even "tolerant" family members frequently encourage "toning down" nonconforming presentations and public opinions out of fear or shame. This secrecy can add to the stress, shame, and guilt felt by the person seeking help. For example, we repeatedly heard, "If my parents find out, they will have a heart attack," indicating that these individuals carry themselves with utmost vigilance and may experience their sexual orientation or gender identity as fatal. As one Arab lesbian woman stated, "My parents are decent, hardworking people, and lived their lives in dignity. I do not want anyone to ever shame them because of me. They do not deserve it. This is why I must be careful. I don't fear them; I fear for them."

Nevertheless, Arab and Middle Eastern LGBTQIA+ individuals are well aware and understand why their family members will not, or at best would struggle to, accept them. They understand that their parents would worry about them and the rest of the family because of the hardships they are bound to experience in our societies, from persecution to violence and discrimination. We recall an individual who, once outed, found a bullet with his name carved on it and a threatening note left at his family house where he lived. Arab and Middle Eastern LGBTQIA+ individuals also understand that their families are exposed to many negative messages about same-gender sexuality and gender diversity and that their faith contradicts their love. As a parent stated once, "It saddens me that we will all be united in heaven while my son won't. I know he is a good boy, and I love him. I just hope that God will receive him in a similar way." We have seen examples of relatively "tolerant" parents rushing to send their children religious scripts after they came out and encouraging them to pray just to "balance things out." Despite their attempt to be supportive, hurtful expressions can still come out. We have seen that many LGBTQIA+ individuals do not immediately equate them with oppression, aggression, or hate.

Not seeing the whole picture can fragment the individual and come across as judgmental, offensive, and hurtful. Professionals working with this population are encouraged to explore how the individual perceives and feels about these comments without making any premature assumptions, especially if the therapist is from an individualistic background. This does not mean that acts of violence, verbal and emotional abuse, and disownment are justifiable or excusable when and if they occur. Instead, it is essential to help the individual see them for what they are and not entertain denial mechanisms.

Navigating Family Expectations and Group Harmony

Respecting and nurturing family ties and group harmony are highly encouraged culturally and religiously in our Arab and Middle Eastern cultures. People in collective Arab and Middle Eastern cultures are rarely encouraged to live authentically if that means not conforming to social, religious, and familial expectations related to sexuality, gender, faith, and other life dimensions. The emotional and psychological pain that might come from losing family love and support is too much for some people to bear, especially those with dominant collective self-construals. Therefore, many struggle with finding the "right" ratio of self-actualization and familial belonging, fearing that a tilt to one side can result in a pricey sacrifice on the other.

Professionals working with this population need to remember and remind the individual that there is no "right way of coming out" that can be generalized across different cultures and demographics; instead, it is a continuous and highly personalized process. It is also important to emphasize that what matters most is the person's safety, thus coming out to people who will support and empower them. Maintaining self-protection is an act of resilience rather than cowardliness. This is especially important because same-gender sexuality and nonconforming behaviors can increase the risk of persecution in some countries. The absence of protective laws can make things very dangerous. Therefore, some LGBTQIA+ individuals residing in Arab countries may feel torn between prioritizing safety by remaining discreet and feeling as though they are lagging in their identity development because of this discretion.

Furthermore, parental blessing is very important in the Muslim and Arab psyche. Its presence or absence is often perceived as an omen that interprets the good and bad that happen to us. This is not a minor detail; it has a powerful impact on the decisions someone can take or abort and how they will feel about these in retrospect. In therapy, many Arab and Muslim LGBTQIA+ individuals fear they will lose their parents' blessings and thus lead an unsuccessful, cursed life. We observed that this sometimes complicates trauma work because the individual can explain traumas as the direct result of the loss of parental blessing and as a punishment from God for their "sinful acts," not as an unjustifiable and undeserving act.

Parental blessing is not just about avoiding what upsets or disappoints parents but also about meeting their expectations. This is very tricky regarding marriage and passing on the family name to children and grandchildren, which is also very important in Arab and Middle Eastern societies. In many Arab cultures, especially tribal ones, marriage is a union not simply between two people but between two families for ulterior motives, such as status, lineage, power, and prestige. Therefore, families approach the topic of marriage as their inherent right rather than a personal decision, which is probably incomprehensible in modern Western and individualistic societies. Many Arab LGBTQIA+ individuals feel tremendous pressure over this topic as they approach marriage age, especially if they are an only child, or the eldest, or the only cisgender "male" carrying the family name. Marriage expectancy starts at a young age in the Arab world; thus, this pressure can extend for a long time. Continuous resistance and avoidance often trigger parents' questions while simultaneously signaling they do not want to know the answer. This tends to be the peak of conflicts, emotional distancing, and the risk of being outed.

Some internalize their parents' pain and disappointment and feel guilty for not "giving them the happiness they deserve" through grandchildren. As one middle-aged gay man stated, "I cannot imagine the day when my parents pass away, and only my name will be written on the obituary, no children, no grandchildren." (In some Arab and Middle Eastern countries, obituaries include not a biography about the deceased but the family tree and lineage of the deceased. The more names, the more honorable the deceased.) Therefore, under these familial, societal, and psychological pressures, it is common to find LGBTQIA+ individuals in heterosexual marriages or in "cover-up marriages'" with another LGBTQIA+ individual from the other sex. For those within heteronormative marriages, a same-gender partner may publicly play the role of a very close friend or uncle/aunt of the children and can be closely involved in providing care for them. While these stories deserve another chapter beyond the scope of the present one, it is important to acknowledge their presence in that unique family constellation and that these individuals are rarely able to honor their true selves publicly, even within the LGBTQIA+ community.

Navigating Arab/Middle Eastern Identities

A prevalent misconception in the Arab and Middle Eastern world is that same-gender sexuality is a foreign concept, imported by the West in order to break down the fabric of society from within. If one scrolls through the comments section on any LGBTQIA+ content on Arab or Middle Eastern platforms, it is impossible not to read comments along those lines. Somehow, sexual orientation and gender identity are treated as "culture-bound syndromes" in our societies, with a persistent denial and ignorance of their presence in our history and literature. This perception as threat is one of the major reasons that aggravate aggression and reduce the larger community's empathy for people who are sexual/gender minorities, and why some claim that the Arab world is not "ready" to promote equal rights.

It is crucial for people in the West and international communities who would like to support sexual/gender minority individuals in the Middle East to be aware of this point. Arab and Middle Eastern countries carry histories filled with trauma, treason, and paranoia, especially with some Western countries that were directly or indirectly involved in the colonization and imperialism in the Middle East. Therefore, "adopting" and politicizing the LGBTQIA+ cause by the West can further feed into the misconception that it is a foreign agenda. It might also expose individuals who are sexual/gender minorities to more aggression and alienation by their communities. One individual beautifully stated, "We have been here long before the Stonewall and before any rainbow flag was ever raised. Our existence needs to be recognized for its own merit and not acculturated to the West." Nevertheless, gaining public and international support is essential in pushing for change. This needs to be through empowering the local LGBTQIA+ community and giving them the resources, experience, power, and space to actualize their existence and identities in their way.

The mentioned misconception is also further fueled by prohibitions of same-gender romantic or sexual relationships by the major religions in the Middle East. Therefore, many Arab LGBTQIA+ individuals live with competing selves, as though they need to choose one part over the other or prove they are "Arab" or "Muslim" enough. Additionally, the limited visibility of Arab queer individuals in this part of the world results in the lack of a clear Arab queer identity. For example, what does a queer Arab/Muslim person look like? Dress like? Live like? Can someone hold all these different identities like a colorful bouquet and represent similar others in the region? Personally, not one image comes easily to our mind.

One thing we know, the Arab queer identity is unique and can only be understood through appreciating the parts that sum the whole. For example, it is not uncommon to find veiled queer, lesbian, and bisexual women who wear their covering out of conviction and not necessarily by force. One trans woman stated that she longs to wear the veil upon completion of transitioning because this is how womanhood and femininity are expressed in her culture and in her mental schema. Two transgender men visited the mosque for Friday prayers in the men's section as soon as they started having facial hair and deeper voices.

We have seen members of a support group for Arab queer individuals choosing an iftar event during the holy month of Ramadan to be among their first outings. There were people from different cultural, religious, and nonreligious backgrounds, some were fasting while others were not. The event was a unique element of community building in our culture, given the significance of this month in bringing people together. It also symbolizes a brave act of ownership of both identities and of collectively figuring out ways to harmoniously synchronize the presence of different identities that the heteronormative community deemed opposite and incompatible. Others have added their own touch to their traditional customs to represent their gender identity and have carried into their chosen families some of their social and cultural rituals, gender roles, values, and systems. It was interesting to observe that even in same-gender relationships, individuals from tribal backgrounds would sometimes choose partners from tribes or lineages of whom their families would have ideally approved.

Furthermore, many Arab and Middle Eastern cultures are still segregated by gender. Ironically, this can add a layer of safety for same-gender couples because the wider community might not suspect or frown on those closely knitted ties. In these cultures, it is not uncommon for same-gender individuals to express verbal and physical affection to each other versus the other gender. In contrast, gender-diverse individuals might have an added layer of struggle and alienation that might not be shared by other gender-diverse individuals in less gender-segregated cultures.

For example, a trans man from a conservative background, before transitioning, attended an all-girls religious school. His friends were all women, and there was limited access or visibility to male friends. It is relevant to explain that women's spaces in conservative cultures are very sacred because they are among the few places where women can wear whatever they want and be themselves without the formality, domination, or inhibition that comes with the presence of men. After transitioning, friendship dynamics were challenging to navigate for this individual. Some female friends now perceived him as a man. They now have to wear their veils in front of him (if they are veiled) or dress conservatively the way they would in front of nonkin men. They also could not explain this other gender friendship to their husbands and families and thus avoided inviting him over or being seen publicly with him. Other female friends chose not to change how they interacted with him and kept the friendship dynamics the same. However, that also implicitly communicated that they did not acknowledge or take his gender identity seriously. Although both were painful, this individual expressed that the latter hurt a little more.

Food for Thought

The queer community in Arab and Middle Eastern cultures is strongly under-represented, misunderstood, and distorted. While some may think it is quashed and nonexistent, others may view it as an oppressed, underdeveloped community waiting to be rescued. Both perceptions ignore the robust diversity and resilience of sexual/gender minority individuals in this part of the world. More importantly, discussing oppression without highlighting resilience and resistance is another form of oppression. The Arab and Middle Eastern LGBTQIA+ communities are ever present and evolving through creating safe places, challenging injustice, redefining social norms, and even advancing the Arab language to develop words and terminologies inclusive of their existence and experience. This community also contains many strong fighters and outspoken activists on diverse topics relevant to our cultures and collective traumas. A close friend once said, "Although there is oppression, we are not oppressed."

Professionals who are interested in working with sexual/gender minorities in this part of the world are encouraged to have in-depth knowledge of the local context, language, history, resources, and day-to-day challenges faced by the local community. This knowledge is gained through literature, stories, academic articles and research, news, and social media, but most importantly through closely engaging with the community (Michli & El Jamil, 2022). Furthermore, knowledge of the historical context, the presence of same-gender relationships, and LGBTQIA+ figures in Middle Eastern, Arabic, and Islamic history, literature, music, and cinema are imperative in bridging the gap between the opposing selves mentioned previously. Individuals tend to be delighted when presented with information about their ancestors in this region, giving them a sense of continuation and recognition. Furthermore, it is essential to study each country's laws and regulations regarding same-gender sexuality and gender nonconformity. As mentioned, this region has great diversity, and different countries are moving in different directions regarding human rights. Therefore, a lack of legal knowledge can endanger both the clinician and patient and can, at least, result in inapplicable treatment plans.

From our experience in the field, it is imperative to assess and differentiate between Arab/Middle Eastern individuals with collective versus individualistic self-construals. We observed that these individuals could experience the weight of the topics mentioned above very differently from one another, even if they were from the same countries and similar backgrounds, and thus might want to manage them differently. Individuals are encouraged to acknowledge and explore the different forms of the LGBTQIA+ community in our region, as it is very diverse and everything but homogenous. Different individuals might find a sense of belonging in one kind of community but not in another.

Following a bottom-up rather than a top-down approach in therapeutic work is essential, as the latter can increase the gap between the therapist and patient. For example, we noticed that introducing and asking about pronouns seemed well accepted by younger LGBTQIA+ patients, those more exposed to Western media and education, and those involved in LGBTQIA+ support groups. It is easy to recognize how their tension decreases in the room, relieved at meeting an authority figure who is respectful and attentive to these details. In contrast, older Arab LGBTQIA+ people, individuals with high internalized homonegativity, and those less exposed to Western media and education experience this approach as foreign and less organic. As one older gay man stated once, "Those words do not represent me, nor are they a language I use in my internal dialogue to think of myself and others. It seems they are best suited for others trying to understand me, but not for me to understand myself." Individuals with internalized homonegativity, especially those wanting to change their sexual orientation or gender expression, might infer the therapist's stance on sexual/gender diversity from those comments, assume the therapist's agenda, and be deterred from continuing therapy. The individual's internalized homonegativity may reflect their adherence to traditional values regarding sexuality and gender, and not necessarily self-deprecation (Rosik et al., 2022). Therefore, it is essential to read the patient's nonverbal reactions to such questions and address how they feel about it in the room. It is also important to follow the individual's language to describe themselves. However, suppose the individual uses derogatory Arab terminologies because they do not know a better alternative. In that case, there is no harm in proposing the more updated terms without forcing it and explaining the reason for this alternative. Therapists must refrain from using derogatory language toward the patient, even if they use it toward themselves.

Mental health professionals working with individuals who are sexual/gender minorities in conservative cultures need to be very aware of their internal stigma. Without deep introspection into our values, beliefs, and attitudes, we can cause harm to others not just in what we say but also in what we avoid saying and in our nonverbal communication. This is important because LGBTQIA+ individuals who have long been exposed to stigma and negative messages can be hypervigilant and skilled at detecting unsafe verbal and nonverbal cues. We noticed that some practitioners with a certain level of stigma choose to cover it up by adopting a color-blind approach, stating things like, "I treat them just like any other patient." They thus turn a blind eye to the unique struggles and needs of individuals who are social minorities and consider their "mere tolerance" a skill when it is the bare minimum. It is an ethical requirement not only to be honest with ourselves about our own stigmas and human limitations but also to work on ourselves through training, education, consultation, and supervision from experts in the field and to explore our stigmas in our own therapy if we wish to work with individuals from the LGBTQIA+ community.

Finally, mental health professionals working with individuals who are sexual/gender minorities need to accept the responsibility of extending themselves and their knowledge outside the clinical room. Anyone who has worked with socially stigmatized people and other vulnerable populations knows that the beauty of working with these populations is that it is unorthodox; it is where psychology, anthropology, social work, faith, and activism meet. Where it is safe to do so, mental health professionals must actively raise awareness and build safe spaces. It is also of great benefit to be involved in outreach programs and in advocating for laws that protect people who are social minorities and vulnerable populations if it is safe to do so.

Conclusion

It is not with the easy seasons of life that most people forge the inner strengths and social support networks needed to weather the harder times; such is the case for LGBTQIA+ individuals. It is easy to conceptualize resilience and well-being as an individual responsibility and choice, but we can fail to acknowledge the social stressors that get in the way.

Stressful internal adaptations (for example, self-rejection, identity uncertainty, insecure attachment, hypervigilance, rumination, emotional dysregulation, substance abuse, suicidality) are normal human reactions to external stressors and can serve as targets for interventions and empowerment. Caring for one's internal stress processes can allow LGBTQIA+ individuals, including sexual/gender minorities who do not identify as LGBTQIA+, to reduce their internal distress and feel more secure in themselves when they cannot immediately change social stressors. As sexual/gender minority individuals, regardless of identity label, strengthen their personal resilience, they are more capable of responding to interpersonal, familial, community, and structural stressors.

"No regrets" is often promoted as a motivating phrase for life purpose and achievement. The reality is that queer lives, by virtue of who we are and what we represent, are the sum total of a lifetime of negotiating complex decisions, boundaries, and obstacles. The obstacles, such as discrimination and lack of support, are regrettable. However, the lives lived are beautiful expressions of the human spirit and can be celebrated as intrinsically and socially valuable.

Chapter 2

Examine Attitudes About Sexual/Gender Diversity

A. Lee Beckstead, Matthew Nielson, Samuel Eshleman
Latimer, Heather Hoffmann, and Eduardo Peres

This chapter was designed to help you understand and examine attitudes that are negative toward sexually/gender-diverse (LGBTQIA+) individuals and attitudes that affirm LGBTQIA+ individuals. We provide questions for exploration, examination, and self-understanding and include a scale to understand a variety of attitudes, motivations, and power dynamics associated with sexual/gender diversity. We'll provide feedback from a traditional/ conservative colleague about the scale. In the end, we highlight current research on the biological and social conditioning effects on sexual/gender diversity and offer an inclusive answer to the question, "Can youth be influenced to become LGBTQ+?"

A challenge in this type of project is that conventional religiosity is perceived as the source of negative attitudes by many within the LGBTQIA+ community, but those same attitudes may be adhered to by other LGBTQIA+ individuals who find the teachings to be a source of truth and guidance. We hope the following and our companion e-resource attend to this enough to help a broad spectrum of conservative and progressive readers.

Safety Issues

We[1] tried to create a balanced viewpoint of sexual/gender diversity. We were fully committed to embracing readers living in out-and-open LGBTQIA+ progressive communities and readers in conservative and traditional communities who are private about their life. We realized we couldn't reach these

---

[1] The following includes guidelines from former coauthors who contributed earlier in the process.

communities without speaking their languages. And we knew we could not represent all perspectives in this chapter. Therefore, we tried to be curious and compassionate about what each coauthor saw as helpful and harmful to the community populations each serves or is part of. We tried to remain open to new experiences and aware of our limitations in presenting the full, nuanced picture of these multifaceted human issues. We hoped to integrate our writings, develop our ideas as a team, and find a common language that incorporates and helps the spectrum of diversity.

On an interpersonal level, we expected we would be respected by each other and see diversity and identities respected. We were not interested in forcing our views on any coauthors or readers. Therefore, we needed to be mindful of our privileges and social positions and their impact on communication. We wanted to avoid the typical labeling and name-calling ways of communicating these issues. We also needed to be open to feedback and accountability. We understood how asking for civility, politeness, and respect in our interactions can also harm marginalized communities by silencing injustice, anger, and hurt and sterilizing conversations of uncomfortable topics. Having difficult discussions can lead to people's civil rights being recognized. Therefore, we encouraged each other to express our thoughts and feelings directly to the coauthor if we had any concerns. As coauthor Peres articulated, "I am an open book willing to be edited and improved, and constructive criticism is always positive (when delivered with kindness and compassion)."

Collaboration typically feels safe with colleagues with similar beliefs. Conversely, when collaborative efforts are made between individuals with politically opposing viewpoints, fear of judgment, distrust, prejudice, and social shaming can make the process more difficult. Our viewpoints and attitudes are personal and based on deeply held developmental experiences. Therefore, we agreed to withhold criticism and not make judgments about each other based on our initial written samples. We realized that coauthors could likely disagree and be able to think of rebuttals for quite a few statements. That's okay. We hoped instead to develop a group culture of appreciation (Okun, 2023) and curiosity about the information that each brings to the table.

If we truly were dedicated to bridge-building and reconciliation efforts, we needed to be aware of when our communication/writing directly or indirectly implied who is good and who is the enemy. To decrease polarization while navigating controversy, coauthor Eshleman Latimer suggested we follow Linehan's (1993) dialectical behavior therapy's *fallibility agreement*:

> We agree ahead of time that we are each fallible and make mistakes. We agree that we have probably either done whatever problematic things we're being accused, or some part of it, so that we can let go of assuming a defensive stance to prove our virtue or competence. Because we are fallible, it is agreed that we

will inevitably violate all of these agreements, and when this is done we will rely on each other to point out the polarity and move to a synthesis. (pp. 118–19)

As we tried to value everyone's opinion, we did not want to tolerate intolerance (Popper's paradox). We agreed to speak up whenever comments or perspectives were discriminatory and tried to be sensitive to how the material would impact readers. We hoped to consider how our content would affect individuals who don't fit our collective ideology or individuals whose lived experiences have been marginalized outside our viewpoint.

We hoped coauthors would act professionally and that we could resolve conflicts by using evidence in the research literature. We agreed that science carries weight and well-replicated effects should carry weight. We also knew that "science" is not neutral because marginalized individuals and communities are often not included and represented accurately. We needed to be aware of how lack of representation has historically harmed and continues affecting marginalized communities. Therefore, we tried to fit what we knew anecdotally/experientially within the existing science. We tried to represent the relative strength of positions and data fairly. If evidence is missing, we agreed to state it and use a consensus approach.

Even though we needed to be concise, we tried to avoid sweeping overstatements and changed vocabulary to be less polarizing. The polarization makes interpreting the research incredibly challenging to sort through. We hope our writing is appropriately tempered and hedged, as we tried to provide nuance as best we could.

Not surprisingly, we had different ways of approaching the topic of sexual orientation change efforts and interpreting the data, which may—at least on some level—be affected by our personal experiences and how this topic affects each of our dispositions (if at all). Those differences are a good thing from a diversity perspective. But, of course, as is the nature of heterodoxy and seeking truth through complexity, it made the process more time consuming with more email and videoconferencing dialogues. We found a common-ground sentiment toward the topic about what needs to be conveyed for all to benefit, with the hope of exploring this topic further rather than reverting to black-and-white conclusions and side taking.

In summary, we were committed to collaboration and accuracy. We believe that the foundation for safe and productive discussions about sexual/gender diversity comes from everyone being curious of different lived experiences and cultural backgrounds and being open to growing together as individuals and as a team. We agreed to have a relentless focus on science, an awareness of who might be marginalized from the scientific literature, a thick skin for disagreement, and an enthusiasm for this new kind of collaboration.

- What would feel safe and unsafe for you exploring your attitudes—and the perspectives of others—about sexual/gender diversity?
- Which viewpoints would be safe and unsafe for you and your loved ones if they were presented in this chapter?
- What do you need from yourself when examining these issues?

If you become emotionally triggered by reading any of the ideas or experiences below, focus on your breath to stabilize yourself, try to take deep and slow breaths, take a break, and decide if you want to continue and which questions and sections to skip.

What Are Attitudes, and Can We Change Them?

Merriam-Webster's dictionary defines *attitudes* as feelings or emotions toward a fact. Our attitudes toward individuals we perceive as "others" and in the "out-group" can range from warm to cold, friendly to hostile, trusting to suspicious, respectful to insulting, and admiring to disgusted (Wright et al, 1997) and wanting to liberate or control them (Benjamin, n.d.). Our feelings/emotions about facts/individuals come from our socialization, viewpoint, mindset, temperament (Bigler & Liben, 2006), and positive and negative evaluations of our own and others' experiences (Tierney et al., 2021).

Kruglanski (interviewed by Rooks & Han, 2021) explained that we form attitudes based on our innate drive to meet two human needs during times of uncertainty: (1) the need for *cognitive closure* (to know what's going on) and (2) the need for *significance* (to matter in some way). Our social narratives tell us how best to meet those needs. This cognitive closure, regardless of whether the conclusion is complete or distorted, and feeling significant, whether negative or positive, can give us a sense of relevance, order, control, and reassurance during conflicts and distress. However, this cognitive closure, through false conclusions, can also create prejudice and thinking traps.

Our social networks, narratives, traumas, and motivation to meet our developmental needs "lock in" and attach us to our attitudes. It's human nature to "seize and freeze" (Kruglanski & Webster, 1996) and fixate on simplistic explanations (for example, *I caused their discomfort*, *I'm bad*, *I'm inferior/ superior*, *They don't belong*, *They are unlovable*). Kruglanski explained that the problem is that we obtain information from different echo chambers: "Same human process, different content, different conclusions."

For example, for some, sexual/gender diversity is a moral issue (a sin, character flaw, strength, social justice ethical issue), a legal problem (a crime, human rights issue), or a psychological phenomenon (an intrapsychic disturbance, an addiction, a gift to the community, a trait that helps humanity evolve) (Katz, 1995). Same-gender attractions and relationships are still seen or experienced by some as moral failures (Gallup, 2022). Some people view a transgender/

nonbinary individual's social or medical transitioning as a sin that violates traditional laws. Others view transition as an act of self-actualization and courage resisting pressures to conform.

Regardless of the variability in perceptions about the morality of sexual/gender identities, social stigma reinforced through laws and institutions harms individuals (Pachankis & Bränström, 2018). Social stigma (Goffman, 1963) marks a group and individual as disgraceful, discredited, and disqualified from full social acceptance due to an attribute or behavior thought to be a disadvantage or a threat to the individual and social order. Individuals with nonheterosexual, queer, or trans/nonbinary identities experience stigma and violence for their self-expression, which plays a role in the individual and those around them believing the individual is inferior, worthless, and a burden and does not belong.

Destigmatizing efforts, in contrast, remove blame and shame and restore worth, safety, and status to a person or group (Clair et al., 2016). Identities, even though stigmatized, can improve resilience in LGBTQIA+ individuals by allowing them to break from social norms and appreciate their own uniqueness of being and outlook (Paz Galupo et al., 2019).

Social contact with individuals from the "out-group" (*intergroup contact*) that allows for perspective giving, empathy, and alliance building to improve relations can reduce prejudice (Cramwinckel et al., 2018), even if the in-group feels threatened and the out-group perceives discrimination (Van Assche et al., 2023). This process of openness, curiosity, questioning, listening for understanding, evaluation, discovery, differentiation, revision, integration, and growth can help us have a bigger picture of ourselves, others, and life. This broader viewpoint can help us be less vulnerable to false and harmful information.

Questions for Exploration, Examination, and Self-Understanding

The following questions are designed for self-exploration to examine our socialization, belief systems, self-concepts, and emotional reactions (our attitudes) about sexual/gender diversity. This self-exploration includes recognizing our privileges, disadvantages, and triggers and how our attitudes about sexual/gender diversity impact ourself and others.

One way to frame questions like these relates to the sources:

- What did you hear about the LGBTQIA+ community from your family/religious institution/faith, peers, and nonreligious experiences? How much of what you heard is congruent with your beliefs, values, and experiences, and how much is discordant?
- What did you hear about the LGBTQIA+ community from the mainstream LGBTQIA+ community and media and entertainment? How much of what

you heard is congruent with your beliefs, values, and experiences, and how much is discordant?

Growing up, how were LGBTQIA+ and exclusively heterosexual cisgender individuals treated similarly and differently, and is that the same or different these days? How were the messages different and similar about White LGBTQIA+ individuals and racially minoritized LGBTQIA+ individuals?

What is your understanding of what causes an individual's sexual orientation and gender expression, and which personal and social experiences influenced your understanding? How much do your attitudes reflect your experiences with one, several, or many LGBTQIA+ individuals and diverse social networks? How much time and energy do you devote to learning about the diversity of LGBTQIA+ individuals (Pantalone et al., 2019), especially immigrants and racialized sexual/gender minority people?

Looking back, which messages and interactions harmed your sexual/gender development? Which messages and interactions were helpful to your growth? How did your disposition and life circumstances make navigating your sexuality and gender challenging and beneficial? How have you grown from these challenges? What is left that needs healing, and what do healing, resilience, and empowerment look like for you? How can your cultural experiences help with healing, resilience, and empowerment?

- Which three to five words would you use to describe how you feel about your sexual orientation and gender? Which three to five words would you use to describe exclusive heterosexuality and traditional gender norms?
- How do you feel about people who are same-gender attracted or gender diverse who do not adopt an LGBTQ identity? What is your attitude toward the idea that anyone's sexual/gender identity needs a label affixed to it in the first place?
- If you have rejected specific messages/assumptions about sexual/gender diversity, what were the reasons? What are/were the reasons for holding onto them?
- Which messages/assumptions are you unsure of and would benefit from exploring more?

Understanding Negating and Affirming Attitudes About Sexual/Gender Diversity

Rather than just a set of negative beliefs, negative attitudes about sexual/gender diversity involve a relational context, as Russell and Bohan (2006) explained:

> An adolescent's saying, "I hate being queer" to a parent has a very different meaning than a bisexual client's saying it to a therapist at a particularly conflicted moment, a lesbian's saying it when the death of her lover goes unacknowledged by her biological family, or a gay man's saying it after

a gay-bashing. To identify all of these utterances as (simply, equally, and unequivocally) expressions of [internalized homophobia] is to ignore the degree to which each utterance and its affective underpinning bespeak not some persistent personality trait but a response to the social circumstances of the moment. To label them all simply as indicative of [internalized homophobia] is to miss this relational complexity. (p. 346)

Russell and Bohan described how internalized homophobia (and transphobia, sexism, biphobia, racism, etc.) can be specific (feeling confused and insecure about your identity, wanting to kill yourself because of how you feel about your identity within your social circumstances, abandoning certain career goals to avoid rejection, avoiding dating, etc.). They described how internalized homophobia/stigma can be more subtle and generalizing (tolerating mistreatment, abusing substances, having brief relationships, etc.).

Russell and Bohan encouraged us to reduce oppression through self-reflection and listening to those who hold minoritized positions in society, including those who hold a different view than our own. If we are compassionate for their pain and resilience, then we are more aware of and accountable for any negating actions from us. This accountability and empathy can strengthen our ability to recognize when and how we are being complicit in negating experiences and, instead, identify when and how we can foster connection, well-being, and growth for everyone.

What's your understanding of the purpose of LGBTQIA-affirmative interventions? Some people believe and fear it means encouraging and even coercing youth and adults into adopting specific gender/sexual values, beliefs, behaviors, and identities that don't legitimately fit them. Many early models of gender/sexual identity development tended to place fully accepting and coming out publicly with an LGBTQIA+ identity and integrating same-gender sexual/romantic and gender-diverse behaviors into one's life as the optimal health outcome. Those who did not identify as LGBTQIA+ were considered at a lesser stage of development. Yet LGBTQIA-affirmative interventions were developed to question (Landridge, 2007), counter, oppose, and challenge the long history of messages prioritizing one life path over another, specifically that an exclusively heterosexual, gender-stereotypical life is superior and that being and acting LGBTQIA+ is inherently deficient, inferior, and doomed.

LGBTQIA-affirmative interventions have two purposes: (1) to counteract the negating environment from historical and current prejudice and oppression against sexual/gender diversity and (2) to counteract the "null environment" from the lack of acceptance, safety, options, and support. Affirmative interventions should remain agnostic about each individual's identity trajectory. The focus is on reducing the effects of minority stress on the person's identity development and health. Affirmative interventions are therefore person-affirmative and assess for minority stress effects on all aspects of the person. Instead of promoting LGBTQIA+ identities, affirmative interventions ideally promote assertiveness, equality/equity, social justice, authenticity, safety, exploration, self-determination, flourishing, and avoiding harm regarding sexual/gender diversity and other socially stigmatized aspects of self.

The American Psychological Association (2009) encouraged providers to use affirmative interventions by attending to the following:

- Provide empathy, support, acceptance, and positive regard for the sexually/gender-diverse (SGD) person;
- Develop a comprehensive understanding of the SGD individual's distress, including the impact of minority stress;
- Empower the SGD individual and counter minority stress by
  ○ Increasing active coping, emotional coping, and cognitive coping;
  ○ Increasing social support and positive community identity;
  ○ Facilitating identity exploration and development of all aspects of self;
- Manage assumptions of how the SGD individual will or should identify or live out their sexual orientation, gender, ethnicity, religion/spirituality, and other aspects of self.

A Scale of Turning Against, Away From, or Toward Sexual/Gender Diversity

We created the following list of negating, accepting, and affirming attitudes about sexual/gender diversity from Riddle's 1973 Homophobia Scale (Riddle Scale, 2022). The first three attitudes *turn against* people who are sexually/gender diverse, in different degrees of intensity, for *hostile control* (dominate, destroy, disempower, etc.) to stop, resist, suppress, eliminate, correct, or erase sexual/gender diversity. The fourth attitude *turns away from* people who are sexually/gender diverse (neutral and uninterested, more interested in cis-heterosexuality). The last four attitudes differ in their degree of effort and motivation of *turning toward* people who are sexually/gender diverse for *friendly differentiation*[2] (affirm, protect, empower, liberate, etc.) to help sexually/gender-diverse people thrive.

The following is not meant to put people or you in a box or reinforce a hierarchy of superiority/inferiority but to represent a continuum of attitudes of various intensities regarding sexually/gender-diverse topics, ideas, and people with various narratives, motivations, and outcomes. A person may feel one way about one aspect of sexual/gender diversity and another way about another aspect. We recognize that these categories may evolve over time, and factor-analytic research needs to be conducted to determine how well these

---

[2] See Benjamin (n.d.), https://lornasmithbenjamin.com/sasb/.

categories map onto current attitudes and motivations within different cultures. Considering our descriptions of these attitudes, how true do they resonate with how you think, feel, and act regarding sexual/gender diversity and LGBTQIA+ individuals?

1. Feel Contempt for/Threatened by Sexual/Gender Diversity and LGBTQIA+ Individuals (*Negate/Turn Against/Attack and Control*)
   a. Attitudes: Everyone is assumed to be exclusively heterosexual or sexually fluid and be better off adhering to exclusive heterosexuality and gender norms. Expressing sexual/gender diversity is believed to be unnatural and wrong for everyone and a choice that threatens social rules, order, and safety (Jewell & Morrison, 2012). In-group harmony is held in the highest regard. Anything is justified to exclude and change/eradicate LGBTQIA+ individuals and their behaviors.
      i. LGBTQIA+ individuals are perverts, freaks, immoral, possessed, dangerous (Arli et al., 2020), and an abomination and doing "devil's work" (Metz, 2022). Children are not safe around them and hearing about their experiences.
   b. Motivations: The purpose is to manage disgust (Ray & Parkhill, 2020), fear, hatred, and aggression (Set & Ergin, 2020) due to hierarchical/minoritizing social norms, stigma socialization, prejudice, sexual/emotional/physical/identity trauma, moral condemnation, moral phobia/panic (Walsh, 2020), erotophobia, feminine devaluation (Hoskin, 2019), or physical limits (aversion/disgust to being sexual with one's nonpreferred gender). Some may believe sexual/gender diversity is evidence of societal degeneration and that it is their divine duty to enforce moral order (Holben, 1999).
   c. Power dynamics: Turn against to dominate or annihilate sexual/gender diversity and stop "the transgender agenda. . . [and] radical sexual ideology" (Perkins, 2022).
   d. The LGBTQIA+ person's self-belief: I will be attacked, punished, and ostracized, and I can't defend myself (Skidmore, Lefevor, Larsen, et al., 2022). I am bad, disgusting, unlovable, sick, wrong, a burden, and unsafe; I don't belong and shouldn't exist. I should change, pretend, hide, or kill myself.
2. Feel Pity and Disapprove of Sexual/Gender Diversity and LGBTQIA+ Individuals
   a. Attitudes: Those who follow social rules are believed to be superior and those who do not are shamed for not maintaining hierarchies and harmony within cultural communities (Choi & Israel, 2016). Those who do not follow gender social rules are considered inappropriate, weird, defective, weak, and deficient. Same-gender sexuality is considered an inferior form of sexuality.
      i. It's their fault they are suffering. They would be happier if they just wouldn't act that way. Men who behave in feminine ways are looking for attention; a real trans man looks and behaves only in

masculine ways; a masculine woman is not a real woman (Schudson & van Anders, 2021). The LGBTQIA+ community pushes themselves into areas where they are not wanted (Krolikowski et al., 2016). LGBTQIA+ people should stop complaining about the way they are treated in society and get on with their lives (Morrison & Morrison, 2002).

b. Motivations: These attitudes manage rejection/stigma by criticizing and blaming sexual/gender minorities for harm instead of social systems and ideologies. The goal is to correct "deviant" behaviors by reinforcing one right way for all.

c. Power dynamics: Exert power over/against sexual/gender diversity to encourage LGBTQIA+ individuals for their and the family's safety to change sexual behaviors and gender expressions that differ from social norms.

d. The LGBTQIA+ person's self-belief: I'm defective and responsible for other people's distress with sexual/gender diversity. I'm an embarrassment and I should strive to be like others.

3. Tolerate and Dislike Sexual/Gender Diversity and LGBTQIA+ Individuals

a. Attitudes: Sexual/gender diversity is believed to be just a phase that the individual will and should "grow out of." Transgender, nonbinary, and nonheterosexual identities are judged as inappropriate or not valid experiences. LGBTQIA+ individuals are considered less legitimate and mature and not given positions of authority.

i. Love the sinner but not the sin (Hoffarth et al., 2018). Being LGBTQIA+ is not a choice, but acting on it is. Same-gender sexuality is a sin, just like any other sin. We all have our trials to overcome. There is too much attention on LGBTQIA+ issues; sexual orientation prejudice is not a problem nowadays (Morrison & Morrison, 2011). I'm fine with LGBTQIA+ people as long as they act normal (Buijs, 2011).

b. Motivations: The purpose is to act friendlier but defend the status quo, restrict and hoard social power, manage personal feelings of uncertainty and ambivalence, and avoid LGBTQIA+ individuals (Cramwinckel et al., 2018).

c. Power dynamics: Justify and maintain systemic beliefs, rules, and rituals that protect power for yourself and those you care about and use power over/against sexual/gender diversity.

d. The LGBTQIA+ person's self-belief: Something is wrong with me. I am not good enough as I am and need to prove myself worthy to belong and be treated well.

4. Accept Sexual//Gender Diversity and LGBTQIA+ Individuals (*Neutral/ Turn Away*)

a. Attitudes: Sexaul/gender diversity is considered a natural fact, but the individual disagrees with and is uninterested in sexual/gender diversity as something to validate and encourage. Cis-heterosexual privilege is denied, which normalizes or ignores violence and silence about sexual/gender diversity in politics and education (Brownfield et al., 2018). The person is unaware, ignores, does not care, or neglects the historical, intergenerational, and ongoing socialized and internalized stigma and pain of marginalization, invisibility, and concealment of social stigma on LGBTQIA+ and exclusively heterosexual, cisgender individuals.

    i. I don't see you as LGBTQIA+; I see you as a person. I can accept you if you don't flaunt it or try to change how we do things. Social change is not my responsibility (Sumerau et al., 2018). People who have the same sexual orientation and gender expression are very similar to one another (Arseneau et al., 2013).

  b. Motivations: The historical and ongoing "null environment" gets reinforced and perpetuates the lack of safety, positive representation, role models, options, and accurate information about LGBTQIA+ people and their relationships. Outlets for safe self-determination remain limited.

  c. Power dynamics: Restrict overt acts of discrimination, rejection, and oppression against sexual/gender diversity and represent an absence or restriction of pro-LGBTQIA+ behaviors (Cramwinckel et al., 2018). Systemic beliefs, rules, and rituals that protect power over/against/away from sexual/gender diversity persist. False and harmful beliefs and discrimination about sexual/gender diversity remain unchallenged.

  d. The LGBTQIA+ person's self-belief: I'm acceptable, freer, and a second-class citizen. I'm allowed to be who I am, but I'm not entirely safe to assert myself.

5. Support and Care about Sexual/Gender Diversity and LGBTQIA+ Individuals (*Affirm/Turn Toward*)

  a. Attitudes: The person feels concern, empathy, and compassion for LGBTQIA+ individuals due to understanding the excess stress and lack of social safety that LGBTQIA+ individuals experience.

    i. "Love is love is love is love . . . , [it] cannot be killed or swept aside."[3] To each their own. Minority stress needs to be reduced for LGBTQIA+ individuals.

  b. Motivations: The purpose is to be curious and learn more about the lives and history of LGBTQIA+ individuals and spend time reflecting on and examining personal discomfort and thoughts, feelings, reactions, and actions about sexual/gender diversity and the diversity of lives of LGBTQIA+ individuals.

  c. Power dynamics: Shift responsibility to each person to self-reflect, ask questions, and examine social stigma and oppressive social attitudes and understand how individuals have internalized these attitudes toward themselves and others.

  d. The LGBTQIA+ person's self-belief: I'm okay/fine as I am. I matter; my feelings, needs, limits, and agency matter. I feel safer being myself.

---

[3] Lin-Manuel Miranda expressed this during his acceptance speech for his 2016 Tony Award.

6. Admiration and Appreciation for Sexual/Gender Diversity and LGBTQIA+ Individuals

    a. Attitudes: LGBTQIA+ individuals and sexual/gender diversity are represented as valuable resources for personal and social growth. Replacing false beliefs and oppressive systems in self and with others is done to restore dignity, honor, and equity.

        i. Everyone is welcome and needed and deserves protection. We're all a bit queer/different. We all can learn and benefit from each other's sexual, gender, and cultural diversity. Being LGBTQIA+ takes strength and creativity.

    b. Motivations: The purpose is to understand the essential roles that sexually/gender-diverse individuals have played throughout history in communities and social development and the mistreatment and abuse they experienced.

    c. Power dynamics: Reexamine what it means to be feminine/masculine and accept, value, and cultivate feminine qualities in yourself and others (Hoskin, 2019). Power is used to make space and center LGBTQIA+ people and gender/sexual diversity in social systems and relationships while promoting LGBTQIA+ subcommunity development.

    d. The LGBTQIA+ person's self-belief: I'm lucky to be LGBTQIA+. I bring value to the community (Russell, 2023). Queer souls are sacred.

7. Protect, Advocate for, and Liberate Sexual/Gender Diversity and LGBTQIA+ Individuals

    a. Attitudes: An intersectional focus is used to consider early, developmental, intergenerational, systemic, and ongoing prejudice and threats and lack of advantages faced by the diversity of sexual/gender minority individuals. Reducing minority stress is prioritized as critical for the well-being of LGBTQIA+ and exclusively heterosexual, cisgender individuals. Social justice and relational healing are considered necessary for individual and community safety. Centering the most marginalized is prioritized to develop empowering strategies for the marginalized to thrive; these strategies will likely also help the community to thrive.

        i. We're queer, we're here, we shall overcome and heal together. Autonomy and consent in relationships are foundational for flourishing.

    b. Motivations: The purpose is to safeguard, stand up for, and restore equality of LGBTQIA+ individuals' dignity, rights, relationships, and lives throughout their life span. The motivation is to grow from examining, understanding, and healing from how social stigma has affected you and others.

    c. Power dynamics: Actively disrupt, interrupt, question, resist, counter, oppose, and dismantle social oppression to liberate everyone, especially marginalized individuals; efforts include trans/nonbinary-affirming lobbying and legislation to reduce the harm of antitrans/-nonbinary societal bias (Singh et al., 2022). Marginalized LGBTQIA+ individuals are centered by representing their grief, losses, strengths, needs, and resilience and helping to remove the obstacles to recovering from minority stress and trauma.

    d. The LGBTQIA+ person's self-belief: I'm safer. I am proud to be resilient and a survivor of hatred and minority stress. I like who I am, and I am not alone.

8. Collaborate with and Nurture LGBTQIA+ Individuals

    a. Attitudes: Sexual, gender, cultural, and other aspects of diversity are considered natural and interconnected parts of society and indispensable resources for personal and community growth. The person treats all LGBTQIA+ individuals and cis-heterosexuals with admiration and normalcy.

       i. Liberation from oppression is a shared responsibility and a transformational process for all.

    b. Motivations: The purpose is to center intentionally and work jointly with people who differ from you and are sexually/gender diverse, especially with individuals who hold several marginalized social identities, to reduce bias, rebalance social power and dignity, and grow together. The intention is to enjoy the synergy and emergent process (brown, 2021) of collaboration with diverse others.

    c. Power dynamics: Actively provide humanizing responses to oppression and mobilize with others to cocreate LGBTQIA+ inclusive and supportive policies within the law, social institutions, and social norms. Power honors group harmony and individual autonomy, accountability, and authenticity. Power is used to create communities and cultures of appreciation and inclusivity (Okun, 2023) that protect the rights and well-being of everyone and do not privilege any one identity or narrative over another (Tan & Weisbart, 2021).

    d. The LGBTQIA+ person's self-belief: I am because of you; you are because of me. We are all sacred, equal, enough, and interconnected (Blume, 2020).

What were your reactions to reading the above? What did we miss, get wrong, or suggest that resonates with your experiences and others you know? Take a moment and reflect on what happened in your body and mind when you read the above attitudes and our descriptions. Take deep and slow belly breaths if you are emotionally triggered.

What are you learning or rediscovering about yourself, others, and these issues? Which questions are coming up about sexual/gender diversity and other aspects of diversity? You may want to reread the above continuum of attitudes and replace "LGBTQIA+" and "sexual/gender diversity" with "traditional religious/faith diversity" or add an essential aspect of who you are and identify with and consider any similarities and differences. Another option is to create your own list of attitudes, intentions, and power dynamics of turning against, toward, and away regarding LGBTQIA+ individuals, religious and political diversity, racial/ethnic diversity, disability, neurodiversity, and other personal and community experiences.

One more thing to note is that research (Fry et al., 2020) suggests we need to counter false messages about the following:

- *Discreteness:* believing clear and discrete distinctions exist between LGBTQIA+ people and cis-heterosexual people, between lesbian and bisexual women, between traditionally religious and nonreligious people, and so on.
- *Homogeneity:* believing people who have the same sexual orientation and gender are very similar to one another; believing people who have the same faith, skin color, or other feature are very similar to one another.
- *Informativeness:* believing that knowing someone's sexual orientation and gender tells you a lot about that person; believing you know a lot about a person knowing their faith, skin color, ethnicity, body size, health, and so on.

Among LGBTQ-identified individuals, one study (Morandini et al., 2022) found that believing in the naturalness (born that way) and discreteness of sexual orientation is associated the highest with people who identify as gay and lesbian and lowest with those who identify as queer and pansexual, with bisexual-identified people intermediate in these beliefs. Overall, research represents the normalcy of sexual/gender diversity and the continuum of gender/sexual experiences, similar to the normalcy, diversity, and continuum of cis-heterosexual experiences. As Dorothy Parker described, "Heterosexuality is not normal. It's just common."

The next section derives from an email response from Jeff Bennion, a colleague of coauthor Beckstead, who provided feedback on the above scale before publication. We reproduce Bennion's thoughts here with his agreement, and we hope readers use the following as an exercise to examine attitudes by providing perspective on the complexity of these issues and exploring your reactions and what fits you and doesn't. What is your understanding of necessary paths forward to resolve attitude conflicts about sexual/gender diversity?

A Politically Conservative/Religiously Traditionalist's Feedback to This Scale

I don't think your scale will resonate with traditionalists and conservatives at all. A fundamental problem I have with characterizing the attitudes of others the way this scale does is that, despite disclaiming any hierarchy, each set of attitudes is then numbered and placed in a rank order. It absolutely *is* a hierarchy. The hierarchy definitely implies which beliefs are harmful and to what degree, and progress is implied based on how far up you have ascended from benighted to enlightened, with intersectionality, social justice, and equity considered the highest ideals. These are all left-wing and progressive values and are not going to resonate with traditional or conservative individuals. The piece also appears to believe that any and all norms are bad (except for the norms of intersectionality and social justice) and that heteronormativity is bad. I would say heteronormativity is vital as a civilizational norm. There has never been a society that has functioned without heteronormativity and cisnormativity as the dominant norm, even those who have included to some degree (ranging from mere toleration to outright celebration) other forms of sexual and gender expression.

Even if I'm mistaken and heteronormativity is bad and needs to be tossed into the dustbin of history, there are certainly others along with me who believe this, and then the question is what we do with people who so believe. Because I do believe it's highly important to create connection and belonging, no matter one's sexuality or gender expression. I can't accept that for those who don't sign on to this scale wholeheartedly that they could not in some way still "turn toward" individuals who deviate from necessary societal norms. Can we only "turn toward" sexual and gender minorities by enthusiastically signing up to the current political goals of the Human Rights Campaign? Or is there much that can still be done in forging connections and belonging even across beliefs and values that may differ?

It looks to me that this scale springs out of progressive/intersectional, queer theory/queer liberation lenses, which has narratives and assumptions that I, and many others, reject. Its focus on power dynamics (which it inherited from its Marxist roots) forces people into zero-sum struggles, in my observation, and I think that's unfortunate.

That can't help but distort the views and beliefs and priorities of those who do not share in that project, in addition to making them look and feel inferior, which can't help but cause defensiveness, which will cause a "turn inward," which will definitely be perceived as "turning away."

Maybe what would help you understand how this feels is to imagine if I, along with other traditionalists who believe that social and sexual norms are vital to the functioning of a healthy society, were to construct a scale from obedience to deviance to perversion and asked people to rank themselves along this continuum based on their behaviors and beliefs. While it would be possible to do so, the fact of the matter is that these aren't values that are important to everyone (though I think they should be, even though this scale would be a *terrible* idea in practice; this is just a thought exercise), and so they would necessarily distort and make the person uncomfortable to be placing themselves anywhere along the scale, even if they could place themselves on the "good/correct" side. In the same way, the entire frame of homopositivity to homonegativity forces people along a scale that presupposes that (a) this is an important value vital to the functioning of a healthy social system and (b) this is the way every-one should see things. It assumes that those who hold homonegative views are going to be harmful or somehow contaminate the progressive/inclusive project. That may be true, but ironically, it's not terribly inclusive of those who disagree.

I think a better frame for "turning toward" is Jonathan Haidt's moral foundations theory (MFT), which shows how people have differing sets of val-ues that they prioritize. It provides more understanding than this scale's frame. MFT talks about how there are tradeoffs, which in my experience progressives resist considering and grappling with. MFT explains how and why people with different moral foundations have different priorities, which then guide their actions and beliefs. It explains many of the disagreements and disconnects we see in our society because we are working from different moral frameworks and priorities. This provides opportunities for discussion as well as broadening our perspective to other moral frameworks that might not be important to us, and maybe never will, but still help explain others' beliefs and behaviors other than "these people hold prejudiced beliefs and that's bad." MFT doesn't require put-ting them in boxes labelled "homonegative" or "marginalized by homonegative beliefs." There's usually more that's motivating the moral foundations among people who hold some of the attitudes this scale considers "turning against." MFT provides a vocabulary and a framework to help people with very different values discuss them and feel understood. That sounds like "turning towards" to me!

Lastly, and I know we disagree about this, but MFT also shifts the locus of control from an external person to the individual, which can be empower-ing. I understand and appreciate the importance of systemic change and how individuals can be agents of social change, but in practice, my observations suggest that focusing on external factors and the need for societal change often increases fragility and reduces resilience in those we are treating in therapy.

I hope that helps, and I am happy to provide feedback because fundamen-tally I share a lot of your commitments, despite the fact that we also have some pretty big disagreements. For more on moral foundations theory, see https://moralfoundations.org/.

- Take a moment, if you would, and reflect on your reactions to this col-league's reactions, assertions, and suggestions. Which do you agree and disagree with and which are you unsure of and curious about? Of those you disagree with, how would you engage with this individual about your dif-ferences, concerns, and hopes? How would you engage with him regarding your agreements and similarities?
- When you "turn inward" when someone has challenged you about gender/sexual diversity, is it (a) for self-reflection to examine your beliefs and con-tribution to conflict/distress, (b) to be self-compassionate about our com-mon humanity to discriminate, or (c) for self-pity and defensiveness? If the

latter, what do you need from yourself and others to reengage in discussions about conflicting attitudes?

- When engaging with others with differing attitudes, how can you remain true to your values while understanding that they are not the only truth and while not promoting a one-fit-for-all framework?

We should clarify that it is not that progressive/intersectional, queer theory/liberation lenses view heterosexual/cisgender identities as bad and that we should hate them. It is the understanding that these are definitions that fit some people but do not fit others. Enforcing cis-heteronormativity as a social norm and trying to force those outside of this norm to conform is what leads to oppression and harm. The problem is when all people are not treated equitably and social power advances people who adhere to cis-heteronormativity at the cost of sexually/gender-diverse people. Normativity is not a one-fit-for-all standard and therefore should not be the singular compass for gender and sexuality. Normativity does not equal normality; the former is about enforcing social appropriateness, and the latter is a description of commonality, although they can be similar depending on where the power resides.

Karl Popper's solution to intolerance of diversity and tolerance of intolerant ideas and actions was to apply rational argument. Only rational arguments are to be tolerated, or irrational arguments are tolerated as long as they do not harm the security and liberty of others (Rawls, 1971). Some disagreements and intolerance have resulted in death when people are dehumanized. A way forward to resolve attitude conflicts may be to clarify universal values and human rights and define what it means to be caring for others regarding sexual/gender diversity.

There is also a difference between engaging assertively and aggressively with those who disagree with us and attack us. Being confronted and questioned about our beliefs and actions is not the same as hostility and violence or being attacked without provocation. We may think the only solution is to make the other person abide by our experiences, beliefs, and values without us bringing a mindset into the interaction that takes into consideration their humanity and integrity and our biases. This mindset levels the field in a conversation so that one side does not dominate. Many times, our interactions with others with different attitudes do not invite conversation and dialogue but rather threats (*If you believe a certain way, I will oppose it*) and impositions (*Change the ideas I don't agree with and focus on the beliefs that I agree with*).

- Which approaches and in which contexts can pursuits of equity, social justice, and intersectionality be used negatively, mainly and especially dealing with diversity and socially marginalized communities?
- You may want to reread the scale above, Bennion's feedback, and our rebuttal, given your additional self-reflection, and note if it has affected your

initial attitudes about these issues. Do reading diverse viewpoints and taking time for introspection and a (mental) step back help you examine and clarify your attitudes and beliefs?

* How can you use the above self-reflection to check for any (potential) prejudice/bias when reading the section below about the causes of sexual orientation and gender identity?

Can Youth Be Influenced to Become LGBTQIA+?

Some believe they must keep children away from LGBTQIA+ individuals and all positive information about their lives and relationships. These restrictions are made for political authority or out of fear that LGBTQ+ people are predatory pedophiles (i.e., child molesters, groomers) (Yurcaba, 2022) and same-gender sexuality and gender diversity are learned and socially caused (like a social contagion) (Gulevich et al., 2018). Some may fear, "Did I make myself LGBT?" or "Did I cause my child to be LGBT?" Based on current research, such fears are most likely unwarranted. Evidence for the social learning and conditioning of human sexual attraction and gender expression is limited (Bailey et al., 2016). Research suggests that *influencing* someone to be attracted to others of the same gender or a different gender or how they express their gender goes only so far.

However, marginalized outliers exist with any general statement (for example, individuals who are not typically included in research samples or are outliers within statistical norms). Therefore, we want to be open to all questions to reduce polarization, invalidation, and bias. Just like the question of whether or not the sexual experiences of *every* individual, just *some* individuals, or *no one* can be socially influenced to heterosexuality or same-gender sexuality, we want to remain open to whether or not *everybody*, *some* individuals, or *no one* will adopt particular gendered expressions and identities by being exposed to that information. For example, increased social acceptance of same-gender sexuality partially—but not completely—accounts for the increases in same-gender and bisexual sexual experiences in the United States since 1973 (Diamond, 2016). Because we do not know, we should remain agnostic about the extent to which social and cultural factors affect different sexual orientations (monosexual vs. plurisexual), different genders/sexes, and gender expression over time.

As the following will suggest, there are multiple pathways to diverse sexual orientations, gender expressions, and identities, and identifying one causal theory is unlikely.

In contrast, the attitude and premise of traditional proponents and providers of sexual orientation/gender identity change efforts (SO/GICE) assume that we are all (a) born cisgender and exclusively heterosexual or (b) born blank slates that are predisposed to develop an undetermined gender and sexual orientation that are highly influenced by social conditioning. Based on this viewpoint, those who desire sex with their same gender or are gender diverse (a) need skills to develop their innate heterosexuality and traditional gender-role competencies or (b) need interventions to decondition the trauma from and repair the attachment wounds caused by parents, peers, and lack of appropriate gender/sexual role models. Some SO/GICE providers believe a same-gender-attracted/gender-diverse individual is weak in character, confused, deceived, addicted, and socially conditioned to go against a heterosexual, gender-normative biological nature and what is most healthy (that is, they are choosing to suffer).

Despite these assumptions, there is not substantial data supporting therapeutic efforts to change a person's sexual orientation or gender identity. Yes, some sexual/gender minority individuals experience change. But the evidence for therapeutic efforts to change sexual orientation or gender is not significant and unlikely to be analyzed (or researched) further due to polarization and ethical concerns with conducting such research.

In contrast, accumulating and converging biological evidence (Bogaert & Skorska, 2020) and objective studies (Gruia et al., 2022) suggest that sexual orientation is most likely predisposed before birth and can be grouped according to sexual attractions toward age and gender/sex: (a) sexual attractions exclusively to adult men (*androphilic monosexual*), (b) sexual attractions exclusively to adult women (*gynephilic monosexual*), (c) sexual attractions to adult men and women or gender fluid/nonbinary/expansive individuals (*ambiphilic, fluid, pansexual, bisexual, polysexual*, etc.), or (d) low/no sexual attractions to anyone (*asexual*). Some are predisposed to be sexually attracted to children, preadolescents, or elderly people (Seto, 2017).

These are not discrete categories and represent a continuum and intersections of attractions and aversions. For example, an individual's sexual orientation may be similar to or different from their romantic and emotional orientations (Schudson et al., 2017). The intensities of a person's sexual, romantic, and emotional attractions and aversions to femininity, masculinity, maleness, femaleness, androgyny, and gender-neutral traits and roles, as well as the person's socialization and cultural contexts, will influence their sexuality and gender expression (Abed et al., 2019).

We highlight below specific mechanisms of how sexual orientation and gender are likely predisposed differently for people before birth.

Prenatal Factors and Sexual Orientation

Current scientific hypotheses of the causes of sexual orientation involve interactions between genes, levels of sex hormones, immunological processes, and the cells of the developing body and brain during different critical periods of fetal development (LeVay, 2016). These variables indicate multiple steps and pathways where sexual orientation and gender development might diverge before and after birth and create differing processes, trajectories, and subgroups (VanderLaan et al., 2022).

Two large-scale, genome-wide association studies (Ganna et al., 2019; Zietsch et al., 2021) found a small (accounting for 8–25% of heritability) additive effect of a range of genes in engaging in sex with men versus women. Interestingly, some genetic variants were related to one's interest in same-gender partners, while another group was linked to openness or risk-tolerance traits (Diamond, 2021).

The prenatal hormone theory of sexual orientation, one of the better-supported biological explanations for sexual orientation, suggests that the degree of androgen (testosterone) exposure prenatally influences neural structures in the brain related to gender/sex partner attraction (Swift-Gallant et al., 2023). More exposure seems to predispose gynephilia (attraction to women/femaleness) and less exposure predisposes androphilia (attraction to men/maleness). Some individuals may have experienced hypo-androgenization prenatally, some experienced typical levels of androgens, others experienced hyper-androgenization, and some experienced both during development (Skorska & Bogaert, 2017).

Another reasonably well-supported idea for prenatal hormonal influence on sexual orientation centers on the fraternal birth order effect (FBOE). Having more older brothers seems to increase the chances of a cisgender man having a same-gender sexual orientation, and between 15 and 29% of same-gender-attracted cisgender men owe their sexual orientation to this older brother effect (Blanchard & Bogaert, 2004). It is hypothesized that mothers develop anti-androgens as an immune reaction from carrying multiple male fetuses. Exposing a male fetus to these anti-androgens alters the fetus's developing brain. Biochemical evidence for this hypothesis was found by comparing plasma from cisgender mothers with an adult gay cisgender son to plasma from cisgender women with no sons and plasma from cisgender men (Bogaert et al., 2018).

The FBOE has been shown in numerous cultures (for example, Gómez Jiménez et al., 2020), in androphilic transgender women (Bozkurt et al., 2015), and with mothers who had miscarriages (Ellis & Blanchard, 2001). A study in the Netherlands found evidence of a FBOE on cisgender women's same-sex sexuality (Ablaza et al., 2022). Other research suggests the FBOE may apply to bisexual cisgender men, although the biological mechanisms might differ (Apostolou, 2019; Blanchard, 2023).

Having more older brothers, being more gender nonconforming, and being left-handed (which is influenced by prenatal androgen exposure) are correlated with gay cisgender men and their preferred sex roles (Swift-Gallant et al., 2017). One study (Swift-Gallant et al., 2019) found four different pathways influencing a same-gender sexual orientation in cisgender men: elevated numbers of older brothers, greater degree of non-right-handedness, elevated gay or bisexual male relatives, and low levels of these biomarkers. These subgroups also differed on levels of gender expression and personality. Cisgender men without these biomarkers conformed the most to masculine gender roles. In contrast, cisgender men with greater numbers of older brothers reported more feminine gender-role expression and agreeableness.

Two strong biological correlations suggest that lesbian cisgender women have more masculinized inner ears and digit ratios (genetic males tend to have a more extended ring finger than their index finger, whereas genetic females show the opposite pattern) than exclusively heterosexual cisgender women (Breedlove, 2017). This digit ratio difference is found also in gay cisgender men and may be due to experiencing high and low levels of androgen prenatally (Manning et al., 2023).

Prenatal Factors and Gender Identity

Research indicates that gender identity can be masculinized by prenatal exposure to testosterone and feminized without it (Roselli, 2018). Gender dysphoria is associated with high levels of prenatal testosterone in individuals assigned female at birth and low levels in individuals assigned male at birth (Sadr et al., 2020). One report of triplets with gender dysphoria suggests a prenatal heritable role (Kauffman et al., 2022). Transgender individuals tend to have similar neuroanatomical, neurophysiological, and neurometabolic features as their experienced gender (Frigerio et al., 2021). However, strong conclusions can't be made, as Doug VanderLaan (personal communication, April 7, 2022) explained:

> The heterogenous sexual orientations of [the trans samples] muddle the interpretation. It is not clear whether the group differences are driven by gender identity or sexual orientation or some combination. Still . . . findings align with hypotheses that postulate trans individuals have a brain phenotype that is somehow intermediate to cis men and women or similar to opposite-sex cis individuals.

Environmental, Systemic, and Hormonal Factors

As you may have noted, some causes that predispose sexual orientation also affect gender identity. Although life experiences and socialization contribute to how we understand and express gender and what type of person we find sexually/romantically attractive, how this happens is complex (Pfaus et al., 2012) and still not well understood.

One or two weeks after birth, we typically experience a minipuberty that involves an output of hormonal changes from the gonads (Becker & Hesse, 2020). Between ages six and 11, many children experience their first sexual attractions and romantic crushes and initiate sex play. Middle childhood might be a time when some develop sexual fetishes (Del Giudice, 2014). Around ages 10 and 12, we experience a phase of sexual development when the adrenal glands release androgens. This adrenal puberty is responsible for pubic hair, body odor, skin oiliness, and acne and occurs during changes in children's cognitive development, which affect their motivation and social behaviors (Del Giudice, 2014). Some children experience this hormonal release at age eight or nine. Puberty, typically between the ages of 10 and 16, is another time of sexual maturation, hormonal changes, and social/systemic influences that affect motivations, gender/sexual identity development, and sexual scripts, depending on the person's temperament, predispositions, options, and circumstances.

Experience and Sexual Orientation

Freund and Blanchard (1993) stated that it is unlikely that we are born with preformed erotic images of women, men, or children. Instead, we are probably born with different sensitivities to particular classes of stimuli (for example, hairiness or smoothness, distinct body odors), and these sensitivities interact with experience to produce finished images of desired objects. Learning and conditioning processes can elaborate on orientation predispositions derived from genetic and prenatal origins. Some aspects of our sexual partners may inherently elicit arousal, but other attributes only do so after a sexual experience with them.

Conditioning is a form of learning that involves associating stimuli and behavior with something rewarding or aversive. Suppose we (repeatedly) experience a pleasant sexual interaction and orgasm with a particular individual. In that case, we may come to be sexually attracted to people who possess similar traits or characteristics. Mate characteristics more critical for successful reproduction (for example, species and sex/gender) may be less easily influenced by experience/conditioning than those less essential for successful reproduction (for example, skin or hair color). Moreover, as Jim Pfaus, a research expert on the role of learning in sexual behavior, has said regarding whom we desire for sex, "The first cut is the deepest." This means that earlier experiences with sexual reward are perhaps most powerful in shaping our later sexual preferences.

Some studies indirectly suggest a role for learning or conditioning in developing partner preference. For example, homogamy—matching of physical and personality characteristics between the other-gender parent and current sexual partner—has been observed with adoptive parents (Bereczkei et al., 2004). Such effects were moderated by the relationship quality with the other-gender parent, arguing against a strictly genetic basis for homogamy. Other studies (Little et al., 2002; Santtila et al., 2009) have found that early experience influences the age of partner preference. For example, men with early sexual experiences desired and had younger partners in adulthood. People born to older parents were more attracted to partners with older faces than those born to younger parents.

One study (Bickham et al., 2007) examined the effects of experience on the gender of partner preference. The researchers compared heterosexual cisgender women who were exclusively heterosexual in their behavior to cisgender women who were mostly heterosexual in behavior and found that experimenting sexually with women and masturbating using images of women before the age of 18 predicted sex contact with women, masturbating to images of women, fantasizing about a female sex partner when having sex with men, and voyeurism directed at women in adulthood. The researchers proposed that since the mostly heterosexual women experienced sexual attractions to men, and since early sexual behavior with men did not differ between the exclusively and mostly heterosexual women, their results argue for the role of sexual conditioning in some heterosexual women.

Another area of research that illustrates the impact of postnatal experiences, and perhaps conditioning, on who we find attractive is work on sexual fluidity. Changes, or fluidity, in sexual attraction can happen over time for some people. Most of the research has been on nonheterosexual cisgender women, but some studies show fluidity in heterosexual cisgender women and cisgender men, although, on average, cisgender women are more fluid than cisgender men (Norris et al., 2015). Some trans/nonbinary individuals report changes in their attractions after hormone/surgical interventions (Burns et al., 2022).

Despite changes in attraction patterns, most fluid people still have a core/stable identity, and when attractions fluctuate, they may do so within a broad range. That is, people became more nonexclusive in whom they found attractive. Little evidence exists that people can extinguish or eliminate existing attractions. When there are reports of intentional attempts to decrease attraction, negative consequences are described (for example, phobic reaction toward one's same gender). What experience/learning seems to allow for *some* people to do is expand the range of who and what they find attractive (Safron & Klimaj, 2022).

Lisa Diamond, who has done much of the work on sexual fluidity, suggested in her 2021 publication that the degree of variation in attraction patterns depends on two factors. The first is individual differences in how fluid people are. Some people may be more sexually conditionable than others, which may be due to their genetics. The second is differences in the likelihood of encountering triggers for fluidity. For example, if you interact with more women than men daily, you might experience stronger attraction toward women, at least temporarily. Also, the more you self-reflect on your attractions, perhaps due to encountering more sexual/gender diversity, the more you may be open to nonheterosexual interactions.

Experience and Gender Identity and Sexual Orientation

Gender identity development can involve cultural socialization of gender stereotypes (Qian et al., 2023) (media, parenting, peer interactions, etc.) interacting with a person's biology and vice versa (Fausto-Sterling, 2000). A few genital surgical mistakes on infants assigned male at birth and a few infants born with a malformed penis provided opportunities to test nature versus nurture effects (Bailey et al., 2016). These individuals' genitals were medically shaped female, and they were raised female; however, most experienced an internal male identity and sexual desires for women. These failed social experiments provide strong evidence that gender socialization has its limits on a person's predisposed gender expression and sexual orientation.

Regardless of rearing, one of the most robust predictors of a same-gender-attracted sexual orientation in adulthood is childhood nonstereotypic gender behavior (Xu et al., 2021). Freund (1974) emphasized, however, that a feminine gender identity is not necessary for the development of male same-gender sexuality and vice versa. Freund and Blanchard tested this in 1983. They found that the emotionally distant relationships of fathers and same-gender-attracted sons relate to the sons' atypical childhood gender expression rather than the sons' sexual attraction to males. Storms (1980) tested whether a gender/sex role or erotic orientation determines a person's sexual orientation. Storms's study suggests that sexual orientation does not necessarily involve gender identity or sex roles but depended on sexual fantasies and erotic feelings. Adults in this study with different sexual orientations did not differ significantly on measures of masculinity and femininity. Rahman et al. (2020) compared the prevalence of different sexual orientations across 28 nations and found that gender norms, roles, and socialization did not affect sexual orientation prevalence rates.

Regarding making a person transgender, some people who detransition and identify again with their birth-assigned sex report that their understanding of gender and sexuality changed after identifying as transgender and that they did not receive adequate evaluation and education from a doctor or mental health professional before transitioning (Littman, 2021). They describe their trans identification as due to bias, stigma, and misunderstanding and from personalizing narratives that "transition will be the answer to all your problems" and learning how to lie to providers for access to medical transitioning (Thomas, 2022). Some report experiencing significant trauma or harassment for being their assigned birth sex and felt great discomfort in their body and assigned gender role (Atlantic, 2018). Some preferred the social rules and activities of another gender, felt more accepted in trans/nonbinary community networks, and disliked the social rules and activities of their same-sex friend-ships. After learning about the positive experiences of others who transitioned, they believed they would feel better identifying as trans and another gender and having a different body (Pique Resilience Project, n.d.). Some regretted socially transitioning and taking steps medically to change their body. They wished they had been supported in understanding their gender distress and exploring a wide range of gender expression and identity.

It is clear that we need more information about the variety of youth who report gender incongruence and fluidity and the various sources of their dis-tress. We cannot lump all youth who report gender diversity and what helps them into the same category. We currently do not know which individual and social characteristics, if any, determine if a gender-diverse child will maintain or change their gender identity. Above all, the experiences and needs of youth and adults who desist or detransition do not invalidate the experiences and needs of the broad spectrum of gender-diverse youth and adults and vice versa.

Similarly, anecdotal reports and fears exist that some heterosexual youth are being misled into falsely identifying as LGBQ+ to feel a sense of belonging because of the increased popularity of and support for sexual/gender diversity in their social media and environments. Others attribute the trend of LGBQ+ identification to social conditions providing more information about the spec-trum of nonexclusive attractions and allowing sexually nonexclusive youth, especially those assigned female at birth (fluid, pansexual, mostly or primarily heterosexual, etc.) another option besides identifying as exclusively hetero-sexual (Savin-Williams, 2021). In fact, despite media claims, adolescent sexual identification has remained stable, with only individuals assigned female identi-fying more as bisexual or unsure (Mittleman, 2023). As with gender diversity, the public needs accurate education about sexual diversity to help youth and adults understand and label themselves accurately.

Other System Factors

Regarding peer influence, social networks seem to have little or no effect on an individual experiencing heterosexual or same-gender attractions. However, social networks may increase youth's sexual activity and desire to have a romantic relationship (Brakefield et al., 2014). While some youth who attend single-sex secondary schools may have increased same-gender sexual experi-mentation, school settings (single-sex vs. coeducational) do not seem to affect their present or ideal sexual orientation (Li & Wong, 2018).

Some believe that bad parenting can make children LGBTQ+. Richard Lippa, research expert on gender, described (personal communication, Octo-ber 16, 2023) the limited likelihood of parental influence on children:

Parents are probably naive and overly optimistic in their expectations about "teaching" and modeling for their children various personality traits, interests, morals/values, sex-typed behaviors, attitudes, etc. And, when they do take credit for such things, they typically ignore the fact that their biological children inherit half their genes by descent from them—that is, the additive effects of parents on children are much more likely to be genetic than social-environmental effects, in many domains.

Research demonstrates that parents' social influence on their children is weak, including the influence of parents' sexual identity on their child's sexual orientation, while the parents' genetics have a strong influence (Bailey et al., 2016; Lippa, 2016; Turkheimer, 2000).

Sexual trauma can influence sexual/gender development and behavior (Rosario & Schrimshaw, 2008). For example, sexually abused boys are likelier than nonabused boys to experience risky sexual behaviors (Lloyd & Operario, 2012). Sexual/gender minority (SGM) individuals are more likely than heterosexual, gender-conforming individuals to be sexually abused (Kalichman et al., 2014). There are explanations for this. For instance, SGM youth tend to be more socially marginalized and rejected and, therefore, in more search of connection than heterosexual, gender-conforming youth. They also likely can't tell anybody about their sexual experiences. These factors converge to make SGM youth more vulnerable and susceptible to perpetrators. Furthermore, childhood sexual abuse can occur for many youth in general before the age of awareness of sexual feelings (Struve et al., 2018). The perpetrator's sexual dynamics can eclipse the child's psychosexual development and leave an early imprint. Attractions and behaviors may be conditioned with flashbacks, adrenaline, anxiety, disgust, shame, anger, and helplessness. Trauma can cause reactive, compulsive sexuality, and such behaviors and feelings could be misunderstood and mislabeled as "homosexuality," "gay/lesbian," or "same-sex attractions." These posttraumatic stress effects may influence the intensity of sexual arousal and phobia and inhibit the child and later adult from freely exploring their sexual orientation and gender expression. Any or all of these factors could be why some believe their sexual abuse caused them to be gay/lesbian/bisexual (Brady, 2008).

People who have a bisexual, pansexual, fluid, mostly straight/gay, and plurisexual+ orientation who are sexually assaulted may have the most challenging time differentiating their trauma-reactive sexuality from their predisposed sexual orientation. Society's binary hierarchy of heterosexuality versus same-gender sexuality and lack of safe outlets for exploration and polysexual affirmation can inhibit their sexual and gender development.

Some individuals believe it is a choice to be a sexual/gender minority. Importantly, Lisa Diamond notes that people who experience sexual fluidity do not see it as choosing their attractions but rather that, in encountering triggers for fluidity, more cognitive openness can lead to more psychological and physical openness. We can decide how we think about, express, and label our sexual orientation and gender. Some of us have more privilege in how and where we express these aspects of ourselves. Above all, it seems like there is a natural limit to how much control we have over these essential aspects of ourselves and others.

Conclusion

The health of individuals who are sexual/gender minorities and those who are exclusively cis-heterosexual will likely improve as we individually and collectively develop more ability to stay engaged instead of reactive with each other. We are all on the same side of trying to figure out all there is to learn about gender and sexuality and experience safety and peace about these issues. We encourage readers to take time to understand and examine their attitudes and reactions so that they can have humanizing dialogues with individuals who have differing experiences, views, and political affiliations. Which behaviors will stop and heal the injustices and traumas about gender/sexuality that have been and are being done?

- Are your attitudes and actions about sexual/gender diversity connecting, disconnecting, liberating, resisting, harming, repairing, disrupting, healing, or something else? What impact and effect do you hope for in response? And then what?
- Are you, I, we seeking win-win, equitable, and nonhierarchical systems for all (secure pluralistic communities that collaborate and promote compassion, self-determination, and health)? If not, why not? What do you think is safer and more effective? What is the end goal?

Affirmative approaches, when not used aggressively but assertively, can reduce prejudice, violence, phobias, and confusion about sexual/gender diversity and promote liberation from false information and discrimination. Affirmative efforts are needed to counteract stigma and oppression experienced historically, internally, and socially and promote well-being for all. Because of the above, we encourage readers to focus on developing collaborative and compassionate agendas about sexual/gender diversity to reduce minority stress and culture wars. What comes to your mind regarding collaborative and compassionate agendas about sexual/gender diversity coexisting with cis-heteronormativity (win-win solutions) for now and the future?

Chapter 3

Develop Emotional Health

A. Lee Beckstead, Kristina Pham, and Lauren Wadsworth[1]

O ur emotional health is influenced by how we evaluate ourselves. We develop these self-definitions in response to how we are socialized and how others think about and treat us (Benjamin, 2018; Singh, 2019). Suffering and fearing rejection, attack, and exclusion for social differences is called stigma stress or minority stress. Internalized stigma related to one's identity can feel like believing you are inferior and defective compared to others. These negating self-beliefs can vary in strength and sometimes be subtle and unconscious (*I wish I weren't me, I'm worthless, I should be like others*). Internalized stigma can often result in self-directed feelings of dislike, shame, guilt, and disgust. This self-rejection impacts emotional health and influences coping behaviors.

We hope this chapter counteracts the effects of internalized stigma on readers' self-definitions and emotional well-being by describing which responses to stigma, shame, and stress are more effective, depending on context. Similarly, readers will learn how to develop self-acceptance and how self-compassion is an affirmative response to social and internalized stigma. Given LGBTQIA+ individuals' exposure to stigma and difficulties in finding safety, this chapter begins by discussing what impedes safety and how we can create safety.

Safety Issues

Experiencing a minoritized but rising identity[2] often involves social safety and emotional health issues. For example, LGB+ youth who experienced harassment

---

[1] Jake Camp, DClinPsy, contributed significantly to this chapter, especially the sections on minority stress and self-acceptance. He ended coauthorship before publication and did not review the final content.

[2] "Rising identities" is a term coined by Dr. Melanie Tervalon (codeveloper of the cultural humility practice) that shifts the frame from "marginalized" to a more empowering/strengths-based lens.

and bullying can be six times more likely to contemplate suicide than their heterosexual peers (Ybarra et al., 2015). Trans+ youth are eight times more likely to consider and attempt suicide than their cisgender peers (Kingsbury et al., 2022). Trans+ youth in Thailand, for example, who were rejected by their families and lack social support are much more likely to consider and attempt suicide (Yadegarfard et al., 2014). LGBTQ-identified young adults raised in traditionally religious contexts tend to have higher odds of chronic suicidal thoughts and suicide attempts than other LGBTQ young adults, and internalized stigma accounts for a significant portion of that distress (Gibbs & Goldbach, 2015). A study involving Filipino lesbian women and gay men (Reyes et al., 2017) found that suicidal behaviors increased due to both experienced stigma and internalized stigma, with current levels of experienced stigma as the strongest predictor of suicidal behavior. Filipino lesbians were more at risk, likely due to sexual minority women being exposed to additional discrimination and victimization. For transgender veterans, trans-specific discrimination and rejection increased their internalized shame, thereby increasing the frequency of their suicidal ideation (Tucker et al., 2019).

These experiences of being rejected, bullied, harassed, or attacked for existing as themselves and not being supported are, sadly, unavoidable for many LGBTQIA+ individuals. A strong part of the invalidating sociopolitical environment tells LGBTQIA+ individuals that they need to change and that their suffering is their fault for being different. A compassionate response to these experiences, however, requires actions and social changes beyond individual coping skills and self-care (Brewster et al., 2013). For example, trans+ individuals in Canada who experienced strong support were 82% less likely to attempt suicide than those without support (Bauer et al., 2015). Protective suicidal factors for trans+ youth include experiencing positive social interactions and having timely access to interventions (McNeil et al., 2017). While one goal of this chapter is to provide tools for individuals to improve their safety and emotional well-being, these studies demonstrate the profound positive impact of not being forced to face such a journey alone. When discrimination is high, even family support is helpful up to a certain point (Lee et al., 2023).

We strongly encourage you to approach this material with a compassionate eye toward what is realistic for your circumstances and ability and remember that minoritized groups are not responsible for "solving" "their" minoritization. Structural social changes need to occur that provide social safety and protect LGBTQIA+ youth and adults from harm.

For example, English et al. (2018) examined the effects of racism and sexual minority stigma on the lives of Black, Latino, and multiracial gay and bisexual men in the United States. They found that racial discrimination and high levels of rejection sensitivity related to their gay/bisexual identity reduced these men's ability to regulate their emotions and increased the likelihood of anxiety and depression. This distress made them more likely to engage in heavy alcohol use. Chronic invalidation increased their emotional arousal, sensitivity, and need to disengage (Kauth, 2022). The study's authors recommended preventative and response measures that include the following:

1. Train educators, clinicians, leaders, and parents to lead discussions and activities to aid youth in reflection and social action to understand and resolve societal oppression.
2. Reduce prejudice through extended positive contact and alliances to improve connections within desegregated school-peer environments.
3. Empower individuals to know how to regulate and process emotions after experiences of trauma and stigma.
4. Promote emotional exploration and take a culturally competent, person-centered approach.
5. Consider the positive and resilient aspects of intersecting social identities, as these cultural and personal strengths can buffer stress and stigma (Bowleg et al., 2016).

Given the challenges of working with others who differ politically, this chapter's coauthors[3] considered how they could create safety for one another. We also wanted to provide suggestions for readers to use during difficult conversations about sexual/gender diversity. We hope these guidelines address power imbalances and prejudice and promote respect and curiosity for differences:

- Assume good intentions and let the person know if there's a disagreement.
- Be open, curious, and respectful when disagreeing and expressing different viewpoints.
- Take time to self-reflect between having a knee-jerk reaction and a response.
- Take time to acknowledge, sit with, and process discomfort.
- Realize limitations, get rest, and consider other viewpoints.
- Treat others civilly and trust that criticism of anything one writes or suggests may be given constructively.
- Do your best not to take things personally or unduly make them about you.
- Check in periodically to ensure our process works well and adjust if needed.

Jake Camp, DClinPsy (he/they; a former coauthor), suggested we adopt a Zen and dialectical philosophy to cocreate a safe and productive environment. They described this philosophy as adopting an attitude that fosters acceptance and living by one's values, that champions the idea that there are and always will be multiple (potentially opposing) perspectives and no one perspective is the whole truth. This philosophy aims for synthesis when faced with differing views and promotes understanding and appreciation of one another's experiences and opinions. A synthesis is not the middle ground, which is a common

---

[3] The following includes guidelines from former coauthors who contributed earlier in the process.

misconception. Rather than it being the gray when one person is thinking black and the other white, a synthesis is like a checkerboard or spiral of black and white (Linehan, 1993). In other words, a synthesis is not a compromise of the two views but an integration, joining, or blending that allows a way forward. Importantly, this also guides us to be nonjudgmental, unattached to outcome, and in the present moment. Such Zen and dialectical processes nurture understanding of the world and the viewpoints of others (whether we agree or not or even if we agree and disagree simultaneously). From this perspective, we recognize we are all fallible and will make mistakes, that we are not expected to be consistent with one another, that we seek a synthesis when differences threaten to divide the group, and that we always know we are exactly where we are meant to be in any given moment.

Regarding safety in reading this chapter, we want to caution you that thinking about negative self-beliefs and past events can be painful. So feel free to skip any questions and self-reflections and go at your speed. Although we don't want to encourage avoidance of considering how these experiences may have affected you, we want to prioritize self-kindness and self-care to respect your current bandwidth.

Understanding the Costs of Minority Stress and Trauma to Emotional Health

Youth is a time to learn how to socialize, date, and negotiate gender in daily life and public spaces (Perez-Brumer et al., 2020). Most sexually/gender-diverse (SGD) youth, however, are learning how to hide, suppress, and lie to avoid discrimination, rejection, and attack. SGD youth may feel—or fear becoming—outcast in their family and community and have no guide, mentors, or connection to an affirming community to learn self-acceptance and how to navigate a stigmatized identity (Hendricks, 2022). This marginalization and structural disregard (Saraff et al., 2022) leave SGD youth vulnerable to prejudice, bullying, and victimization and a greater risk for depression, posttraumatic stress, substance abuse, loneliness, and suicidality than their exclusively heterosexual, cisgender peers (Day et al., 2017; Johns et al., 2020).

Experiences of minority stress and victimization can be experienced as *societal invalidation* (Cardona et al., 2022) and *queer pain* (rejection for being sexually/gender different). Any difference where you do not fit the expected picture of cis-heteronormativity will likely be less understood and thus less validated and more teased, harassed, or bullied. Invalidation may include messages like "You don't like dolls, they're for girls," "You shouldn't walk that way," and "This is just a phase you're going through." While invalidation is not specific to SGD individuals, they will have increased exposure to invalidation associated with their diversity, alongside everyday invalidation experienced by the majority. This chronic excess invalidation makes it challenging for SGD youth and adults to understand and value their internal experiences and who they are in relation to the world. Chronic invalidation results in internalizing invalidation (*Something is wrong with me*). Societal invalidation and self-invalidation make it difficult to express our needs to others, making it more likely that others will further invalidate us. When we conceal our gender and sexuality, others will likely reinforce our concealment and validate this version of our expression while accidentally (or perhaps purposely) invalidating our authentic self. Fears regarding authenticity can lead to avoiding circumstances that could lead to acceptance. All this impacts well-being and the ability to find validation and provide self-validation.

If you want to spend time with self-reflection, here are some questions to consider:

- How much do the above descriptions of minority stress and trauma relate or not relate to you?
- How would you describe your emotional experiences growing up with social (un)safety, (in)validation, discrimination, and understanding of yourself and your sexuality/gender?
- What did you most need growing up about sexuality and your gender?
- What helped you survive your childhood and feel good about yourself?

One study (Nicholson et al., 2022) found that minority-stress exposure is associated with changes in the Default-Mode Network of sexual minority individuals, the brain area affecting our sense of self and social beliefs. This research suggests that minority stress affects us similarly to how adverse life stressors, relational traumas, and traumatic events can have lasting harmful effects (Herzog & Schmahl, 2018). One harm results in negative self-beliefs (cognitive closures/distortions). We can develop these thinking traps and emotional wounds not just from minority stress but also from the small rejections to the big traumas that many can experience. Here are some examples of negative self-beliefs from life stressors (Shapiro, 2017):

- *I don't exist/matter; my needs/feelings don't matter.*
- *I'm not safe; I'm going to be annihilated.*
- *I'm powerless and have no choices.*
- *I'm bad, ugly, defective, and responsible (inadequate, not good enough).*
- *I'm broken/a freak/damaged.*
- *I'm not worthy of care.*
- *I'm different, inferior, and don't belong.*

When triggered, negating self-beliefs cause distressing emotions and human reflexes to control distress (for example, attack, avoid, fawn, ruminate, dissociate, collapse).

Danielle Spratley[4] described how trauma affects our mind-body, emotions, and relationships in this way:

> One thing that comes up for me is how fear lives in the body after trauma and how the (my) body feels uneasy in (relative) safety and love because it's waiting for the next trauma—and so, when it comes, it compounds on all the other trauma that lives there and still neeeds to be exorcised. And this turns safety and love into things to be feared, because they are distractions from the vigilance my body lives in. It is one way (my) fear makes the (my) body pliable to trauma and makes connection and belonging seem like danger.

A colleague of coauthor Beckstead, Sandra Forti, described the costs of trauma, minority stress, and general stress in this way (personal communication, May 17, 2021):

> Neuroscientists have identified in the last few years the brain's Default-Mode Network and how much that area of the brain creates or carries our sense of self but also causes a "constricting knot" when it informs us in limiting and biased ways. Identity and self-worth informed by distorted reflections and categorical rejections by caregivers, family members, peers, abusers, and/or culture can create deeply held beliefs in one's worth. These negative beliefs can limit psychological growth and restrict the development of a value system that enhances one's life.
>
> This self-limiting "knot" exists in the mind and is lived in the body and keeps the focus on trauma and survival. The idea of "loosening the knot" is that we need to change that Default-Mode Network to free ourselves from the conclusions we came to due to the trauma of living from our authentic self. Freedom from this focus allows the discovery of a true self that can generate values and actions that are flexible and congruent with an evolving self. Developing a mind-body connection and an evolving meta-view of life, existence, and humanity or, in other words, a spiritual perspective appear to be essential features of this healing and self-developmental process.

Self-negating reactions and adaptations are similar to how misinformation can be programmed and stored in a computer. There's nothing wrong with the computer. It's doing its function. Similarly, the mind-body can do many wonderful things, and we all have unique genetics and temperament in responding to life. The "bad" programming and stress cause problems, not the operating system, computer, or person. Another analogy is considering how food lacking nutrition can affect the body's functions. But lack of equity in resources leaves many unable to buy food, let alone nutritious food. To improve functioning, we must separate what we put into the mind-body from the mind-body itself.

In contrast to minority stress and trauma, feeling good about ourselves involves developing self-affirming beliefs (Pittinsky et al., 2011) and feeling them on an embodied level. Research shows that simply having fewer or less

---

[4] Quoted on https://www.whitesupremacyculture.info/fear.html.

intense negative attitudes about sexual/gender diversity is not the same as having affirming attitudes (Mayfield, 2001). To feel good about ourselves, we must examine self-negating internalized beliefs while cultivating internal affirmation.

We invite you to pause and consider how much you relate to the above. Here are other questions and actions to consider, at your own pace:

- Which self-negating beliefs affect you the most, where do you feel these beliefs in your body, and how strongly do you feel this way about yourself? What's your understanding of when and from whom you learned to think this way about yourself?
- How do these self-negating beliefs affect your internal state, body, and coping? How much do they inform your daily activities?
- What would you prefer to believe about yourself, including what you wish you had heard when you learned the negative self-belief(s)? If someone you cared about thought this way about themselves, how would you want them to respond to themselves? How would they need to think about themselves to respond to themselves in this caring way? You may not believe the positive self-belief, so what would you prefer your future self believes? Which self-beliefs empower you? Here are a few examples: *I have worth and add value, I'm different and belong, I'm okay/fine as I am, I'm equal to others, I just am* (Litt, 2016), *I did the best I could with what I had, Their reactions are not about me, I'm responsible for my well-being, I can trust myself, My body belongs to me, I'm worthy of care, I can now make choices that fit best for me* (Benjamin, 2018).
- When you express self-affirming beliefs to yourself, what impact do you notice on yourself, if any?
- Do you notice any internal blocks or resistance to describing yourself in this affirming way? If so, consider acknowledging this reaction as having a function in the past (and maybe still in the present or future) to protect you. Consider allowing this reaction as you reaffirm what you would prefer to believe about yourself, even if you want to believe you are learning a new way to think about yourself. This self-affirmation is not about making you feel a certain way but providing self-direction, similar to living by your chosen values. If you have the bandwidth, consider exploring the fears you have of not thinking about yourself in the old way and how valid they are currently. What do you need from yourself and others to think about yourself in the affirming way?
- Which actions can you take to reinforce your preferred empowering self-beliefs, values, well-being, and connections with others?

Research suggests that minority stress and trauma can disconnect a person from others (Mereish & Poteat, 2015) through the following structural-systemic, institutional, community, familial, and interpersonal processes (Pachankis & Safren, 2019):

- Prejudice, stigmatization, invalidations, marginalization, (fear of) harassment, attack, or ostracization

- Lack of social safety, inclusion, and positive options and role models
- For gender-diverse individuals, sexism, transmisogyny, cisgenderism, gender-performative stress, gender-role dysphoria, social dysphoria (misgendering), inadequate health care, and no access to congruent bathrooms, among others

Minority stress and trauma disconnect a person from their self via these internal processes:

- Internalized self-stigma, self-rejection, self-shame, self-blame, self-attack, and self-neglect
- Stigma consciousness, anticipation of and vulnerability to discrimination and victimization, expectations of rejection, vicarious stress, rejection sensitivity, feelings of being a burden and not belonging, acceptance concerns, need for acceptance
- Insecure attachment, fear and avoidance of intimacy, preoccupation about earning intimacy
- Contingent self-worth
- Negative body image, disordered eating
- Distrust with and dissociation from one's body, feelings, needs, limits, and desires
- Identity harm, conflicts, concealment, inauthenticity, and uncertainty
- Worrying and ruminating about rejection, attack, and appeasing
- Hypervigilance/monitoring, social anxiety, and generalized anxiety
- Emotional dysregulation, anxiety, and depression
- Avoidant coping
- Loneliness
- Sleep difficulties
- Substance abuse/disorder to disengage from rejection, self-rejection, and anxiety/depression
- Sexual behaviors that put the person's health at risk
- Moral distress and loss of one's spiritual center and meaning and purpose in life

Bourn et al. (2018) suggest that the best predictor of suicidality (the ultimate disconnection from self and others) is insufficient coping resources to handle emotional suffering from self-rejection.

- We invite you to pause and consider which of the above minority/trauma stressors impact you and which ones you have resolved or are developing resilience to cope with.

Overall, when we are seen as "the other" and discriminated against, this takes a toll on our body's stress inflammation and causes wear and tear and "weathers" our bodies. This *weathering hypothesis* (Diamond et al., 2021) helps explain how chronic invalidation, lack of social safety, and disconnection from self and others affect our stress levels, emotional coping, and bodies.

Any action and resources that help us connect to ourselves, our body, and others can help liberate us from oppression and self-rejection and help our bodies and communities be more resilient. Next, we highlight some principles and options that might help you connect to yourself and others and be more resilient to life's challenges.

Coping With Stress and Minority Stress

The Buddha taught that suffering, pain, loss, and vulnerability are normal aspects of being human. Life can be difficult, unsatisfying, and uncertain. It's normal also for us to judge and stay attached to our expectations of how life *should be*. Labeling normal life stress as "clean stress" and differentiating it from the "dirty distress" that we create may help us recognize and accept what we can't and can control (at least in the moment) and reduce our suffering (Hayes & Strosahl, 2004).

We create "dirty distress" by rejecting ourselves, others, reality, life, and everyday stress. Here are some examples:

- Criticizing, berating, or hating ourselves or others for acting a certain way
- Taking responsibility for others' feelings and distress that we did not cause
- Blaming ourselves when others are upset by their insecurity or judgments about us
- Feeling bad when we can't act perfectly and make people happy or not angry
- Avoiding rejection by sacrificing what we like and doing what others do or want
- Judging ourselves as inferior or weak when we experience stress and can't "fix it"
- Ruminating and worrying about rejection and what is out of our control
- Neglecting self-care, including not nurturing our body, interests, and meaning in life
- Suffering from addictions

Being emotionally triggered is normal, human, and "clean stress." Our immediate reactions to triggers are outside our control unless we avoid or coerce situations. But avoidance reinforces incompetence and prejudice. Trying to control something outside our control results in anxiety, frustration, and depression. Panic attacks are an example of "clean" and "dirty" distress. They happen when we hyperfocus on, misinterpret, fear, and fight physical sensations (*I can't handle this, What's wrong with me, I have to control this, I'm going to die*) and add tension and threat to an activated nervous system that might already be overstressed, instead of calming and reassuring ourselves.

Our negating reactions may come from our human reflexes, cognitive distortions (thinking traps, prejudice), need for significance, and how we have coped previously. For example, we may want to figure out and know why something stressful is happening or why someone acts a certain way. Some may blame themselves or others to feel some control and relevance and make sense of what they can't understand (for example, *If my child is gay, I must have done something to cause it*; *If that person is upset about my gender expression/ sexuality, I must have caused it*).

We invite you to pause and reflect on the following:

- What are your reactions to what you just read? What fits and does not fit with your experiences and others you know?
- What happens in your body and mind when you are emotionally triggered by rejection?
- Notice how you judge and react to your experiences, triggers, and different types of life stress and how this judgment affects your experience.
- If you were to describe the primary cognitive closures/thinking traps and ways you create "dirty distress," which labels would you give them?
- How well can you differentiate your experience of "clean stress" from your judgments and self-negation?
- How do you want to feel about yourself, life, and others during "clean stress" and "dirty distress"?
- Which values and empowering self-beliefs and behaviors do you want to reinforce?

Acknowledging and accepting "clean stress" and taking responsibility for our happiness may help us refocus on what's essential and realistic to live through "clean stress." Accepting and adapting to "clean stress" can help us grow from adversity (*How can I learn from and use this?*). Being open and curious about the present moment (*I don't know if this is good or bad; I wonder what will happen*) (Ballard, 2021) keeps us alert and safer than narrowing our perspective with judgments.

Acceptance during emotionally difficult moments comes from developing **psychological flexibility** (Hayes et al., 2004; Matos et al., 2017), which is the ability and intention to (a) notice when we are emotionally triggered and (b) regulate our breathing to (c) acknowledge the facts of the moment and (d) assess and understand the present situation to (e) make a decision based on our values, needs, and current resources. Psychological flexibility allows us to tolerate stressful situations instead of avoid them and refocus on what we want, can do, are responsible for, and hope will help the future.

Research suggests that developing psychological flexibility can reduce believability of negative thoughts about sexual orientation (Yadavaia & Hayes, 2012) and reduce shame and work stress for sexual minorities (Singh & O'Brien, 2019). The opposite is psychological inflexibility (thinking traps, prejudice), which causes avoidance of stigma-inducing events (Matos et al., 2017). **Experiential avoidance** can have more influence on a person's depression than their negative self-stigma (Gold & Marx, 2007).

More "clean stress" will likely happen. Which life challenges and minority stressors are you most afraid of facing? Developing a life philosophy, intended purpose, and new skills to respond to stress may help you feel more confident and trust your ability to handle what comes.

Adapting to "Clean" Minority Stress and Reducing "Dirty" Minority Distress

Minority stress is a mix of "clean" and "dirty" distress. For example, being a sexual/gender minority individual means meeting fewer similar people to date and connect with (clean stress). Many social systems block safe social outlets and opportunities (clean stress). Being alone can involve the clean stress of boredom and lack of support and wanting to share our experiences with someone (Litt, 2016). Being alone can also trigger shame from believing we are a failure, unlovable, or not good enough (dirty distress). Our judgments about being alone and different cause increased suffering. Clean stress is difficult enough. Blame and shame can help us feel some control, predictability, and relevance but add more distress when unjustified, misplaced, and disempowering.

We each have our "pile/burden" of clean stress. Some of us have a larger pile/burden and some a smaller pile/burden due to any of the following life circumstances:

- The time/location/community in which we were born
- Our parents' personal and intergenerational traumas, resilience, genetics, temperament, and social status and their/our upbringing
- Historical and current social advantages and disadvantages
- The mistakes our caregivers and we made and make and will continue to make
- The accidents, traumas, and illnesses that happen to our loved ones and us
- The pain of rejection, aging, loss, grief, and more

As mentioned, being a sexual/gender minority individual involves clean stress. Here are examples:

- Exclusively heterosexual, cisgender individuals comprise most of our families and communities. They will likely not fully relate to and understand our sexual/gender experiences and may have untreated shame about their stigmatized experiences. Because we are a social minority, it will be normal to be the only sexually/gender-diverse individual in the room or group.
- Some on the bisexual/fluid/pansexual spectrum may believe others can choose to deny their same-gender attractions and flourish.
- Betrayal and loss are painful when family and community members reject and don't support us.
- Integrating and resolving cultural, religious, family, and personal conflicts is complicated.

- Being a minority means forging our own path, even if it conforms to social norms.
- Same-gender/queer couples may need to grieve not having biological children with the one(s) they love and need more effort and support to raise children.
- For some, gender-body dysphoria and social dysphoria are persistent and distressing.

These challenges also include our existential powerlessness and aloneness. No matter how much we try to change life, ourselves, and others, we still have little control and are alone with specific issues. Differentiating clean stress from dirty distress may help you examine what is true and not true about yourself and life—or at least acknowledge what you/we don't know.

Understanding Coping Options and Outcomes

In general, we have three coping tasks during a stressful situation: survive it, regulate our emotions, and solve the problem, if possible (Stanisławski, 2019). How we cope will depend on our temperament and resources, and what we were taught about what a problem is and what to do about problems and emotions. Many cultures, social institutions, parents, and individuals reinforce that same-gender sexuality and trans/nonbinary expressions are a problem to stop or fix. Others reinforce that traditional religions and conservative cultures are a problem to stop or fix. How each group copes with the threat and stress from the other group reinforces "culture wars" that never resolve. This negating interpersonal dynamic is termed "turning against" in relationship counseling terms (Lisitsa, 2023). *Turning-against coping* can occur between two people in a relationship and within a person (for example, an inner critic using shame to motivate the person to be perfect). The "problem" is not solved because it is the wrong problem. Unjustified blame, neglect, violence, and disconnection are the problems, and emotions continue to get dysregulated. Similarly, we may get stuck or feel helpless, demoralized, and exhausted repeating the same reactions and not know more effective ways to respond to stress, including minority stress.

Stanisławski (2019) developed a coping circumplex/scale for stress that identifies four coping strategies: (1) being problem focused, (2) being problem avoidant, (3) using negative emotional coping, and (4) using positive emotional coping. Stanisławski found these coping strategies combined predictably to end in four possible outcomes:

1. *Effectiveness* comes from problem-focused, emotionally affirming, and person-centered strategies. Examples include dividing complex problems into realistic goals; seeing the big picture and context; thinking creatively about a problem; using your strengths and values to address problems;

acknowledging, accepting, and respecting limits and needs and adapting (grieving); using anger to protect and set limits; developing self-acceptance and self-compassion; examining shame/guilt and reinforcing accurate self-beliefs; seeking support; appreciating yourself when you accomplish a goal; giving yourself and others room to be human and make mistakes; recognizing you and others are more than mistakes; seeking collaboration and win-win solutions; and ending a toxic relationship and seeking others for mutual connection.

2. *Preoccupation* comes from problem-focused, emotionally and personally negating, and defensive strategies. Examples include reinforcing binary, all-or-nothing options; denying a part of reality; minimizing/dismissing needs/limits; blaming yourself and trying to fix something out of your control; being frustrated about what is happening; wanting revenge and holding a grudge; staying hypervigilant as a way to protect yourself; shaming yourself or another into submitting to expectations; belittling someone to build up yourself, focusing only on the negative aspects of a situation or person (venting and complaining); hating someone or something you can't change; replaying in your mind mistakes and rejection; taking responsibility for how others think of you; seeking external validation; trying to get approval from people who cannot give it; comparing yourself unfairly to others; and getting angry at yourself for doing the same coping.

3. *Helplessness* comes from problem-avoidant, emotionally and personally negating, and defensive strategies. Examples include avoiding triggers; not taking responsibility and accountability for your needs, limits, and actions; concluding you must be unlucky or cursed; thinking about suicide; and disengaging from others and your needs.

4. *Pleasure/joy/hedonia* comes from problem-avoidant, emotionally positive, and disengaged strategies. Examples include using distraction or humor to transcend difficult moments, taking a break from distress, and using food and other substances to feel better.

Using substances and distractions continually to avoid problems and difficult emotions results in preoccupation, addiction, and helplessness. In contrast, Stanisławski (2019) defined positive emotional coping to solve a problem as "being kind and understanding to oneself as one tries to solve a problem on one's own regardless of success and the use of cognitive transformations that enable the elicitation of positive emotions and calming down (through reinterpretation and humor)" (p. 9).

Developing an Assertive/Affirmative Response to Distress and Minority Stress

Understanding Stanisławski's coping options can increase our awareness not of how a person is broken or deficient but of how the systems are broken and deficient and of how the person is responding is ineffective. It's not about the person; it's about the coping methods they learned and adapted to and how social systems affect them, which is a normal human concern. We may also be mistaken about "the problem" and "the solution." What do you think is the problem to solve when you're rejected and discriminated against? Gain people's approval, educate them, change their minds, avoid them, attack them to feel better, attack yourself to act better, use substances to disengage, find other supports, or address the shame you may feel believing something is wrong with you?

Suppose we want to respond from the most humane part of our brain during stress, including minority stress and conflict. In that case, we need to learn and practice coping skills that help us engage, connect, and turn our attention to ourselves and others. This means using acknowledgment, acceptance, curiosity, compassion, and creativity to help us adapt and grow.

We adapted Stanisławski's coping circumplex to apply to coping options for minority stress. We'll use *assertive/affirmative coping* to describe problem-focused, emotionally engaging, person-affirming strategies that involve turning toward the problem, accepting reality as it is, and promoting diversity. Assertive/affirmative coping involves acting lovingly and powerfully toward ourselves and others and doing behaviors that help us connect with ourselves and others. Examples include valuing aspects of ourselves that others cannot or don't; connecting to our truth about ourself to reject what is being falsely projected on us; and using humor to respond to absurdity with absurdity, get perspective, and disempower abusive power (Truszczynski et al., 2022). Coping assertively to stress and affirmatively to minority stress means a person wants to add to reality instead of deny, fight, prevent, or overcome reality. Assertive/affirmative coping provides an emergent process (brown, 2017) of openness, authenticity, validation, and discovery (*possibilities thinking*) (Ginwright, 2022) rather than being controlled and restricted by expectations.

In contrast, *aggressive coping* refers to using negative coping, being expectation focused, and hating yourself and others for being different. Examples of turning-against efforts include trying to stop feelings, violating your or another person's limits and personhood, shaming another person or yourself into compliance and thinking/feeling a certain way, pushing yourself or another person to accomplish more to prove worth, forcing an experience or coercing a relationship to meet expectations, and trying to change yourself or another person. These aggressive efforts typically result in disconnection, preoccupation, insecurity, and burnout.

Passive/avoidant coping applies to disengaging and turning away from a situation/problem, others, and ourselves. People can be outward facing for validation and direction and surrender their power to others, resulting in exploitation, helplessness, disappointment, and resentment. We can distract ourselves from thinking negatively, but this does not help us develop more self-affirming and self-empowering ways to think and act (Huynh & Lee, 2023).

Passive-aggressive coping may occur when a person has limited power to confront someone or change a situation but feels responsible and tries to gain control indirectly. Passive-aggressive coping differs from problem-solving and dreaming. It can involve wishing someone was different, worrying about rejection, sulking and pouting to coerce relationships, trying to get people's approval by suppressing one's needs and limits, and using addictions to avoid shame and feel more in control.

Our coping techniques and strategies can be nonlinear, including the possibility of adopting multiple, opposing approaches at the same time (Giwa, 2022). Above all, self-acceptance and self-compassion are assertiveness skills for all of us to have in life. We'll describe them in more detail below.

Developing Self-Acceptance

Acceptance of ourselves and our identities is essential to our well-being. As sexual and gender minorities, fighting the reality of our sexual orientation and gender expression tends to cause a significant increase in shame and suffering. The aim of increasing self-acceptance is to feel more congruent with who you are and become free from the pain caused by societal rejection and the internalization of such stigma. "Acceptance" can feel wrong for some people who have been socialized to believe that "acceptance" means relinquishing all control, giving up and giving in, and allowing harmful behavior. Instead, "acceptance" means acknowledging the facts and realities of a situation/yourself/another person and making decisions based on those facts and what one needs to move forward in life. As Huber (2003) explained, we don't gain the power to change our circumstances through acceptance; we develop the ability to determine our experience of those circumstances, which may lead to more practical changes.

What Is Self-Acceptance?

Queer culture and scientific literature often mention self-acceptance as the opposite of shame and the process of healing from rejection and stigma (Arístegui et al., 2018). Many related self-resilience concepts are also helpful, such as *self-esteem* (how we feel about ourselves) and *self-pride* (how well valued our identities are to ourself). Self-acceptance in the context of sexuality and gender means choosing to accept and cultivate comfort with the stigmatized aspects of our sexuality/gender as part of who we are (Camp et al., 2020). Notice that we describe this as a choice. We would argue that we have to choose to accept most things in life, especially when others do not accept them and are incongruent with mainstream stories of what we "should" and "shouldn't" be. Acceptance is not a passive stance and tends not to happen automatically.

By acceptance, we do not mean liking or feeling pride. Self-acceptance may lead to pride and liking (Cass, 1979). But, this process is about (a) acknowledging the facts/reality of our gender and sexuality, (b) making a choice to accept the facts regardless of their strengths and limitations, (c) questioning and replacing self-negating judgments about our sexuality/gender, and (d) giving space to consider and make choices about our gender/sexual experiences so that they are meaningful and safe aspects of our lives. Along those lines, religious conceptualizations of self-acceptance and stigmatized gender/sexual identities are being developed to promote the concept of "grace to self" (Yarhouse et al., 2023).

* What does providing grace to yourself about your sexuality and gender mean to you?

Finally, self-acceptance is a lifelong process that will probably be everchanging. We may accept our gender/sexual identity and reject other aspects of ourselves as we age. It is vital to see self-acceptance as an essential journey to embark on and enjoy rather than an end goal. It can be considered a life value—the direction we move in (or aim to move in) rather than the actual destination and a worthwhile endeavor to help us live a more meaningful life. Research suggests that self-acceptance is associated with higher levels of other positive life processes, such as self-kindness, self-esteem, connection with others, and connectedness with the LGBTQIA+ community (Camp et al., 2020) and lower internalized stigma, self-criticism, depression, and anxiety (Camp et al., 2022).

Self-acceptance ultimately allows for celebrating and delighting in our own and others' authentic ways of being and relating (termed *pro-being pride*) (Benau, 2022), which can heal relational trauma. Similarly, celebrating and delighting in our own and others' sexual/gender diversity (*queer pride/joy*) can heal queer pain and gender/sexual minority trauma.

What Gets in the Way of Accepting Yourself?

Self-invalidation is the practice of dismissing and rejecting one's experience. As mentioned, we learn self-invalidation when others communicate that something is "wrong," "bad," undeserving, and inferior about ourselves due to stigmatized personal characteristics. This invalidation becomes personalized and internalized, resulting in self-oppression (Skerven et al., 2019). Self-invalidation can increase a person's emotional vulnerability due to being dysregulated with shame/guilt, anxiety, envy, anger, disgust, despair, and more. Emotional vulnerability makes it harder to practice self-acceptance because these emotions feel intolerable, confusing, and justified. It is difficult to accept ourselves (and not turn against or away from our experience) when we feel "out of control" regarding our emotions and distress/pain level.

Shame results from self-invalidation and is painful due to rejecting ourselves. Shame makes sense when we have done something harmful that we should reject and stop doing. Feelings of *justified shame* alert us that we did something harmful. Alongside *justified guilt*, justified shame keeps us accountable to ourselves and others and helps us live by our values and morals. Germer (2023) described shame as an innocent wish to be loved. We can resolve justified shame and guilt through appropriate action (learning skills to replace harmful behaviors, making amends to those we have harmed, etc.). Feelings of shame made sense years ago when we were developing as humans. The uncomfortable feelings reduced the likelihood of us repeating unsafe behaviors or revealing information that would get us kicked out of our tribe/family, which we depended on for food, shelter, and survival. In modern society, this is more complicated. Yet many cultures, leaders, and caregivers continue to use shame to motivate others to comply.

Justified shame from doing something harmful differs from *unjustified/ misplaced shame* and believing we are bad, defective, inferior, and unlovable because we did something harmful or because someone convinced us that we did something harmful. Heterosexism and negative judgments toward stigmatized identities provide a chronic message that being different is bad and will lead to rejection from family and society. This, in turn, means we internalize the possibility of rejection, which elicits shame, anxiety, and a need for acceptance and approval.

We typically react to shame in four ways: attack ourselves, attack others, withdraw, or avoid (Nathanson, 1997). Shame urges us to attack or pressure ourselves to overcompensate, live up to unrealistic expectations, and hide our identity from ourselves and others. Shame causes us to avoid reminders that we are LGBTQIA+ and reject that part of ourselves to reduce the discomfort of shame and the real threat of societal rejection. Rejecting ourselves, withdrawing, and avoiding reminders stop our identity development by blocking our access to connection and role models and safe expression for these parts of ourselves. This creates cycles of shame and nonacceptance.

Continual invalidation reinforces internalized shame, emotional pain, and more rejection. When we do not fully accept ourselves, we are vulnerable to society's subtle and direct messages that we are undesirable and inferior (called *microaggressions*). We may cope by suppressing ourselves to fit in and inadvertently (or perhaps consciously) send negating messages to "nonconforming" queer people and rejecting the "nonconforming" queer parts of them. This rejection blocks connection and self-acceptance and reinforces unjustified shame. Social support and acceptance have a direct relationship with the degree of self-acceptance that we build (Vincke & Bolton, 1994).

What Can We Do to Develop Self-Acceptance?

Mindfulness skills have a good track record of improving acceptance and self-acceptance (Rodriguez et al., 2015). Mindfulness, however, is not just a tool but a way of being that is fundamental across different Buddhist practices to promote insight, self-care, liberation, and enlightenment (Comas-Diaz & Lian, 2023). Linehan (1993) conceptualized mindfulness as a set of skills for accepting emotionally challenging, uncertain moments. These skills can apply directly to the self-acceptance of a stigmatized sexual/gender identity. First, we'll describe *what* to do regarding mindfulness and then *how* to practice mindfulness regarding your gender and sexuality. Remember, we are all different, so you do not need to do self-acceptance as suggested. Explore what works for you.

Step 1, Observe: Notice where you are currently in your self-acceptance journey about your gender and sexuality. How does this level of self-acceptance feel to you? Where are you in terms of healing from past rejections, invalidations, trauma, and prejudice? What are the facts about your sexual orientation, sexual expression, gender, and gender expression? How do you feel about your sexual orientation, sexual expression, gender, and gender expression? Notice when and why you accept and reject your gender/sexual experiences and how acceptance and rejection affect your body and well-being.

Step 2, Describe: Which three to five words would you use to describe your gender experiences and sexual experiences? How would you describe your relationship with your gender/sexuality? Take time to observe, label, and describe how evaluations and judgments affect your emotional state, actions, and relationships. If you have conclusions, opinions, thoughts, and emotions, name them as such (for example, *I just had an evaluation-thought that I like that part of myself*). You can use this naming skill alongside the nonjudgmental skills (described below) to label your sexual orientation and gender authentically.

Step 3, Participate: Use your observations and descriptions to understand what, if anything, you want to do about your self-acceptance. What do you need and need to do, if anything, about your gender and sexuality? What do your gender expression and sexuality need from you? Maybe you want to continue observing and being curious about your sexual/gender experiences, or you want to learn more about gender and sexuality or develop more assertiveness to express your sexuality, gender, and other aspects of yourself more authentically.

Now, we'll describe *how* to do these three mindfulness skills.

Step 1, Nonjudgmentally: Nonacceptance is linked to negating self-judgments, so it can be empowering to notice when you are rejecting and judging yourself unjustly and separate from judgments by refocusing on the facts. Some find it helpful to name the judgment as a judgment (*I just had a judgment that . . .*) and refocus attention on factual descriptions. You can even include a positive judgment with this process (for example, judgment: *Everyone thinks I look ridiculous when I go out in . . .* , and factual description with a positive judgment: *I am worried that people will judge how I look, and I feel good wearing this and want to do it anyway*).

The important thing about judgments is that we all have them and likely always will. Therefore, the task here is not to prevent judgments from happening within yourself or within others. The task is to practice noticing and observing the judgment (***cognitive defusion***) (Hayes, 2022) and reframing the meaning of your experience to reduce the emotional intensity. Doing so reduces negative rumination and allows more empowering information and positive reappraisals to come into our awareness (Chan et al., 2020).

Step 2, One thing in one moment: Practice focusing on one thing at a time. Consider setting aside time during your day or week to practice acceptance and self-acceptance. We all multitask, as modern life requires, but focusing on one thing in one moment allows for more engagement, insight, and understanding of the realities of the present moment. Suppose your mind wanders, and it will, including worrying about uncertainty in the future about your gender/sexuality or perhaps into past difficult memories. In that case, notice and *kindly* bring your attention back to this moment and the task. Sometimes saying, "Thank you, mind," helps to acknowledge that the human mind wanders and you are honoring your mind and humanity when it does.

This practice of ***intentional attention***, of deciding where to put your focus (for example, on some aspect of your inner experience or some aspect around you), allows us to gain control of what we attend to, including noticing and detaching from prejudice and internalized stigma and refocusing on what we prefer to believe about ourselves and which actions to take aligned with this belief and our values (Flentje, 2020; Salvati et al., 2019).

Step 3, Effectively: This is a powerful skill and reference point to guide action. It suggests evaluating whether our actions are effective and aligned with our needs, limits, values, and goals. When choosing how to participate in the world, we can ask ourselves if our intended action or path is effective and, if not, if we want to reroute. For example, research indicates that ruminating about rejection is a normal response to minority stress but also results in depression (Sarno et al., 2020). Noticing you are ruminating, understanding its ineffectiveness in stopping rejection, and shifting to problem-solving how you want to respond when someone rejects you will be more effective in developing confidence and recovering from any potential rejection.

How Do We Act Opposite to Internalized Shame and Nonacceptance?

As noted above, distinguishing between justified and unjustified shame is essential, as there are many circumstances in which shame is functional. If we act opposite to justified shame, we will continue to harm ourselves and others. If we act opposite to unjustified shame, we can build internal resilience to handle unjustified social rejection. Each individual must evaluate if any part of their gender expression and sexuality violates their or someone else's personhood and, if so, learn skills to be more respectful to themselves and others. We can change our behavior and choices, but changing fundamental parts of ourselves can be extremely difficult, if not impossible. In changing essential aspects of a person, shame is likely unjustified. Even if shame is justified, using humiliation and self-invalidation to change behavior is unlikely to produce long-lasting change. We all deserve to be who we are, feel equal to others, and determine what that means for ourselves to live a meaningful life. When shame is unjustified or ineffective, we want to soften it with facts and reassurance.

This is not to say that just because there is a risk of social rejection, and the potential justification for your shame system to warn you of this risk, that you need to act in line with what this emotion is telling you to do (usually to hide). Instead, it is a warning alarm to prompt you to evaluate current safety conditions (Laliotis, 2021) and choose how you want to proceed. In many cases, where the risk of harm is low or you feel empowered to develop your identity and promote social change, it can be essential to do the opposite and be "out and proud" in whatever way that feels authentic to you.

To navigate shame and know when and how to intervene, we need to know what shame and rejection feel like in our body (this invites *observing* and *describing* mindfulness skills, described above). Often, shame produces activating sensations, such as worry, nausea, heaviness, a knot or punch in the stomach, shoulder and neck strain, throat tightness, blushing, or other uncomfortable body sensations. Shame also comes with an urge to be small, hide our face or body, freeze, collapse, avoid eye contact, and disappear. Some people get angry and defensive and demean others when they feel shame (we call this secondary anger). Withdrawing and avoiding situations, topics, or people because we don't want to feel unjustified shame is another indicator to intervene and practice self-acceptance and self-encouragement.

As emotions are a whole system/body response, when we experience an emotion such as shame, this will also produce changes in thinking, body sensations and physiology, and action urges. Therefore, each of these parts of the emotional experience can be a cue to which emotion you are feeling and a potential element to consider should you want to reduce or increase the intensity of the emotion. To reduce the intensity of an emotion, we need to shift our body to do the opposite of the body signature of that emotion. This works well because our mind and body are one well-connected system. Changing one aspect of the system or emotion signature in the body will affect the rest of the system.

To act opposite to unjustified shame, perhaps start by sitting confidently but relaxed, back straight, shoulders down, chest raised, jaw unclenched, and breathing as deeply and slowly as possible. Use your breath to stabilize you and keep your voice tone steady and clear. Offer yourself a half smile (this is gold!). A half smile is moving up the outer sides of your lips as though you are about to smile. It doesn't need to be visible as long as you can feel it. What do you notice happens in your mind-body when you breathe deeply and do a half smile? As Thich Nhat Hanh (2005) described, "Breathing in, I calm body and mind. Breathing out, I smile. Dwelling in the present moment, I know this is the only moment" (p. 114).

The next step is to do the opposite of what the feeling of unjustified shame tells us to do (opposite to the action urge). So don't hide; make things public if you can safely do so. If it is not safe, then internally acknowledge your worth. If it's socially safe enough, don't apologize for who you are, and don't fight who you are, but question and reject unjustified societal attitudes or at least take time to examine their impact on you. Talk with others about the harms of minority stress. Name your sexual and gender identity authentically and provide kindness to yourself.

Self-acceptance and disclosure are challenging decisions, as we need emotions like shame to keep us safe and in "the group" should that be necessary for our survival. At the same time, we do not want to reinforce unjustified shame, and we may have a role in changing harmful societal norms. This is your decision, and know that whatever you do, you are exactly where you need to be, and your efforts are enough.

Finally, keep doing it. Opposite action works in the moment and needs to be returned to and repeated. This will not happen automatically, at least not initially; you will need to choose repeatedly to take this road until it becomes overlearned. Responding to shame with increasing self-acceptance will connect you to yourself and others more authentically. Building a compassionate community for yourself and others is the ultimate continuation of acting opposite to stigma.

Responding to Stress and Minority Stress With Self-Compassion

Self-acceptance can foster a kind and caring position toward ourselves in situations where we feel distressed, different, inadequate, and a failure (Neely et al., 2009). Neff (2003) described self-compassion as developing a loving, connected presence toward ourself that is mindful of our judgments and distress, helps us respond to ourselves with kindness, and recognizes the common humanity of our actions and suffering. Self-compassion involves being kind and generous toward ourself instead of critical and withholding. Brach (2019) described self-compassion as recognizing when we are suffering, allowing what is happening inside us to be as it is, investigating and being curious about what is causing our suffering, and nurturing ourselves with what we need based on that self-awareness. Self-compassion can mean providing self-soothing to help us face and tolerate pain. It can be an act of self-compassion to do a mindful body scan at any moment to be more aware of any physical tension to release and relax.

Developing Self-Compassion to Reduce Sexual/Gender Stigma

Self-compassion is related to better outcomes for our mental health, well-being, and relationships (Beard et al., 2016; Neff et al., 2017). Specifically, some research shows how self-compassion can make it easier to come out about our sexual/gender identities as it reduces the fear that we will be self-condemning if others reject us (Crews, 2012). Self-compassion can buffer the harmful effects of discrimination, oppression, and self-stigma (Brown-Beresford & McLaren, 2021). How much do the following (Raes et al., 2011) fit you regarding your gender/sexuality?

- When I'm going through a tough time about my gender/sexuality, I give myself the caring and tenderness I need.
- I get angry with myself when I fail to meet expectations about my gender/sexuality.
- I try to understand and be patient toward aspects of my gender/sexuality that I don't like.

Self-pity is different from self-compassion. How would you describe the two? Self-pity can involve feeling bad about ourselves instead of for ourselves and judging ourselves as inferior, defective, and pathetic because we suffer (for example, *I deserve to suffer* vs. *I matter, have inherent worth, and deserve care*). Self-compassion involves wanting to understand and care about our suffering and connect to others who suffer like us. As such, self-compassion can be a vital coping mechanism to address mental health disparities for sexually/

gender-diverse (SGD) individuals (Helminen et al., 2023). Stigma messages are one component of mindfulness that can be noticed and responded to with self-compassion (Vigna et al., 2018). Not only can self-compassion address the negative beliefs of self-stigma, but it can also reduce anxiety and depression and our sense of disconnectedness and loneliness for being SGD (Chan et al., 2020). With self-compassion, we understand that everyone has prejudices and suffers. This connection to humanity can prevent negative comments from feeling like an inadequacy of the individual and more about the vulnerability of we diverse humans.

Developing Self-Compassion in Rural Communities

The experience of SGD individuals in a rural environment cannot be assumed to be the same as the experience of individuals in an urban environment. Equality for SGD individuals in urban environments has seen improvement in recent years, but this progress has not extended to large amounts of the population (Meyer, 2016). The experience for those in rural communities still often consists of stigma, fear, marginalization, and invisibility (Rosenkrantz et al., 2017). The reason for this can be seen in the differences between liberal/progressive versus conservative/fundamentalist values, which tend to correspond to population density, with rural areas tending to be more conservative. The rural environment is also more likely to promote conservative religious values, leading to isolation and stigma-inducing events for SGD individuals. Rural SGD individuals may also not relate to the liberal/progressive activities of urban LGBTQIA+ communities.

The type of support and social messaging offered, if any, may also vary significantly from the urban to the rural environment. Urban SGD adults tend to have greater access to like-minded individuals to connect to, both in person and on the internet, which may influence self-acceptance and their ability to develop intimate relationships. Research (Leedy & Connolly, 2007) on LGB+ cisgender individuals in rural settings indicates that many conform to the expected standard of the community to decrease being a target of assault or being ostracized from their small community, as they also have to figure out on their own how to find similar others safely. In addition to this lack of safety and support, trans/nonbinary individuals needing medical options for transitioning may suffer more due to the lack of providers who are willing and able to be educated in gender-affirming care (Movement Advancement Project, 2019). Youth coming out in the rural environment will likely have an experience that is very different from the experiences of youth coming out in an urban environment due to these conflicting social values and lack of safe resources and outlets (Dahl et al., 2015).

In a rural community with little social support for the SGD individual, learning to use self-compassion as a coping mechanism can be critical to addressing mental health disparities. Self-compassion can provide internal support and validation to reduce the internalization of stigma messages, unjustified shame, and self-hatred and improve self-esteem. Self-efficacy is crucial to self-determination, especially during adolescence, and self-compassion is a valuable tool in rural communities because it can be strengthened through practice. Plus, individuals with a stigmatized identity are likely to feel a disconnect in a rural environment between their religious/social identity and their SGD identity. Using self-compassion to develop one's spirituality can be a way to reduce anxiety for sexual minority individuals (Lassiter et al., 2022).

The rural community college is one area of focus for cultivating self-compassion for the SGD population. There can be a difference in experience for a rural versus urban LGBTQIA+ college student experience. This difference in experience also extends to the college environment when comparing the four-year institution to the two-year institution. SGD students have lower retention rates than their heterosexual, cisgender peers due to the campus climate (Garvey et al., 2018). Stigma-related events in the classroom and on campus can keep LGBTQIA+ students from attending class. Although the college campus is often more liberal, the community college campus leans conservative in a rural environment. The lack of resources experienced in the rural community extends to the community college campus in those communities.

Nguyen et al. (2018) noted a lack of resources for marginalized communities at two-year colleges compared to four-year institutions. This lack of resources is even more likely in the conservative, rural community. The lack of resources and trained support staff designated for SGD students or even a specific LGBTQIA+ resource center at community colleges leave the SGD students without support or a community (Zamani & Choudhuri, 2016). When the community college is in a rural community, this means the student lacks support at the college and in the community. Due to the lack of resources at two-year institutions, the SGD community is at a higher risk than their heterosexual peers of not transferring to a four-year university or completing their degree. Minority stress significantly deters the pursuit of education, especially in the community college environment.

Teaching self-compassion in schools is ideal for building internal and social resilience (Vigna et al., 2018). It is an inexpensive humane intervention that a person can cultivate through practice. Self-compassion is beneficial due to connecting to the suffering of all humanity and decreasing the tendency to personalize stigma-related events.

Conclusion

Systems of social power, privilege, and oppression shape our developmental experiences, options, health, and intersectional understanding of ourselves (Moradi & Grzanka, 2017). More action and resources are needed to address social oppression and reduce its effects on self-definition, emotional health, and coping. We hope the ideas, experiences, and skills presented in this chapter and our companion e-resource increase your ability to use assertive/affirmative coping to respond to stress and minority stress, especially with more self-acceptance, self-compassion, and social connection.

Chapter 4

Develop Your Sexual/ Gender Self-Knowledge

A. Lee Beckstead, S. Candice Metzler, Pichit Buspavanich, Elizabeth Morgan, and Marty A. Cooper

This chapter will not tell you who you are. Instead, we'll present many questions and experiences for your exploration. We'll suggest different ways that people label their sexuality and gender. We'll describe how to understand sexual orientation, including fluidity, bisexuality, and asexuality, and which aspects of sexuality can be changed. We'll describe ways to understand gender and gender identity, role, and expression. We hope the definitions we provide for these concepts are precise and inclusive enough to clarify what is true for you and what is not. We hope this understanding will help you make informed life decisions and help you talk with others about your experiences. Getting clearer about your sexuality and gender may help you find others like yourself for connection and mutual understanding. Even if you are clear about your sexuality and gender, we hope this chapter increases your knowledge of and empathy for individuals whose gender and sexuality differ from yours.

Cocreating Safety About Sexual/Gender Diversity

We coauthors (and others who contributed to an earlier draft) expressed the following safety guidelines to inform our process and reduce prejudice in our writing. We hope these common-ground safety guidelines help you know what you need for yourself and with others regarding sexual/gender diversity.

- We will reduce friction by abstaining from forcing each other's perspectives and experiences into frames that fit our biases. I intend to try to understand each of you from within your framework. I trust you will do the same for me.

- We need to integrate research, theory, clinical practice, and personal experiences to create a well-rounded picture of who sexual and gender minorities are in the world.
- Clarity of terms is essential, even ethical, for these issues, especially to understand what we can and cannot change about sexuality and gender.
- Be patient with each other while we work at seeing each other's perspectives and understanding each other's language and work at finding our common ground.
- I hope to assume positive intent and learn from others' differences in perspective.
- I would like criticism to be delivered thoughtfully rather than in a demeaning way.
- Knowing that some people can be difficult to work with, I remind and challenge myself to return to a mindset of compassion and pursue outcomes that transcend my personal interests and reflect a broader perspective.
- Everyone would benefit from their sexual orientation and gender identity being understood and given the same dignity and legitimacy as another's.

We therefore agreed to avoid unsolicited questions, judgments, and comments about each other's sexuality, relationships, body, and gender expression.

Ultimately, "Don't yuck someone's yum." Expressing disgust or disapproval about someone's sexuality, sexual orientation, gender identity, or gender expression will not make that person like what you like or stop liking what they like. Shaming them may cause unnecessary harm by reinforcing the individual's internalized self-rejection. Turning against someone's gender/sexual expression may have the good intention to prevent or stop harm, but the relational dynamic leaves both individuals unaware of each other's experiences.

It may be helpful to "turn toward" a "yuck" response with acknowledgment and curiosity of how a person's "yuck" response defines that person's limit (what is wrong for that person) rather than describing what the person is rejecting or that the attraction is wrong for the person who likes it. This statement does not imply ignoring or allowing sexual attractions that harm others (rape, lust murder, zoophilia, sex with individuals younger than a given age, etc.). It means that shaming someone about their sexual attractions or lack thereof or their gender expression is ineffective in changing the individual's sexual orientation or gender identity.

For example, it may feel disgusting and unnatural for some exclusively heterosexual men to experience or think about sex with men, as it is disgusting and unnatural for some exclusively same-gender attracted men to experience or think about having sex with women. As sex researcher Alfred Kinsey described, "The only unnatural sex act is that which you cannot perform." We encourage you to examine your reactions to others' experiences and consider the impact on them and you, as you also consider which sexual, gender, faith, and cultural expressions best fit you.

- Which safety guidelines would you add to make it as safe as possible and productive for you and others to read the following?
- What do you need from yourself to feel safe enough to explore your gender identity, sexual orientation, and sexual identity? Do you need permission, patience, protection, accuracy, or more options that fit you?
- What's most important for you, and what are your limits regarding gender, sexual orientation, and sexuality?
- What do the people in your significant relationships need from you and themselves as you explore these issues?

Some discomfort is possible and perhaps okay when exploring these issues. However, some may have trouble exploring who they are because of fear, uncertainty, embarrassment, and losses from being a person with a stigmatized gender identity, sexual orientation, or sexuality. It may not be safe for you to explore these issues with others. You may be concerned about what others think or how they will treat you differently and respond to your experiences and desires.

You may benefit from spending time alone as you explore these issues. Paying more attention to yourself may help you identify your reference points of likes, dislikes, needs, limits, and necessities and evaluate whether these are yours or "rogue points" given to you by others and life experience. Do these reference points still fit you, and do you still agree with them? You may benefit from talking with people you trust, including those who will give you various viewpoints on gender and sexuality.

As you learn more about yourself and these issues, we encourage you to go as far as you want and explore what is safe and healthy for you. Having self-consent and learning your needs and limits will help you enjoy your desires. This ownership, self-knowledge, self-awareness, and process of learning may help you understand more about your insecurities, aversions, and phobias and what you need to feel more secure and comfortable about your gender and sexuality.

We also recognize that the following is limited by the current research base, which has privileged monosexual, predominantly White, cisgender male experiences, and will be constrained by our biases and understanding of the current research. Carl Dybdahl[1] described the problems with biased research and researchers:

Research can serve various purposes. Let's consider two in opposition: figuring out the truth versus producing propaganda. Ideologically biased people argue

---

[1] Former coauthor.

that social science is all about propaganda and that truth-seeking is dead. Insofar as that is true, presumably, the debate is just about which side of the propaganda you should support since eliminating the bias in a field that consists solely of bias makes no sense. On the other hand, one might argue that the purpose of research is not the production of propaganda but to seek truth for the safety and well-being of everyone. However, researchers along the political spectrum may use truth-seeking as an excuse for producing propaganda and not realize how their ideology prejudices their research and the research they support.

The starting point for opposing ideological bias should be humility to look at the views and arguments of yourself and your allies and work to throw out the things produced by bias. This is partly because these are the easiest things to intervene on and partly because this legitimizes one's position as *actually* searching for the truth. Doubling down on one's own bias in critique of bias is self-defeating.

We hope more researchers prioritize truth-seeking and accuracy over ideology and deception. Therefore, we hope more researchers prioritize the inclusion of voices and experiences of those with lived experience in the research area/subject in order to minimize bias.

Next, we highlight how individual and institutional prejudice and community segregation and marginalization can harm identity development and well-being.

Blocks to Identity Development Related to Sexual/Gender Diversity

For some individuals, their sexual orientation and gender are like their hair and eye color, easy to categorize. For others, their sexual and gender experiences do not fit the norm, and they may not be treated fairly or see themselves socially reflected accurately, positively, or fully. The minority stress model (Brooks, 1981) postulates that individuals from stigmatized groups are exposed to unique and excess stresses that add wear and tear to their bodies and minds related to race/ethnicity, gender, sexual orientation, sexuality, disability, faith, and other identities. Research supporting the minority stress theory counters assumptions that LGBTQIA+ individuals suffer because there is something wrong with them and they are inherently deficient (Borgogna & Aita, 2023). In this intersectional model, LGBTQIA+ individuals' development and emotional/physical health are reduced due to coping with (a) *social minority stressors*, such as prejudice, discrimination, invalidation, isolation, violence, and lack of safety and options, and (b) the person's *internal stress adaptations*, such as expecting and ruminating about rejection, violence, or loss; concealing and suppressing self-expression and authenticity, and thinking they are worthless and inferior due to internalized stigma.

Social minority stressors and internal stress adaptations can make it difficult for a person whose sexuality, sexual orientation, gender identity, and gender do not fit cultural norms to know themselves and feel secure with others.

We may also have different ideas of what "LGBTQIA+" means. To ensure we're all on the same page, we must differentiate culture and prejudice from one's understanding of these terms. As Michelson (Kolodny & Michelson, 2015) explained,

> Just because you're attracted to other men or you enjoy the physical act of having sex with other men, whether it's easy or it's genuinely attractive to you, that is very different than saying, "I'm a gay man," or "I'm a queer man, and I partake in the cultural totems of being part of that community." I don't know that they have to line up exactly. What I'm more interested in at this point is if any of this happens because of internalized homophobia.

If we don't have a clear view of ourselves and others and have language, options, safety, and a life vision that fits us, then we can get misled about labels, choices, and possible futures. Similarly, if we want concepts such as gender identity and sexual orientation to be useful for communication, education, ethics, and morality, then we need such terms to be accurately inclusive, clearly defined, and mutually understandable.

Biased, Limited, and Subjective Terms and Labels

An option for many (for example, identifying as a man or woman) may distract and limit other individuals. This exclusion is due to binary (either/or) terms not fully capturing everyone's experiences and definitions. Binary gender/sexual labels (for example, *boy/girl*, *woman/man*) may feel different and be expressed differently than nonbinary gender/sexual labels (for example, *lesbian tomboy, nonbinary lesbian, primarily straight masculine woman, pansexual man assigned female at birth, asexual gay transmasculine, heteroflexible, woman with XY chromosomes, soft butch, boy who sometimes wants to be a girl,*[2] *two-spirit woman, lesbian-leaning kind of bi-romantic grey/demi asexual*) (Galupo et al., 2017).

- How do you define what a man, woman, and nonbinary individual is, and what characteristics or factors do you use to determine and explain any differences?
- What's your understanding of how a cisgender individual differs from a transgender individual and an intersex individual?
- Are your definitions different from who is a "real man" and "real woman" and who is "trans/nonbinary/intersex enough"?

---

[2] A line from the musical *Everybody's Talking about Jamie*. See https://en.wikipedia.org/wiki/Everybody's_Talking_About_Jamie for more information.

- Which images come to mind when considering a *typical* man, woman, or nonbinary individual?
- Are these images different from what is an *ideal* man, woman, or nonbinary individual?

Some think that if they are not masculine/feminine or male/female enough compared to the "ideal/typical man/woman," then they are trans/nonbinary+. Some may believe they are another gender because they experience similar attractions as that gender (*If I like boys, I must be a girl*). Their experience of their gender/sex is misaligned and different from the stereotypes of their assigned birth sex. Some may reject being labeled according to their assigned birth sex because they don't see themselves fitting in with the stereotypical gender traits and status of their assigned sex (*If that's what a man is, I'm not that, I'm not womanly/feminine, so I must be a man, I don't want to be vulnerable like girls/women*, etc.).

There might be confusion and different ideas about what it means to be sexually/gender diverse. We consider someone **gender diverse** when their internal and social experience of their gender traits, expression, and appearance are not stereotypical for others assigned their sex at birth. Similarly, someone who is **sexually diverse** means their sexual orientation, sexual experiences, or sexual relationships are not stereotypical for others assigned their sex at birth.

Body diverse is also something that needs clarity and acknowledgment. Gender and sexual-orientedness are ultimately based on a stereotype (medicalization/creation stories/religion) of the body that many of us actively participate in because it is all we have been taught and known. Perhaps as a consequence, we see and exist in a seamless world where we do not recognize bodily differences or consider the significance that such diversity does exist. Humans go to great efforts to conceal, confuse, and erase specific expressions of sex development that do not fit the stereotype. Everyone has an experience of their body that has been subjected to speculation and demarcation before being born and is part of an intimately personal experience as we each develop our own sense of gender identity and sexuality.

- Which descriptions and images come to mind when considering the term *sexuality*?
- Which descriptions and images come to mind when considering the labels *gay, lesbian, bisexual, transgender, nonbinary, queer, intersex, asexual,* and *aromantic*?
- Which gendered expectations and stereotypes do you associate with each term?
- How does racism affect your viewpoint (Patel, 2019)?

Some people feel LGBTQIA+ community norms are too limiting or extreme for them. *Gay, lesbian, queer,* and *nonbinary* can come with political connotations aligned with creating a counterculture or challenging dominant narratives. That is why some people either adopt or reject such labels. For others, these social labels describe their connection to a diverse community representing inclusion, pride, creativity, and strength. A person can define *gay* and *lesbian* as simple adjectives to describe anyone sexually attracted primarily or only to same-gender individuals. Some women call themselves gay rather than lesbian.

Queer has historically meant a "perverted deviant" (Cervini, 2020) but has pivoted more affirmatively to refer to being different and "not straight." *Queer* as well as *same-gender* remove the biological binary of "same-sex" or "opposite-sex" and can be used for nonmonosexual, fluid sexualities, and nonbinary genders. *Trans+* and *transgender* imply a broad spectrum of individuals who don't identify with their assigned birth sex or expected social gender role and expression. Historically, the identity *transsexual* was a category of transgender and applied to those who benefited from medical interventions to reduce the incongruence and internal aversion between their experienced gender and sex characteristics. Some still use this term to describe themselves.

If you are turned on sexually or romantically to some degree by women, men, and genderfluid/nonbinary individuals or a person regardless of their gender/sex, then you could label yourself *bisexual, fluid, pansexual, panromantic, queer, bisexual leaning heterosexual/lesbian, mostly gay/straight, primarily heterosexual/gay* (Savin-Williams, 2016), *heteroflexible,* or some other plurisexual/polysexual orientation label. Or you could decide not to use a label to avoid boxing yourself into others' ideas. Some individuals who experience attraction to men and women still label themselves heterosexual/straight or gay/lesbian. Many use the label that applies to their relationship (heterosexual or gay/lesbian/queer) rather than their sexual orientation.

Cisgender and transgender categories can create a binary system and limitation for those whose experience of their gender, gender expression, and pronouns fit better with nonbinary terms, such as *genderfluid, genderqueer, third gender, gender outlaw* (Bornstein, 2016), *gender creative* (Ehrensaft, 2011), *gender expansive, agender, gender warrior* (Feinberg, 1996), or *androgynous.*

- Do each of the above terms mean the same to you? How do you think they are different and similar from each other and to your gender identity, traits, roles, and appearance?
- If you were to embody any of the above terms, how do you think you would experience and express yourself? Which of those terms, if any, would better fit you and come closest to describing your experience of your gender?

For some, *bigender* refers to individuals who experience their gender as binary male and binary female simultaneously or at different times. *Androgyne* refers to a person with a blend and mix of traits associated with masculinity/

femininity and maleness/femaleness. *Androgyne* may also refer to someone whose physical appearance lacks gender traits or who prefers to minimize or obscure traits that could be identified as masculine or feminine and prefers not to label themselves. This is common when people do not feel safe with labels for themselves and perhaps are early in their gender exploration.

Various Sources of Distress Related to Sexual/Gender Diversity

The following highlights how people can get shamed, confused, and anxious about and question their gender and sexual orientation. We provide these differing experiences so that those who struggle with psychological distress can get the help they need. We do not want to imply that something is wrong with sexual/gender diversity. We hope the following provides ways to understand a person's distress with their sexuality or gender or both. It's essential to understand the sources of distress associated with gender identity, gender expression, sexual orientation, and sexuality to know what to change, what to accept, and what to develop.

For example, some people assigned male at birth seek genital removal with no explicit desire to present as female, some experience body dysmorphia, while others suffer from gender dysphoria (Wibowo et al., 2023). Current data (Wibowo et al., 2022) suggest that some wish to resolve a *body-integrity incongruence* (making their body match their internal representation). Others may feel plagued by their libidinous thoughts and seek a psychological *"eunuch calm"* by becoming nonsexual. Still others may experience sexual arousal at the idea of being castrated, where castration itself is an extreme form of *sadomasochistic paraphilia* (Recorder et al., 2020).

Research suggests that reinforcing rigid, hypermasculine gender roles (men should fight and dominate, boys don't cry, men should never show their tenderness or look weak, etc.) can be a factor in some men rejecting their worth and the validity of being a man (del Pino et al., 2022). Some men believe they are unqualified to be a man because they believe men must act and look a certain way (*precarious manhood*) (Vandello et al., 2023). Similarly, some women feel compelled to prove their womanhood and femininity. For men, restricted gender roles can create *gender-role conflicts* of guilt, shame, depression, fear of expressing emotions or others expressing emotions, discomfort with affection and intimacy, sexual dysfunction, and coping with health-risk behaviors. Some heterosexual, cisgender men with hypermasculine ideas may be anxious about being gay or being aroused by male erotica and consequently experience a self-protective anger (fear and disgust; *homophobia*) against male intimacy (Hudepohl et al., 2010).

Traditional masculine gender roles (authority, leader, competitor, protector, provider, etc.) and traditional feminine gender roles (helper, caretaker, nurturer, homemaker, etc.) may fit and feel authentic to some individuals regardless of their assigned sex or gender identity. What would you gain by expanding your idea of gender and gender expression? Many times, cis/trans men who are held captive to stigma and stereotypes want more emotional intimacy, while cis/trans women want equal social power (Sweet & Reigeluth, 2018).

Some individuals who fear and constantly question that they might be lesbian, gay, or bisexual (LGB) may be suffering from *sexual orientation obsessive-compulsive disorder* (SO-OCD). These individuals are typically exclusively heterosexual, but people who are sexual/gender minorities can suffer their version of SO-OCD depending on how anxious they are about their sexual orientation and if they use compulsive behaviors to manage their anxiety. About 10% of those who suffer from OCD also suffer from SO-OCD (Williams & Farris, 2011). Some suffer from pedophilic-OCD by constantly questioning, checking, and fearing that they may molest children, even though they have no sexual desire for children (Bonagura et al., 2022). Some may fear that any aesthetic attraction and appreciation of the beauty of children or same-gender people indicates they are pedophiles or LGB or will make them pedophilic or LGB. Some may mistake their anxious feelings for sexual arousal, given the physiological similarity (Penzel, 2007), and mistake their compulsion to check as indicating their sexual interest.

Some people with SO-OCD may try to relieve their anxiety by avoiding same-gender and LGB individuals and situations. Those who suffer from SO-OCD may also feel shame for being unable to control or change their thoughts and feelings, much in the way LGBTQIA+ individuals with internalized stigma may experience shame about not controlling their unwanted sexual feelings and gender expression (Williams et al., 2015).

Treatment for SO-OCD is similar to other anxiety and obsessive-compulsive disorders by using safe exposure to people and settings that trigger the fears while preventing compulsive responses and tolerating uncertainty. For example, the individual may carry around photos of attractive same-gender people and encourage their mind and body to respond (Intrusive Thoughts, 2017). The individual may learn to notice and observe when they *fear being LGB* and differentiate this physical experience from when they *feel sexual interest*. As Williams (2008) described, "A person with internalized homophobia usually has some positive feelings about homosexuality and will enjoy same-sex fantasies, whereas the person with [homosexual OCD] dreads the thoughts and finds them intrusive" (p. 201). Exposure and self-reflection may help individuals be curious about and better know their sexual orientation and desires rather than be distracted by obsessions and compulsions.

The following paragraphs point out how definitions and criteria for gender dysphoria have been imperfect/problematic and have led to false positives (Jorgensen, 2023). We do not want the following examples to undermine the legitimacy of the experiences of trans+ and nonbinary individuals and gender incongruence and fluidity. We hope it helps readers who experience gender distress understand if any of the following fits them and what they may need for resolution.

Many reasons exist why someone would want to be treated as a different gender, be unhappy in their assigned gender, hate their body, or want to avoid being a woman, man, or nonbinary person. They may feel wrong or unhappy in their expected gender role, feel shame about their sex characteristics or feel that their body is incorrect, or want to dissociate or escape from their body. For example, an individual who experienced complex trauma from sexual abuse, rejection, and neglect about their gender and sexuality may have a strong desire to be a different gender or no gender or be treated as another gender or no gender. This gender incongruence, however, may be experienced differently from those who have a clear sense of their gender but experience distress due to the contradiction with their sex characteristics and body appearance. A strong desire to be the other gender may be experienced as wanting to escape the negative feelings associated with sexism, trauma, and their body and to be treated better or to express the gender role that fits them (for example, *I didn't want to be male, I wanted to be able to be masculine*) (Deleted, 2021; Heyer, 2019).

Some individuals with dissociative identity disorder may experience "gender incongruence" but may not be transgender (although some may be). Their incongruence and distress are due to experiencing separate internal identities with different genders that may be unaware, or mostly unaware, and phobic of each other. Some people experience dissociation, depersonalization, or derealization (seeing themselves from outside their body or perceiving things around them as unreal) due to gender/sexual/physical trauma and feel phobic about thinking and looking at their body because it triggers unprocessed trauma.

Some people experience dissociation or depersonalization due to the incongruence/distress with their internal gender and sexed body (***gender-body incongruence***); some experience dissociation or depersonalization/derealization from both gender/sexual/physical ***trauma*** and gender-body ***incongruence***.

Gender-body incongruence is a term coauthors Beckstead and Metzler developed in consultation with others[3] to specify individuals' (a) incongruence between their experience of self and specific sex characteristics of their body and (b) the level of physical distress caused by the incongruence. Their suffering is inherent to the incongruence and will be triggered when they are reminded

---

[3] See ReconciliationAndGrowth.org.

of gender-physical discrepancies. Gender-body incongruence means a person's physical sexed body and gendered appearance do not align with the gender they perceive themselves to be and want to be perceived as. Gender-body incongruence is about the relationship with one's body as much or more than it is about someone else's perception, considering most people will never see those parts of the body.

Others who experience themselves as gender incongruent (their internal sense of their gender does not align with their assigned birth sex) do not suffer from their natural gender diversity but from how others perceive and treat them and their gender expression. They may experience incongruence between their experience of self and expectations to adhere to a specific gender role according to sex assignment (*gender-role incongruence*). Gender incongruence does not necessarily imply distress or indicate the reason for any distress; hence the need to differentiate gender-body incongruence from the other ways people can suffer from gender stigma.

As will be described later, distress from gender-body incongruence differs from gender-role incongruence, which differs from *gender shame/trauma*. They all differ from *body dysmorphia*, although they have commonalities. For example, people with body dysmorphia are preoccupied and distressed about their attractiveness and appearance. In contrast, people with gender-body incongruence are preoccupied and distressed about discrepancies between their gender and sex characteristics. They may be anxious about which gender they appear to be to others. An individual could struggle from both body dysmorphia and gender-body incongruence due to gender shame/stigma and feeling inferior due to not having the body type of the ideal man/woman. Being unable to defend oneself from possible social attack for being gender diverse adds to the unease.

Personal/social incongruities and social stigma may lead a person to *internalize gender stigma* and feel uncomfortable and embarrassed by their gender identity, gender, and gender expression. Unaddressed gender trauma from past or ongoing distress from gender-role or gender-body incongruence will also affect a person's gender distress. Although these sources of distress may be difficult to differentiate, the distress from gender shame/trauma, gender-role incongruence, body dysmorphia, and internalized gender stigma are based on prejudice, anxiety, phobia, trauma, minority stress, and unjustified guilt/shame and may be reduced using psychological and social interventions (Pachankis et al., 2023).

Gender-body incongruence is a physical condition in which social transition and medical interventions are considered to reduce personal/social incongruence and distress. For example, research on outcomes of top surgery among transgender and nonbinary-identified adolescents and young adults designated female at birth reported improved chest dysphoria, gender congruence, and body image satisfaction as compared to a control group, suggesting the potential for improved psychological outcomes postsurgery for those who suffer from chest-gender-body incongruence (Ascha et al., 2022).

Defining Gender and Developing Gender Congruence

Similar to sexuality and sexual identity, gender identity has many components. The American Psychological Association (2023) defines *gender identity* as a "person's psychological sense of their gender," defines *gender* as "the roles and self-identity associated with sex (i.e., what it means to be/identify as a woman, man or nonbinary [person] in a specific culture)," and defines *biological sex* as the "biological features that have been associated with being male, female, or intersex." This definition allows a person's subjectivity of how they experience, think, and feel about their gender compared to how others describe and express gender, along with the objectivity of how their assigned biological sex affects them.

Tate et al. (2014) conceptualized a person's gender as involving the person's

1. *birth-assigned gender category* (biological sex characteristics)[4]
2. *current gender identity* or gender self-concept (how the person experiences and thinks and feels about and labels their gender)
3. *gender roles and expectations* (gendered traits based on culture)
4. *gender social presentation* (expression and appearance)
5. *gender evaluations* (attitudes about gender and gender diversity), which can influence gender identity and expression

An individual can experience congruence, harmony, conflicts, dissonance, or discordance between these five components. They may or may not be distressed about any incongruence.

- Are your gender definitions based on gender-role expression (how much a person acts masculine/feminine based on cultural definitions of a typical/ideal man/woman) or on sex characteristics (how much a person's body and appearance look like a typical/ideal man/woman) or both (gender/sex) (van Anders, 2015)?
- How much do you identify with your sexed body and the stereotypes and expectations associated with your assigned birth sex?
- How rigid are your definitions, and how much do your answers restrict or expand options for self-expression for yourself and others?

---

[4] Sex assignment is not always based on biological characteristics. Birth-assigned gender does not necessarily match biological sex characteristics because there could be some chromosomal or hormonal differences that don't manifest in (notable) external genitalia differences.

A person's *gender category* is typically assigned at birth (or before during ultrasound) based on the appearance of external genitalia. When external genitalia are ambiguous or atypical, other indicators *may* be used to assign sex. Gender is considered by many to be *sex assigned at birth*. However, this reinforces a biased ideal and current system that needs to be challenged and changed to benefit the whole. The language suggests gender is rightfully based on a medicalized system of categorization that erases noncompliant sex development and intersex people from legitimacy. Gender is clearly not based on sex assigned at birth because gender is a construct based on a combination of social, institutional, and personal factors. Gender is constructed differently in other cultures, which has been the case throughout recorded history. Gender is a social construct associated with the body experienced at both the individual and societal levels. Sex assignment is a medical process based on a formula that is inconsistent and varied in how it is applied and ascribed to the human body. Our system of sex assignment is being used to maintain an unrealistic view of the body, gender, and sexuality as a consequence or goal.

Believing chromosomes are the defining criterion for gender because they fit the majority and are culturally reinforced is considered a "social" choice. The concept of gender/sex needs to be inclusive of everyone and is therefore a nonbinary construct and spectrum, or at least bimodal and mosaic, to represent this variability (Hyde et al., 2019; Strkalj & Pather, 2021). For medical reasons, an individual's sex assigned at birth is male, female, or intersex, but their gender identity indicates their level of identification with certain genders (Ho & Mussap, 2019).

An individual's gender identity is influenced by historical and current social constructions and by the individual's internal sense of which gender category feels (or categories feel) authentic (Hyde et al., 2019). Gender identity means how an individual interprets and labels their experience of their gender, which may be shaped by cultural stereotypes, self-awareness, self-knowledge, and negative/positive evaluations about themselves, others, and gender.

Gender roles are rules about how people of certain genders are supposed to act. For example, there are traditional gender roles, traditional European gender roles, progressive gender roles, and more. *Gender-role orientation* is our level of affinity or aversion to expressing specific gender roles. Your gender-role orientation includes how much you like, dislike, or are neutral about representing yourself in masculine, feminine, or androgynous ways, depending on your culture. *Gender expression* is how we show others our gender and gender-role orientation, defined by our culture's behaviors, interests, and traits.

As mentioned earlier, an individual will experience gender-body incongruence when their physical sexed body and appearance do not align with the gender they want to be perceived as by themselves and others, and the discrepancy causes internal distress. The distress is inherent to the incongruence between their body and experienced gender. Gender-role incongruence happens when an individual is expected to act according to specific gender roles and live with a gender expression incompatible with the individual's gender-role orientation and authentic gender expression, and doing so causes internal distress. The distress is socially instigated and inherent in the social interaction. Someone who suffers from gender-body incongruence or gender-role incongruence can suffer *social incongruence* when someone misgenders them and treats them as their assigned birth sex. A person will suffer gender shame/trauma from social stigma, discrimination, rejection, neglect, or violence for not fitting in with gender expectations and feeling inferior and inadequate about it.

Gender stereotypes and restricted gender schemas are often central to the development of distress with one's gender, gender expression, gender-role orientation, sexual orientation, and sexuality. It is also natural after sexual trauma for a person to hate and fear their sexed body. Some prefer how their bodies looked before puberty because they were less vulnerable to sexual harassment and abuse. Some prefer how their bodies looked before puberty because their sex characteristics were mostly congruent with their internal sense of gender. Some experience both types of disturbances about their sex characteristics. Body dissatisfaction, sexism, anxiety, transphobia, homophobia,[5] and trauma can be part of the distress that trans/nonbinary people experience, along with gender-body incongruence.

- If you are distressed about your gender and body, what about the way your body currently is limits your sense of authentic living and loving?[6]

Gender-body incongruence, gender-role incongruence, social incongruence, and gender shame/trauma can lead to ***internalized gender stigma*** when the person internalizes rejection, turns against and away from themselves, and feels inferior, wrong, and deficient. Some people who experience gender-body incongruence, gender-role incongruence, or social incongruence decide to live incongruently due to traditional religious/cultural values or their social circumstances and still feel equal to others (they experience little or no gender shame/stigma but gender neutrality or pride instead).

Personal/social gender congruence, therefore, is the degree to which (a) a person's gender, gender identity, gender-role orientation, sex characteristics, and gender expression align with what feels authentic and healthy to that person (Kozee et al., 2012) and (b) the person is socially safe in expressing themselves in this way (Wu et al., 2021).

---

[5] Transmasculine and transfeminine individuals can be inaccurately perceived as gay or lesbian because of gender stereotypes.

[6] C. Johnson, personal communication, May 22, 2023.

With these definitions, gender identity remains a "fuzzy" and subjective concept and can mean different things for different people, given the variability in how people experience their gender and their attitudes and beliefs about gender. This subjective definition requires communication and curiosity about how each individual experiences themselves. A meaningful and objective definition for a person's gender may involve the person's degrees of (a) resonance, (b) dissonance, and (c) fluidity with embodying male and female sex characteristics (broad shoulders, flat chest, muscles, penis/testicles, deep voice, and hairiness compared to breasts, hips, vagina, smooth skin, long hair, high voice, etc.) and acting masculine and feminine according to the individual's cultural gendered expectations. Each experience of gender (for example, man, woman, nonbinary, gender expansive, agender, bigender, genderfluid, etc.) may indicate different levels of resonance, dissonance, and fluidity with maleness/femaleness and masculinity/femininity. A person's gender identity (the internal sense they have about their gender, as well as the beliefs they have about gender and their gender) will affect their gender expression.

- How much does the above fit your experiences with gender?
- How do you define *gender*, *gender identity*, *gender dysphoria/incongruence*, and *gender euphoria/congruence*?
- How do you define *sexual orientation*, and what does sexual congruence/incongruence mean to you?

Defining Sexual Orientation and Developing Sexual Congruence

The American Psychological Association (2024) defined *sexual orientation* as multidimensional and a person's "often enduring pattern of emotional, romantic, and/or sexual attractions to men, women, or both. It also refers to an individual's sense of personal and social identity based on those attractions, related behaviors, and membership in a community of others who share those attractions and behaviors." Coauthor Beckstead has asserted the need to define sexual orientation separately from the broader term *sexuality* and differentiate a person's sexual attractions from their emotional attractions, romantic orientation and experiences, motivational desires, relationship diversity, and social identity and affiliation. A person's *sexual identity*, similar to gender identity, has aspects that are objective and subjective and may indicate their sexual attractions or sexual activity or both and how the individual thinks and feels about and labels their attractions and experiences. Beckstead asserts that separating sexual attraction from sexuality and sexual identity may reduce confusion in the legal, professional, and clinical debates between proponents and opponents of sexual orientation change efforts (SOCE). Without clear definitions of sexual orientation, proponents and opponents of SOCE can talk past and misunderstand each other.

For example, a same-gender-attracted individual, monosexual or plurisexual, who changed their behaviors to match heterosexual norms could argue and promote that they changed their sexual orientation. With a multidimensional definition of sexual orientation, someone could declare their sexual orientation is fluid by transitioning away from a gay/bisexual identity and limiting their sexual fantasizing about same-gender individuals; avoiding situations that trigger same-gender attraction and arousal; reducing their same-gender sexual behaviors to rarely or never; feeling less desire, arousal, or interest in acting sexually or romantically due to a reduction of sex drive or social or personal prohibitions or changes; restricting themselves to heterosexual sexual behaviors; developing their romantic or emotional feelings for their heterosexual spouse; rejecting an LGBQ identity for political, religious, or social reasons; developing a heterosexual identity (or ex-gay, heterosexual with same-gender attractions, sex addiction survivor, no label, etc.); or limiting their social networks to exclusively heterosexual people.

None of these shifts in sexuality and sexual identity indicates a change in the individual's sexual attraction capability to different genders.

With a multidimensional definition of sexual orientation, "sexuality change" (changes in desires, behaviors, or social affiliations) can be mislabeled as "sexual orientation change" (changes in sexual attraction capability), and people may be misled into believing everybody's sexual orientation is fluid. Beckstead asserts there is too much "noise" and variability in multidimensional definitions of sexual orientation to know what can be changed and for whom. For instance, one study found that changes in self-reported sexual orientation (or identity) were unrelated to changes in sexual arousal (Gruia et al., 2022).

Because a substantial number of sexual/gender minorities report a variety of harm from trying to change or suppress their sexual/romantic attractions and experiences or gender expression, it's essential to understand what can be changed and developed regarding a person's sexuality and gender identity.

Terms such as *monosexuality* and *plurisexuality/polysexuality* differentiate individuals whose sexual attraction capability (sexual orientation) remains relatively constant (for example, exclusively same-gender- and other-gender-attracted individuals) from those whose sexual attraction capability (sexual orientation) is fluid and dynamic throughout their life. Plurisexual/polysexual individuals seem to represent a distinct sexual orientation from monosexual individuals (Rullo, 2012; Slettevold et al., 2019). We'll highlight below the various aspects of sexuality, also known as a person's *sexual script* (Simon & Gagnon, 1986) or *lovemap* (Money, 1986).

- How would you describe your sexual script or illustrate your lovemap?
- What is the sexual script or lovemap of your ideal or current lover/sex partner(s)?

Defining Sexual Attraction

One way to define sexual orientation is by assessing the intensity of the person's *sexual attractions* (positive emotional states of sexual interest and arousal) (Chivers et al., 2010). Sexual attractions can involve fantasies and desires to be sexual with someone, although not always. Sexual desire is different from sexual attraction and physical arousal. An individual can be sexually attracted but have no desire to act on the attraction due to low arousal, lack of energy, or social circumstances. An individual can be physically aroused but not want sexual intimacy.

If you have ever experienced sexual attraction to a person, then your sexual orientation is *allosexual*. If you have never experienced sexual attraction to a person, then your sexual orientation is *asexual* (Bogaert, 2004) or on the asexual spectrum of low sexual attraction and excitement.

If you are only sexually attracted to adult women/femaleness, then the scientific term for your sexual orientation is *gynephile*. Sexual attraction to femininity (as defined by your culture), regardless of a person's sex characteristics, is termed *gynesexual/gynosexual*. If you are only sexually attracted to adult men/maleness, then the scientific term for your sexual orientation is *androphile*. Sexual attraction to masculinity (as defined by your culture), regardless of a person's sex characteristics, is termed *androsexual*. If you are sexually attracted to men/maleness/masculinity and women/femaleness/femininity, then the scientific term for your sexual orientation is *ambiphile*, or *bi/poly/plurisexual*, *pansexual, omnisexual*, or *fluid* may fit you if you are attracted to people of all genders, depending on how important gender and sex characteristics are for you. In this way, sexual orientations can be categorized (for example, androphile, gynephile, bisexual, pansexual, fluid, asexual), and any changes would be categorical (for example, from androphile to gynephile or from bisexual/fluid to gynephile/androphile).

Men sexually attracted to adult men (androphiles), by definition, are not sexually attracted to children (Bailey et al., 2021). Despite prejudice about gay men being pedophiles (Herek, 2018), same-gender-attracted androphiles are *not* to be confused with same-gender-attracted *pedophiles* (individuals attracted to prepubescent children) and same-gender-attracted *hebephiles* (individuals attracted to pubescent children).

Categories can be helpful, but sexual orientation categories are not discrete categories and are best represented on a continuum with intersections of romantic, emotional, and social attractions and aversions. Within each category and between categories, there are a multitude of unique combinations of sexual attraction, particularly as different criteria are used to identify it, such as genital arousal, cognitive awareness, and fantasies/desires, as well as intensity with which the attraction is experienced. A categorical understanding of sexual orientation allows a description of the sexual attraction capability of the individual. These categories do not, however, tell us the strength or causes of such attractions and the reasons for any reported changes (Cantor & Fedoroff, 2018).

One way to assess sexual attraction capability is by assessing physical arousal to sexual stimuli. For example, the genital arousal of lesbian cisgender women and heterosexual and gay cisgender men tends to match their reported sexual identity (lesbian, heterosexual, gay) and be category specific: toward only women or only men (Chivers et al., 2007). Bisexual+ people can demonstrate a range of arousal, sometimes more same-gender or another-gender, with strong arousal to bisexual erotic material (Cerny & Janssen, 2011), and be less gender specific than exclusively gay cisgender men and cisgender lesbians (Rullo et al., 2015). In contrast, asexual individuals can experience a sex drive underlying their masturbatory behaviors that is diffuse with no direction toward gender or connection to others (Yule et al., 2017).

Cisgender women and transgender men tend to have an automatic genital response to sexual activity, regardless of the gender involved in the sexual activity; their genital arousal may not necessarily represent their sexual identity. As Chivers et al. (2004) noted,

> A self-identified heterosexual [cisgender] woman would be mistaken to question her sexual identity because she became aroused watching female-female erotica; most heterosexual [cisgender] women experience such arousal. A self-identified heterosexual [cisgender] man who experienced substantial arousal to male-male erotica, however, would be statistically justified in reconsidering his sexual identity. (p. 741)

Although cisgender women's sexual attention is impacted by contextual cues and the intensity of sexual stimuli (O'Kane et al., 2022), they show a stronger genital response to their preferred gender when sexual cues consist of static images (Bouchard et al., 2015). Farr et al. (2014) demonstrated that sexual minority cisgender women have a sexual orientation despite the high degree of variability in their sexual attractions. Research on transgender men's sexual arousal showed a mixed pattern of responding more strongly to their preferred gender than to another gender, identical to cisgender men's sexual arousal, and responding sexually to men and women similar to cisgender women's arousal (Raines et al., 2021).

Overall, asking someone what turns them on when or if they sexually fantasize tends to provide self-concordance with a person's genital arousal and sexual attraction (Chivers et al., 2010). The power dynamics, process, and ending of the person's sexual fantasies will likely describe what age and type of gender/sex turns them on and their sexual script/lovemap and preferred gender expression and role.

Labels that individuals select for themselves might fit with these overall patterns, but others do not like to label their sexual orientation and some choose multiple labels. Others select a label such as "questioning" or might fluctuate in labels they select even when their underlying sexual attractions do not change.

Defining Sexual Aversion

Coauthor Beckstead (2012) noted from his qualitative study on 50 individuals who tried to change their sexual orientation through traditional religion and psychotherapy that some who failed to change reported experiencing a physical aversion and disgust to being sexual with their nonpreferred gender, including their spouse, even though they loved their spouse. Because of this discrepancy, Beckstead suggests that a definition of sexual orientation include not just what gendered sex a person is attracted to but the person's degree of *sexual aversions* (negative emotional states of sexual dislike/disgust) to men, women, and nonbinary individuals. Sexual aversion differs from internalized social phobia (homophobia, bi-phobia, transphobia, etc.), which may be reduced with accurate information and positive social contact.

Freund et al. (1973) first explored sexual aversion in gay cisgender men, examining if it represented anxiety or a phobia toward women. Their findings did not support this assumption. However, subsequent research by Freund et al. (1974) revealed gay cisgender men subjectively rated feelings of disgust toward pictures with breasts and vulva. Recent studies indicate that the intensity of *physical sexual aversion* (disgust, discomfort, avoidance) can differentiate individuals attracted exclusively to one gender from those attracted to more than one gender (Ebswort & Lalumière, 2012; Israel & Strassberg, 2009; Lippa, 2012; Mahaffey et al., 2011; Morandini et al., 2019; O'Handley et al., 2017; Semon et al., 2017; Tassone et al., 2019).

Dehlin et al. (2019) discovered that sexual minorities with higher physical and emotional aversion toward other-gender sexuality and lower emotional attraction to an other-gender spouse were more likely to be divorced or in separated mixed-orientation marriages. The degree of sexual aversion may limit one's ability to tolerate, enjoy, and engage sexually with one's nonpreferred gender, depending on various factors like sexual attraction, sex drive, and emotional components.

Defining Romantic Orientation

Some people's sexual orientation may differ from their romantic orientation and have different functions. Clark and Zimmerman (2022) found that 89% of allosexual individuals (people who feel sexual attraction to others) had a romantic orientation that matched their sexual orientation. In their study, 96% of heterosexual participants, 81% of gay/lesbian participants, 71% of pansexual participants, and 64% of bisexual participants had concordant sexual and romantic orientations. Among asexual individuals (people who have never felt sexual attraction to anyone), 37% also identified as aromantic. Diamond (2003) proposed a dual system of (a) *romantic love* that is more person-oriented and (b) *sexual desire* that is more biological-sex-oriented. Some individuals may develop romantic love or nurturing feelings for their long-term partner(s) even though they have decreased sexual attraction, arousal, desire, and even physical aversion for the aging body of their partner(s). Some people prefer the term *affectional orientation* instead of sexual orientation to ensure their intimacy does not get reduced to sexual behaviors. Some people may confuse romantic orientation with emotional orientation when their relationships are emotionally intimate and physically demonstrative but not sexual (for example, a bromance).

How do you define romance? What are your ideas and feelings about romance, and what feels romantic to you? Romance may mean having crushes and infatuations, falling in love, feeling erotic passion, wooing or courting someone, or experiencing emotional bonding. Many studies have demonstrated associations between romantic relationship styles and parental attachment styles (Diamond et al., 2010). Thus, an individual's romantic orientation may be developmentally and socially influenced and involve emotional needs, attachment wounds, levels of trust, bonding styles, internalized social phobia, and companionship desires. Li et al. (2022), for example, found that negative attitudes toward LGB individuals and positive attitudes toward traditional Asian values on family continuity strongly affected LGB and heterosexual Chinese individuals' romantic orientation.

When you're in a romantic relationship, how much do you worry about relationship commitment and being rejected, abandoned, controlled, or emotionally smothered, and how much do you dismiss and avoid feelings? Your answers could indicate how much your predominant *attachment style* is secure, preoccupied, avoidant, or chaotic. This attachment style may influence how you feel getting romantically close to men, women, and nonbinary individuals.

Romantic aversion due to disliking being romantic with your nonpreferred gender is different from *romantic insecurity/phobia* due to attachment style and past attachment wounds and from *internalized social phobia* and negative attitudes about being romantic with men, women, and nonbinary individuals.

- How much do you desire versus dislike being romantic with women, men, and nonbinary individuals?
- How much do you fear rejection versus feel secure being intimate with women, men, and nonbinary individuals?
- How much would you fear social rejection and feel embarrassed versus comfortable if others knew you were being romantic with women, men, and nonbinary individuals?

Overall, an individual's *romantic orientation* may involve their (a) romantic attractions, crushes, desires, and preoccupations and (b) aversions, disgust, insecurities, distrust, and avoidance related to men, women, and nonbinary individuals.

- How much do your romantic and emotional orientations, mood, and relationships affect your sexual attractions and sexuality?

Understanding Fluidity

It's easy to confuse "changes" in sexuality (for example, sexual identity and behaviors) with "fluidity" of sexual orientation. Research describes sexual fluidity as variable and inconsistent instead of malleable and changeable, with shifts in attractions and experiences spontaneously occurring for some individuals (Diamond & Rosky, 2017). The consistency for pluri/polysexual individuals is the inconsistency of their attractions, behaviors, and identity (Slettevold et al., 2019). The consistency for monosexual individuals is their consistency of attractions, behaviors, and identity. Diamond et al. (2017) defined sexual fluidity as heightened erotic "sensitivity to situational, interpersonal, and contextual influences which may facilitate shifts in sexual attraction, behavior, and identity" (p. 193).

Safron and Hoffman (2017) hypothesized that most cisgender women, due to their nonspecific genital arousal, have a unique system and motivational incentive that is more sensitive and shaped by social context and experience. They suggested that this unique orienting system may provide a strong enough feedback loop of emotional and romantic experiences to enhance preferences and orientations. This orienting system explains how relational factors, such as romantic attachment, context, or changes in the ovulatory cycle, may affect women's sexual choices and identity more than arousal (Diamond & Wallen, 2011; Manley et al., 2015). Similarly, sexual fluidity may describe how some individuals discover their sexual nonexclusivity due to changes in circumstances, exploration, self-identification, and an expansion of sexuality (Katz-Wise et al., 2016).

Rieger et al. (2013) examined bisexual-identified cisgender men's sexual arousal patterns and found one group of men were aroused by men and women, but this was true only for those who were more curious about sexually diverse acts. The second group of bisexual-identified cisgender men had arousal patterns similar to gay-identified cisgender men and lower sexual curiosity than those sexually aroused to men and women but higher curiosity than heterosexual and gay-identified cisgender men. The sexual arousal patterns of heterosexual and gay-identified cisgender men were little affected by their sexual curiosity. These researchers concluded that at least two groups of cisgender men identify as bisexual, depending on their sexual arousal and personality.

Assessing Sexual Orientation, Romantic Orientation, and Internalized Self-Stigma/Pride

Here are some questions that might describe a person's sexual orientation and romantic orientation and the person's negating or affirming attitudes associated with these orientations:

- How would you describe in three to five words how sex would be for you in general with men, women, and nonbinary individuals?
- Think of the type of men, women, and nonbinary individuals whom you admire for their beauty or think are emotionally attractive. Rate on a scale from 0 to 10 the degree of your sexual attraction to those individuals. Sexual attraction means being "turned on," aroused sexually, and erotically interested in another.
- Rate on a scale from 0 to 10 the degree of your sexual aversion (sexual dislike to disgust) with being sexual with women, men, and nonbinary individuals.
- Rate on a scale from 0 to 10 the degree of your social phobia (negative attitude and fear of embarrassment/shame) about being sexual with women, men, and nonbinary individuals.
- How do you define romantic attraction, aversion, and security/insecurity? How much are you attracted or opposed to being romantic with men, women, and nonbinary individuals and to your partner(s) if applicable?

If any of the above descriptions include negative associations and reactions, consider recognizing your physical and psychological limits as you also consider addressing shame and phobias associated with attachment insecurities, trauma, loss, minority stress, and other factors.

- How would improving your emotional health affect, if at all, your sexual and romantic attractions, aversion limits, and attachment phobias (your sexual and romantic orientations)?

Acknowledging Other Aspects of Sexuality

Sexual interests, such as fetishes, preferences, and "types" (Zhang, 2022), differ from sexual orientation, which is the range of genders/ages you want to join you in your sexual interests. Sexual preferences can involve the dynamics and gender roles that erotically turn you on. For example, some gay/bisexual men view themselves as "sides" who enjoy same-sex sexual intimacy but not anal sex (prefer masturbating together) as opposed to others who experience themselves as "tops," "bottoms," or "versatile."

Some people prefer new and exciting sexual stimulation (*sexual sensation seeking*). This disposition for novel stimulation can lead to unsafe sexual practices and substance use. For example, research shows that greater sensation seeking in gay men is associated with greater expectations about the sexually enhancing effects of substances, which in turn is associated with greater unprotected anal intercourse (Kashubeck-West & Szymanski, 2008). Unexpectedly, less sensation seeking is also related to more substance use during sex for some gay and bisexual men, possibly to cope with internal conflict, which in turn is associated with more risky sexual behavior. Elevated levels of both sensation seeking and *sexual curiosity* were found for bisexual cisgender women and men; only bisexual cisgender women reported elevated levels of *sexual excitability* (Stief et al., 2014). Sensation seeking is positively associated with resilience markers of life satisfaction, positive affect, and less stress due to problem-focused coping for those who had experienced trauma (McKay et al., 2018). Therefore, a disposition for sensation seeking may increase resilience by decreasing stress and increasing an individual's resources to manage adversity.

- How much do you seek out sexual stimuli and are easily turned on by sexual stimuli and when you see an attractive person, and has this changed for you throughout your life?
- How much is monogamy, nonmonogamy, or polyamory and fetishes/kink an integral part of your identity and the way you live life best?

Van Anders (2015) also noted the importance of factoring *partner-number preference* into a person's sexuality. How many sexual partners do you prefer to have over a period of time and when you are being sexual? An individual's desires for *companionship* may differ from their sexual and romantic orientations and sexual partner number. Companionship can involve wanting a committed partnership to bond emotionally and share the ups and downs that are part of life.

- How much do you desire companionship and a partnership and with which type of person(s)? How important is it for you to experience sexual and romantic aspects in your companionship(s) and partnership(s)?
- How many sexual/romantic partners and companionships do you prefer?

Multidimensional definitions of sexuality and gender may help us understand how aspects of sexuality and gender can be *branched* and joined together with enough sexual/gender integrity and manageable conflict, as adaptations of incongruence and fluidity. Interventions may be used to empower aspects of sexuality (for example, mindfulness, sexual attitudes, sexual self-concept, motivations for sex, assertiveness, social support, self-awareness, self-acknowledgment, sexual skills, etc.). Interventions may be used to reduce the effects of attachment insecurities, trauma, and minority stress on a person's sexuality. Reducing internal and social distress associated with gender, sexual, and relationship diversity and noticing the impact on the person's health, relationships, and sexuality will be more effective and safer than trying to change their gender and sexual orientation.

Conclusion

A person's sexual orientation involves the degree and fluidity of their (a) sexual attraction and (b) sexual aversion to maleness and femaleness (physical sex characteristics) and (c) sexual attraction and (d) sexual aversion to masculinity and femininity (characteristics and social roles described by their culture for women, men, and genderfluid/nonbinary individuals). A person's sexual orientation may be similar to or different in degrees from their romantic, emotional, and social orientations. Some individuals' sexual/romantic orientations are not specific to sex characteristics and gender roles but contextual, relational, and individual.

A person's sexuality has many components: sexual, romantic, emotional, and social attractions and aversions; beliefs; attitudes; values; motivations; desires; skills; behaviors; social identity; preferences; needs; and comfort/satisfaction with commitment, performance, and different sexual expressions and activities. These components may be influenced by the person's biological sex, gender identity, gender role, sex drive, and social and personal options.

A person's gender involves the degree and fluidity of their (a) resonance with and (b) dissonance to maleness and femaleness (gender-body congruence) and acting masculine and feminine according to their cultural gendered expectations (gender-role congruence).

How an individual thinks and feels about and expresses their gender and sexual orientation (sexual/gender identity) may be influenced by the following:

- Their current relationships and outlets of expression
- Their sexual and gender identity exploration and development and level of self-awareness, self-acknowledgment, self-concept, and the level and impact of attachment, trauma, minority stress, cultural norms, prejudice, internalized stigma, and moral aversion on sexual, romantic, and personal development
- The social constructions that limit or expand the individual's cognitive and emotional prohibitions and permissions about sexuality, romance, and gender expression
- Their willingness, need, and ability to ignore, tolerate, compartmentalize, buffer, reframe, and cope with any short- and long-term incongruence

Therefore, an individual's degree of *personal and social sexual-orientation/ gender congruence* involves the fit, conflicts, branchedness, and authenticity between the above aspects and the degree of distress/satisfaction with any expression and differences. An individual has some influence in changing many of these components but likely not all.

Chapter 5

Find Peace With Religious, Sexual, and Gender Conflicts

Edward (Ward) B. Davis, Tyler Lefevor, Sulaimon Giwa,
Jeanna Jacobsen, Jeff Paulez, Samuel Eshleman Latimer,
Annelise Parkes Murphy, Helen Harris, Janet B. Dean,
Jay Tekulvē Jackson-Vann, and A. Lee Beckstead

For many sexual/gender minority (LGBTQIA+) individuals, sexuality, gender, and faith are sources of inspiration, comfort, grace, joy, conflict, and pain. We hope this chapter helps you understand your relationship with spirituality, faith, religion, and sexual/gender diversity and clarify what provides you with resilience, health, and meaning. We emphasize questions for exploration and provide options to address identity conflicts. We also offer a few stories of people who have found peace within themselves and socially. We hope this information helps you with your self-determination, identity exploration and development, and well-being.

Getting Started (or Continuing) on Your Journey

Knowing how to take the first or next steps on your identity journey can be challenging. Often, it is helpful to begin by describing your life needs and conflicts. What is vital for you regarding religion, faith, spirituality, gender, romance, and sexuality? What are the most prominent conflicts you feel among and about (a) your romantic/sexual identity (how you publicly and privately identify and experience your romantic and sexual orientations and romantic and sexual expression); (b) your gender identity (how you publicly and privately identify and express your gender, which may be different from your sex assigned at birth); (c) your relationship identity (how you publicly and privately identify your relationship system, such as monogamous, polyamorous, open, swingers, etc.); and (d) your faith identity (how you publicly and privately identify your religion, spirituality, and purpose in life)?

- Considering which words describe your sexual, gender, relationship, and faith identities and needs, what is essential to your well-being?
- What might have caused and fueled any conflicts and distress?

Navigating Conflicts Among Your Sexual, Gender, and Faith Identities

Often, conflicts stem from negative messages about gender, sexual, and faith diversity or a lack of positive options or both. You may have grown up in a conservative religion and family that criticized and rejected people with expansive or nonnormative sexual or gender identities. Heterosexuality might have been championed as the only permissible sexual orientation. In the same way, identifying with your birth-assigned sex or living by binary gender roles may have been held up as the only acceptable gender identity and expression.

You may understandably internalize these messages and feel unwelcome, unacceptable, or unloved. Internalization is the process by which we believe the statements others have told us about ourselves, or similar people, and agree they are justified and true. We "swallow" the cultural beliefs and norms without processing them cognitively or emotionally. Because of these internalized messages, you might treat certain aspects of your sexuality or gender as unwelcome, unacceptable, or unlovable. You may also feel like specific pathways of identity integration (identifying as both LGBTQIA+ and religious or spiritual) are not options for you.

Whatever the case, if the situations in this chapter resonate with you, you may be experiencing what is called *identity conflict*. Identity conflict happens when someone feels they have important parts of themselves that are irreconcilable with each other (for example, being gay and Muslim, being transgender and Jewish). Identity conflicts can lead to negative psychological, spiritual, physical, and relational consequences (for example, anxiety, depression, negative religious coping, fatigue, concealing, and social isolation). Yet conflicts, incongruence, and divergence among a person's gender, sexual, and faith identities do not always involve distress, especially if safe options are available. Identity conflicts without distress are called living a *branched* sexuality (van Anders, 2015), gender, and faith. Unfortunately, identity conflicts, social rejection, internalized self-rejection, and a lack of options can lead some individuals to self-hatred, dissociation, and self-injurious thoughts or behaviors—even suicide.

You may just be embarking on your journey of identity exploration. Identity exploration involves developing self-understanding, learning more about options, and evaluating various pathways and possibilities for identity resolution. Identity resolution refers to the process by which you accept the different parts of yourself and pursue harmonious integration—or at least a satisfactory balance—of any current identity conflicts. The very resolution of the identity conflict brings up identity integration, which contributes to the positive coherent experience of self and general well-being.

It can be challenging to decide how you want to pursue peace among the different parts of yourself that may feel in conflict. Yet, in the midst of it all, chances are that you exhibit a lot of strengths and have resources you can draw on for help (Rosenkrantz et al., 2016). Compassion can help you treat yourself with the same kindness with which you treat others. Your commitment to honesty and integrity can help you be open and truthful with yourself, others, and your higher power/purpose (whatever that means for you). Patience can help you endure difficulty, accept paradoxes, and embrace uncertainty. Creativity can help you develop innovative solutions for yourself and expand your perspectives and possibilities.

Common Strategies for Resolving Identity Conflicts

Experiencing sexual, gender, and faith conflicts without resolving them causes distress (Lefevor et al., 2023). People tend to use one of four strategies to resolve conflicts:

1. Some reject or alter their sexual identity, sexuality, or gender expression and prioritize their religious identity.
2. Others reject their religion or change how they think about and live out their religion and spirituality.
3. Sometimes people compartmentalize their sexual, gender, and faith identities to be "out" at school or work but not in their faith community or family. In contrast, some people are not "out" about their faith identity in their LGBTQIA+ community and relationships.
4. Other individuals find ways to integrate their sexual, gender, and faith identities personally and publicly, such that people in all spheres of their life know about these identities (Pitt, 2010; Rodriguez & Ouellette, 2000).

As people continue their journey of identity development and resolution, they often move from strategy to strategy throughout their lifetime (Yarhouse et al., 2018).

- Which strategies have you experienced the most, and how have they affected you?
- What feels off-limits for you now about any of the identity strategies mentioned (or any you may have considered)?
- Which identity strategy feels best for you now in your life? What about during future phases of your life?

Research on these strategies indicates there are benefits and drawbacks to each one. For example, rejecting one's gender expression and sexual orientation can and often does lead to self-rejection, emotional pain/suffering, shame, and suicidality (Bourn et al., 2018). Some people who reject a sexual/gender minority identity also deny their sexual attractions, gender expression, and personhood, which may fuel some of the earlier-mentioned health problems. At the same time, individuals who reject a sexual/gender identity may experience a strong sense of attachment and support from their family, religion, spirituality, higher power/purpose, and faith community (Dehlin et al., 2015). Experiencing a sense of belonging in one's religion and family can reduce suicidal thoughts by reducing the person's internalized shame (Skidmore, Lefevor, Golightly, et al., 2022). Even so, some individuals who reject their sexual orientation and gender expression may be more likely to engage in hidden same-gender sexual experiences, which can cause them intense shame, guilt, distress, or difficulty. Some, unable to sustain the rejection of their sexual/gender identity, may resent the family and faith they feel contributed to their self-rejection, internal conflict, and religious or relational trauma (Cole & Harris, 2017).

One benefit of rejecting or adapting one's religion or spirituality comes from the person exploring and borrowing from diverse spiritual and religious paths and creating an individualized spiritual practice (Beagan & Hattie, 2015). LGBTQIA+ individuals are twice as likely to identify as religiously unaffiliated than exclusively heterosexual, cisgender individuals, with some LGBTQIA+ individuals identifying as "spiritual but not religious" (Pew Research Center, 2015). LGBTQIA+ individuals who reject or adapt their religion or spirituality tend to report greater resolution of internal conflicts, no change in or lower mental health problems, and a better quality of life than those who abandon or feel abandoned by their faith and family. These results can vary depending on how LGBTQIA+ individuals reject or adapt their faith. Adapting their faith may include exploring religions and faith communities that have changed and become welcoming and accepting. Some benefit from forms of spirituality that do not require the existence of a god/deity to provide meaning.

It can be challenging for those not immersed in a religiously conservative community to understand why someone identifying as LGBTQIA+ would not just leave and find an open and accepting community. Yet, for many LGBTQIA+ individuals, these communities have played an influential role in their development and remain an important source of support and sustenance. Additionally, the families and friends of those who identify as LGBTQIA+ may be deeply involved in these communities, so leaving the faith community and social network could be a profound loss and place some LGBTQIA+ people at significantly higher risk for isolation and health problems. People who leave their religion can also experience rejection by religious family members, friends, coworkers, and their higher power. That can be quite traumatic, resulting in intense loneliness and greater internal conflict and distress (Grigoriou, 2014; Lefevor et al., 2020). Yet remaining and "hiding" who one is can also be a profound loss and process of grief. This elevates the urgency of the current movement for many faith traditions and denominations to have conversations about more inclusive and supportive policies, practices, and doctrines (Harris et al., 2021).

Another strategy people use is to compartmentalize their sexual/gender identity from their faith identity. This strategy allows individuals to have separate spaces to explore and express themselves. This strategy can often be a transitory approach that leads to another resolution strategy at a later point. Over time, this process can include various successes and failures with integration, often leading to finding a supportive faith community or eschewing faith affiliations altogether. Compartmentalization can be helpful because it fosters self-exploration and validation in spaces perceived as safe for expressing an essential part of one's identity. However, some drawbacks include fragmented support, greater internal conflict, internalized sexual/gender stigma, and mental and sexual health problems (for example, depression and lower use of condoms) (Ryan et al., 2017; Severson et al., 2014).

Studies have found that the best health outcomes tend to be exhibited by people who can publicly integrate their sexual, gender, and faith identities. In research (Yarhouse et al., 2018) with Christian sexual minorities with more theologically conservative beliefs in U.S. colleges, finding a way to "hold" and value their religious and sexual experiences was more common than rejecting either. Finding ways to integrate them was healthier than compartmentalizing them. Identity integration may not be a realistic goal for some people, given their community's views toward sexual/gender diversity and their views concerning religious beliefs and practices. Research with LGBTQ+ Latter-day Saints found less than 5% of participants reported integrating sexual/gender and faith identities (Dehlin et al., 2015). Individuals who openly identify as both LGBTQIA+ and religious can risk being misunderstood and marginalized in both their LGBTQIA+ communities and religious contexts (Cole & Harris, 2017). If so, the risk of belonging nowhere can be significant. Some find a faith community that is welcoming and affirming as multiple faith groups are prioritizing inclusion (Harris & Yancey, 2021). Some faiths provide religious rituals, lay leadership, and employed leadership to everyone with sexual/gender minority identities (Harris et al., 2022).

Some LGBTQIA+ individuals prefer to find or stay in faith communities that provide support, encouragement, and mentorship as they follow their own deeply held, religiously conservative values around sexuality and gender. Integrating one's sexual/gender identity with faith identity may be a somewhat longer process for those with more traditional values, yet some are able to do so (Yarhouse et al., 2018). During this developmental process, these individuals are likely to have difficulty with affirming positions and also expectations to change their behaviors, yet eventually determine that their sexual orientation and gender expression will not likely change.

If this is where you find yourself, know there are multiple ways to hold together your sexual/gender identity and conservative faith. Some people will experience a call to vocational singleness (celibacy) and may even take vows of such with their faith communities.[1] It feels important to name that a call to celibacy is not a good fit/preferred option for all sexual minorities holding conservative religious beliefs, just as a call to celibacy is not for all heterosexual people holding conservative religious beliefs. There are costs to committed celibacy (Yarhouse & Zaporozhets, 2019), but some people have found these needs met through spiritual friendships (Hill, 2015), monastery-like living and service, and LGBTQIA+ organizations with similar religious values. For others, mixed-orientation marriages may be a viable option. In these mixed-gender marriages between one straight, cisgender individual and one LGBTQIA+ individual or when both experience same-gender attractions or identify as LGBTQIA+, spouses sometimes can experience intimacy and marital satisfaction comparable to other forms of marriage, particularly if they have a high degree of relational commitment (Kays et al., 2014) and a low degree of sexual aversion to the other gender and one's spouse (Bridges et al., 2019).

As the broader culture shifts toward more LGBTQIA+-affirming views (Pew Research Center, 2015), more sexual/gender minorities seek acceptance and meaning within their faith communities rather than leaving. Others are becoming more spiritual than religious, which might include practicing a more personal form of spirituality rather than maintaining involvement with a religious community or tradition. Research suggests LGBTQIA+ individuals often receive more health benefits from a more personalized spirituality than from participation in a faith community (Lefevor et al., 2021).

As you consider your identity resolution and development, several factors often help with this process: (a) accepting and liking yourself; (b) having support from family, friends, and people in your faith community; and (c) being part of a faith community that is affirming of sexual and gender minorities' experiences (Yarhouse & Carr, 2011). Self-acceptance may be the key factor. Research has found that LGBTQIA+ individuals who accept all of themselves, even the parts they wish were different, have better mental health than those who struggle with self-rejection (Dean et al., 2021). In addition, social support

---

[1] For example, see the testimony and ministry of Pieter Valk, executive director of Equip, at https://www.pieterlvalk.com/ and https://equipyourcommunity.org/.

from family, friends, a higher power, and a faith community facilitates good mental health by fostering self-acceptance. You learn to accept yourself as others accept you. Interestingly, this seems true regardless of your religious beliefs about sexuality and gender.

One way to practice self-acceptance is through self-compassion practices (Neff, 2023). Each component of self-compassion (appreciating your common humanity, treating yourself with kindness, and practicing mindfulness) overlaps with religious and spiritual traditions. For example, one study (Severson et al., 2014) on Christian Latino men who had sexual relationships with men found that they offered themselves compassion by emphasizing that "nobody is perfect; we are all sinners." This expression is a Christian way of verbalizing common humanity: "For all have sinned and fall short of the glory of God."[2] Self-kindness is honored within most faith traditions as the divinity's grace and love for all creatures (Kumpasoğlu et al., 2020). Within Christianity, kindness is one of the fruits of God's Holy Spirit.[3] Many Indigenous cultures emphasize treating all living things, including ourselves, kindly because we are all equal, sacred, and interconnected throughout time (Blume, 2020). Meditation and contemplation are widely accepted within most faiths and are examples of mindfulness. For example, looking for the sacred in each moment and interaction is an Indigenous spiritual activity and mindful way of living (Blume, 2020). Research suggests mindfulness promotes internal and social integration (Siegel, 2014).

- How can self-acceptance and self-compassion become part of your spiritual/ life practice and how would it affect your security in yourself?

Another option for identity exploration and development is cultivating a *quest orientation* (Malty & Day, 1998), which involves approaching life open-mindedly and humbly. This approach appreciates nuance and uncertainty and resists the urge toward clear-cut, oversimplified, and one-size-fits-all answers (Hill et al., 2012). People with a quest orientation are aware of how rigidly held beliefs and expectations can block understanding, connection, and growth. They are open to changing their views and actions to adapt to the complexities of life. This open-minded search for truth is associated with mental health benefits and reduced prejudice and discrimination (McFarland, 1989). A quest orientation helps us use doubt, confusion, and loss to question our belief systems, higher power, and purpose in life. Asking questions is as important for self-development and relationships as seeking answers. Some individuals, guided by a quest orientation, embrace the freedom to metaphorically "fly to fly," not requiring a landing recognizable to outsiders. While conventional wisdom insists that quests must reach conclusions, for others solace is found in the

---

[2] Romans 3:23.
[3] Galatians 5:22–23.

ongoing process of the quest itself. This curiosity and openness can promote a sense of awe and wonder for self, everyone, and everything. A quest orientation, therefore, can help people appreciate and grow from complexity and be flexible to adopt compassionate ways of experiencing life, especially during uncertainty.

Stories of People on Their Journey of Identity Exploration and Resolution

The following are stories of people who have used various strategies for resolving conflicts among their sexual, gender, and faith identities. These stories are based on compilations of experiences from people we have encountered in our clinical practice, empirical research, and personal lives. We have situated each story within a specific faith and cultural context, but each one is applicable across a wide range of faith and cultural contexts. Each name and story is fictitious and not connected to any specific individual.

- As you read the following, pay attention to your internal reactions and reflect on which experiences do and do not overlap with yours.
- Which strategies would be helpful or harmful to you in finding resolution and peace with your sexual, gender, and faith identities?

Taylor: A Christian Sexual Minority at a Conservative Christian College

Taylor is a 21-year-old White cisgender man and an undergraduate student at a conservative Christian college. He grew up in a conservative religious home, in which his personal and family life centered on the Christian faith. Taylor always felt grateful that his faith provided answers about God, life, and himself. But, during middle school, he began noticing that he was only romantically and physically attracted to his male peers. Over time, these attractions intensified. He never felt comfortable enough to tell his parents or friends. On his own, he tried to figure out how to reconcile his conservative faith with his experiences of same-gender attraction. Taylor found books and online resources about the topic. Yet all his reading never really helped, especially because much of the information was negative or contradictory. What helped the most was when Taylor met other students like himself once he started college. Taylor began attending a weekly student group where he and other Christians who experienced same-gender attraction could share their stories and support one another. He developed deep and meaningful friendships with other Christian sexual minorities like himself. Everyone started the group with some conflict between their faith identity and sexual/gender identity. Over time, many found increasing inner peace after exploring and living out the sexuality, gender, and faith that best fit each of them. Yet one of Taylor's friends died by suicide and had been talking about how hard-lined and isolating his family and congregants' families were treating him. This friend's death was a wake-up call for Taylor and his friends to prioritize finding value in themselves and investing in relationships with people who treat them accordingly, regardless of their sexual/gender/faith identity.

Some of Taylor's friends decided to adopt an LGBTQIA+ label and began referring to themselves as "gay Christians." A few others tried dating heterosexual individuals. Taylor took a different approach. After years of prayer, reading, reflection, and extensive conversations with his fellow group members, friends and family, and psychotherapist, Taylor made up his mind. He decided that, at least for now, the best strategy for him was to stay highly engaged with his Christian faith and only share about his same-gender attractions in spaces and relationships where it felt safe and relevant to do so. Taylor wants next to explore whether celibacy fits him and how he will respond to his sexuality and romance in relationships.

Alex: A Muslim Transgender Woman

Even when she was three, Alex knew she was different. Although she was born in a male body, she never felt at home in it. Alex's parents tried their best to love her, but they couldn't understand why she never was interested in typical "boy stuff." Despite this, Alex was always interested in her family's Muslim faith. She actively participated in devout prayer and became heavily involved in their mosque from a young age. Her family's Muslim faith and religious community had clear, strict roles for boys and girls. So Alex worked hard throughout her childhood to avoid transgressing gender boundaries. When she failed, she experienced painful rejection and criticism from others, including her parents. Year after year, Alex tried desperately to fit in, fearing she might lose her family, community, and even her eternal soul if she didn't. She wore a fake smile and tried not to let anyone see inside.

As a young adult, Alex did what all "good" Muslim men do: she married a woman and had children. For 10 years, she lived dutifully as a devoted husband, father, and Muslim. But no matter how much she tried, it always felt like a lie. Alex grew severely depressed but didn't talk about it with anyone. She was often irritable and felt guilty for not being closer to her children and spouse. Eventually, things got so unbearable she attempted suicide. After that, Alex entered psychotherapy. For the first time, she disclosed that she had always felt she was a woman. Throughout psychotherapy, Alex grew in self-understanding, self-acceptance, and self-compassion. She eventually decided she couldn't pretend anymore.

Alex secretly began experimenting with more feminine gender expression. She started connecting with other transgender and gender-expansive people—first via online chat rooms and then in person. In time, Alex felt increasing internal peace, support, affirmation, and empowerment.

Eventually, Alex decided to come out to her spouse. Her wife responded harshly and went immediately to their imam, who tried to convince Alex to disavow her gender identity and conform to her birth-assigned sex and conservative Muslim expectations for masculine gender expression. At first, several people in their mosque offered support and understanding until Alex began trying to participate in sex-segregated religious services that aligned with her gender. The more Alex challenged conservative gender roles and expectations, the more she experienced social pressure to live as a man. Her imam repeatedly urged her to stop sinning through her gender identification and nonconformity. Alex's wife threatened to leave and take their children.

Despite this heart-wrenching threat, Alex could no longer play the role of living as a man and knew she needed to live as a woman for her own sake. She chose to leave her spouse but do all she could to maintain close relationships with her spouse and kids. Because of how her imam and religious community treated her, Alex left her mosque and childhood faith. She is now thriving as a secular woman.

David: A Bisexual Jewish Man

David is an Orthodox Jewish man in his early 30s. He has always been very close with his family and still lives in the Orthodox Jewish community where he grew up. For as long as he can remember, David has been sexually and romantically attracted to both men and women. But David grew up in a religiously observant Orthodox Jewish family, synagogue, and community. Any form of same-sex sexual and romantic behavior was strictly forbidden. David always felt he had to hide his interest in boys to survive. He dated girls and prayed fervently that G-d would remove his attraction to boys. David tried his best to follow the path and practices his Jewish family, community, and tradition prescribed. Yet no matter how hard David prayed or how many times he repented of having sexual/romantic thoughts about other guys, it never changed David's feelings and attraction toward men.

During his twenties, David started dating men without revealing his religious beliefs and spiritual practices to them. Despite his desire to share this aspect of himself, he found it challenging to disclose this information. Furthermore, he never informed his family and religious community about his relationships with men. In short, David kept his romantic life and his religious life separate. Despite his uncertainty about what G-d wanted for him, he was confident that he didn't want to be alone. He acknowledged that some men he dated were a better match for him than the women he had dated. David currently manages to compartmentalize his romantic and religious lives quite effectively. However, there's an occasional concern that his family or religious community might discover this compartmentalization. He wishes he could openly discuss the highs and lows of his dating experiences with them. Sometimes, the fear arises that if he falls in love with a woman, he won't be able to share his whole self with her. Alternatively, if he falls in love with a man, he worries about keeping it a secret or potentially ending the relationship. The future appears uncertain for David, and, for now, he feels the need to explore and navigate these two aspects of his life separately.

Maria: A Lesbian Latina Catholic Woman

"You can't make me leave. I belong here, too." That is how Maria felt. As a Latina who had grown up in a conservative Catholic family and church, she loved her religion and her faith community. However, at age 20, Maria fell in love with Beth, who was also part of Maria's church. Maria never expected it or planned it. She even fought against it. But Maria's love was as authentic and powerful as her love for God, the church, and her family. Maria felt intense guilt and shame over her feelings, primarily whenever she and Beth engaged in romantic and sexual behavior. Maria contacted her priest to confess her perceived shame and sins with Beth. Her priest was kind but firmly warned Maria to avoid all temptation and stop seeing Beth entirely. Maria reluctantly agreed. She spent months engaging in strict religious observance. She worked hard to avoid Beth, but she missed Beth terribly. Maria's grief and longing were so intense they became almost unbearable. Finally, Maria couldn't take it anymore and decided to start seeing Beth again.

Maria and Beth eventually got married. At first, they stopped attending church. But Maria missed their religious community and the religious rites she loved so much. Maria knew many LGBTQIA+ people who had abandoned their religion and worried she might have to do the same. Yet, through much prayer and reflection, Maria realized her spiritual relationship was with God and was not dependent on others. So Maria returned to church, along with her wife. She knew their church wouldn't allow them to participate fully in congregational life, but at least she could attend mass as frequently as she wanted. Maria's nonreligious LGBTQIA+ friends told her she should leave her church or change religions and find one more welcoming and affirming. Yet she could not because she had grown up in the Catholic Church. Catholicism was the only religion within which she could imagine raising any future children. Maria just no longer believed her love for Beth was a shameful sin.

Over time, Maria's congregation became more accepting and supportive. There still were sermons that made her want to cry. But her priests and fellow congregants gradually became kind, welcoming, and affirming toward Maria and Beth. Maria also saw how some youth in her church looked up to her and her relationship with Beth. The visibility of their lives and relationship let these youth know they were not alone and could be both Catholic and LGBTQ+. Maria believed God loves and accepts everyone as they are, and she was determined to show that love passionately—through her Catholic faith and marriage.

Questions for Your Identity Development

Anecdotal stories and research can offer helpful information but cannot dictate your choices. Too often, a single narrative is held up as the path every person must follow. Each person's life path is unique, including your own.

- Of the examples above, which aspects and experiences do you most resonate with and why?
- Which strengths did you see in each example, and what would you wish for each person?
- How would you write about or describe your sexual, gender, and religious history and development?

The following questions can guide you in your identity exploration and, hopefully, help you find deeper peace. Check out our resource list online[4] if you are struggling.

Questions for Exploring Your Gender Identity

1. What does your gender mean to you? When did you first notice and identify your gender? How has that shifted or remained constant throughout your life? How do gender and gender roles fit into your life story, family/cultural history, relationships, and identity?
2. How much does your sex assigned at birth reflect your gender identity? How much does your gender identity reflect your current gendered physical body?
3. How do you experience and express your gender? How might that be different if you felt less tension, emotional distress, or societal expectation? How supported do you feel in expressing your gender? How does your gender expression fit and not fit with social norms? How much do your family

---

[4] At https://findingcongruence.com/.

members' and peers' gender expressions fit and not fit with social norms? How do gender social norms affect those you know?

4. When you express your gender authentically, what helps? What do you need from yourself and others to express your gender more authentically? How do you imagine living your authentic gender expression would feel? How open are you to changing your views on gender and how you might express your gender?

5. What more do you need to learn about gender and your gender expression?

Questions for Exploring Your Sexuality

1. How would you describe (in just a few words) your sexuality? How similar are these descriptions to how you want to feel about your sexuality? How open are you to changing your views on sexuality or your sexual expression, and what is realistic in changing aspects of your sexuality?

2. Who are you romantically, sexually, emotionally, spiritually, and socially attracted to? Are you romantically, sexually, emotionally, spiritually, and socially averse to any specific genders? When did you notice your attractions or lack thereof and any aversions?

3. Have your attractions or lack thereof and aversions changed or remained constant? Will your attractions or lack thereof and aversions change in the future? Which sexual orientation label(s) resonate and fit your sexual attractions or lack thereof and aversions? How do you identify privately? Publicly? Why?

4. How do you experience and express romance and sexuality? What do you enjoy, and what are you concerned about, if anything, regarding your sexuality and how you express romance? Are you more passionate or nurturing or both? If you felt less distressed, limited, or conflicted about romance/sexuality, what would you do differently? If you were at peace with your spiritual and sexual values, how would you relate with your partner(s) or potential partner(s)?

5. How do passion, sexuality, and companionship fit your life story and identity? What has led to that? What do you hope it will lead to? How vital are sexuality, romance, and companionship to you? What have been the most meaningful romantic and sexual connections you have had? What was so significant about them? What does all this tell you about yourself?

6. What more do you need to learn about sexuality and your sexuality?

Questions for Exploring Your Relationship Style

1. Which aspects of singlehood, monogamy (sexually closed relationship), nonmonogamy (sexually open relationship), and polyamory (multiple intimate relationships) appeal or not appeal to you?

2. How does your LGBTQIA+ identity intersect with your views on these relationship styles? Do any align with your spiritual values?

3. How do LGBTQIA+ and religious/spiritual/cultural spaces and events influence your exploration of these relationship styles?
4. What support networks exist within your LGBTQIA+ and faith communities to engage in singlehood, monogamy, nonmonogamy, or polyamory?
5. What are your thoughts on societal expectations and judgments about singlehood, monogamy, nonmonogamy, and polyamory?
6. How might discrimination and marginalization impact your decision and ability to enjoy singlehood, monogamy, nonmonogamy, and polyamory?
7. How would you navigate issues of representation and visibility enjoying singlehood, monogamy, nonmonogamy, and polyamory?
8. Is there a connection between your spiritual journey and being single or in a monogamous, nonmonogamous, or polyamorous relationship?
9. Are there specific considerations from your spirituality that you want to integrate into your relationships?

Questions for Exploring Your Faith

1. How would you describe (in just a few words) your religion, spirituality, faith, or purpose/meaning in life? How vital are religion, faith, and spirituality to you? How do they fit or not fit into your life, relationships, and identity? How strong is your conviction of what you believe? How open are you about your convictions with others? Which religious, spiritual, and faith experiences have influenced your identity? In which ways does your religion affect your spiritual life and vice versa? How open are you to changing your views on spirituality, religion, and faith and your private and public religious/spiritual practices?
2. Which doctrines, rituals, and practices were important to you growing up? Which ones did you not believe in and how did that affect you? Which limitations and strengths did you find within your religion and faith growing up? In which ways does your family's faith impact your life and development?
3. What are the historical representations of sexual/gender diversity in your community and tradition? How would you describe your religious/spiritual heritage about sexual/gender diversity? What are the times when your religion/spirituality supported your sexuality/gender (and vice versa)? How have your faith and spirituality influenced your beliefs and behaviors regarding sexuality and gender (and vice versa)?
4. What are your current religious/spiritual motivations? What were they when you were younger? How do these affect your health? What role do spirituality, faith, and religion (or nonreligion/-spirituality) play in your well-being? What is joyful about your religion, faith, spirituality, or purpose/meaning in life? How do your religion, spirituality, faith, or purpose/meaning in life help you and others? When others view you living your faith, spirituality, religion, or purpose in life, what do you hope inspires them?

5. How do you see your spiritual gifts and faith purpose? What or who helps facilitate your spiritual growth? How would you describe spiritual-sexual-gender wellness? What are the qualities of a spiritually healthy person?

6. What is sacred in your religion, faith, spirituality, and purpose/meaning in life? How does your religion or spirituality sanctify aspects of you, others, and life that are not to be defiled? What does it mean to you to defile something or transgress what is sacred? How may spiritual transgressions be repaired and redeemed?

7. How do you describe your higher power/purpose and your relationship with your higher power/purpose (if you have one)? Which strengths do you get from this relationship? Is your relationship based on openness, compassion, and trust regarding your sexuality/gender or on punishment, anger, and insecurity? How much do you wonder if your higher power has abandoned you, or do you question your higher power's love for you? How much do you seek and experience your higher power's love and care regarding your sexuality and gender?

8. What is your relationship with religious texts, if you have any? How much do you question or adhere to them? How does this affect your life positively? Negatively?

9. What are your cherished religious/spiritual symbols, holidays, rituals, songs, images, and experiences? Which make you happy, give you comfort and peace, help you cope during adversity, or remind you of positive memories? What inspires or moves you about this symbol or practice?

10. Who were the spiritual, religious, and faith leaders and role models who played a part in your development? How supportive and compassionate are your religious leaders toward you for experiencing sexual/gender diversity? How much does your relationship with your higher power guide your spiritual/religious experiences above any person or religious leader? How much do you trust your faith leaders to guide you to what is best regarding your sexuality and gender? How often do you disagree with your faith leaders, and where are the areas of agreement between you and these leaders?

11. How much do you believe your religion/spirituality is the correct faith and tradition for everyone? For you?

12. How has (or would) "coming out" and telling others about being LGBTQIA+ influenced your religious, spiritual, and faith beliefs and purpose/meaning in life and vice versa?

Questions for Exploring Internal Self-Conflicts

1. When considering your sexuality, gender, relationship style, and faith/spirituality, do any hold greater value or importance? If so, how? Why? What led to that?

2. How well do your sexuality, gender, relationship style, and faith fit together? What are their places of harmony and unity? What are their areas of tension and dissonance?

3. How will your faith influence your sexuality, gender, and relationship style in the future? How will your relationship style affect how you live out your sexuality, gender, and faith?
4. Which beliefs and practices from your religion, cultural gender norms, and sexual experiences do you want to keep, which ones don't fit you, and which ones do you want to redefine for yourself and keep exploring?
5. How would you describe your self-esteem and self-worth? How satisfied are you with yourself? How much are you living true to yourself? How do these feelings influence the internal conflicts you experience surrounding your sexuality, gender, relationship style, and faith?
6. Are you using your religious/spiritual practices to "spiritually bypass" and avoid engaging with feelings, self-stigma, and psychological and relational difficulties? If so, how does this affect your well-being and ability to find help (Ahmad et al., 2023)?

Questions for Exploring External Conflicts

1. What have your family, friends, religious community, and faith tradition taught you about sexuality, gender, and relationship styles? What has the LGBTQIA+ community taught you about your faith? Which beliefs and attitudes about sexuality, gender, relationship styles, and faith are yours? Which ones do you hold because others have told you that you should?
2. How might your family, friends, and faith community respond to you if you chose an LGBTQIA+-affirmative path? What is the evidence they will react this way? What would you need (from yourself, others, and your higher power) to help you handle any negative reactions you might face?
3. Who are your primary sources of emotional and spiritual support? Are there any conditions for their support? How might you function if they no longer supported you? What would you need from yourself and others if you lost their support? How might you feel and function if they offered you their full and unconditional support?

Questions for Exploring Possibilities and Pathways of Identity Integration

1. What feels like an ethical spiritual sexuality (Helminiak, 2004) and a gender-expansive spirituality to you?
2. How can your faith beliefs and practices help you cope with the difficulties of being LGBTQIA+ in your faith communities and being religious/spiritual in your LGBTQIA+ communities?
3. If you are trying to change your sexual orientation, sexual experiences, or gender expression, how do the strategies you're using affect your well-being, self-development, faith, and sexuality/gender expression? Would any of the following help you with your identity conflicts and resolution?

    a. respond to your self-expression with more acknowledgment, acceptance, curiosity, self-compassion, and grace

    b. question shame and develop self-appreciation and self-respect

    c. consider your sexuality/gender and faith as complementary and meaningful to you

4. If you focused on increasing your existential and eudaemonic well-being, what helps you feel good about life, live a purposeful and fulfilling life, pursue your potential, contribute to society, feel happy and in good spirits, and give your life meaning (Tan, 2005)?

5. If nothing held you back, how would you resolve the current conflicts among your sexuality, gender, relationship style, and faith? What is hindering you from doing that? How would life be different if you followed that path? What might help you do so?

6. Which personal and interpersonal skills and community resources would help you explore and integrate? How do those compare with your current internal and external resources? Which resources might you need to bridge this gap?

7. Ten years from now, what would you hope your life looks like regarding sexuality, romance, gender, relationship style, and faith? Who and what can help you journey toward that? How so?

8. What is and is not in your power to change regarding (a) your sexuality and romantic desires, (b) your gender, and (c) your religion and spirituality? Of the things you can change, what do you want to change? Why? How? What will help you accept, adapt, and find peace with what you cannot change?

9. What are the core values that guide your life? How can they guide your identity exploration and development? How might they hinder your identity resolution?

10. Who are the most supportive people in your life right now? How can they help you in your journey toward peace? How might you broaden and deepen your support network? How much might you be overrelying on particular people? How much might you even be overrelying on a higher power without having enough spiritual and emotional support from yourself and others?

If you are interested in exploring more of these aspects of yourself, consider asking the above questions to others who believe differently than you do. Like an anthropologist, see where your curiosity leads you to understand other people's faith cultures, chosen identities, and spiritual journeys. How are their responses similar and different from yours, and how can they help you develop your meaning in life? Which aspects of this "other" faith would you want to include or not include in your life purpose and what is important for you?

Conclusion

Hopefully, these stories, strategies, and possible options will help you on your life journey toward more health, wholeness, and flourishing. You deserve inner peace and fulfillment. You have infinite worth, beauty, and value. And your story of religion/spirituality, faith, sexual, and gender diversity is worth telling—even if it is still a work in progress.

References

Abdurasuli, K. (2020). Scientific research against LGBT propaganda. In *Student of the year 2020: XIII International Research Competition* (pp. 352–54). ICNS "Science and Education."

Abed, E. C., Schudson, Z. C., Gunther, O. D., Beischel, W. J., & van Anders, S. M. (2019). Sexual and gender diversity among sexual and gender/sex majorities: Insights via sexual configurations theory. *Archives of Sexual Behavior, 48*(5), 1423–41. doi:10.1007/s10508-018-1340-2

Ablaza, C., Kabátek, J. & Perales, F. (2022). Are sibship characteristics predictive of same-sex marriage? An examination of fraternal birth order and female fecundity effects in population-level administrative data from the Netherlands. *Journal of Sex Research, 59*(6), 671–83. doi:10.1080/00224499.2021.1974330

Adichie, C. N. (2009, October 7). *The danger of a single story* [Video]. TED. https://www.youtube.com/watch?v=D9Ihs241zeg

Ahmad, S. S., McLaughlin, M. M., & Weisman de Mamani, A. (2023). Validation and test–retest reliability of the Spiritual Bypass Scale in Muslims and implications for psychological help-seeking attitudes and self-stigma. *Spirituality in Clinical Practice, 10*(1), 62–73. doi:10.1037/scp0000300

American Psychological Association. (2009). *Report of the American Psychological Association Task Force on Appropriate Therapeutic Responses to Sexual Orientation.* https://www.apa.org/pi/lgbt/resources/therapeutic-response.pdf

American Psychological Association. (2021). *APA resolution on sexual orientation change efforts.* https://www.apa.org/about/policy/resolution-sexual-orientation-change-efforts.pdf

American Psychological Association. (2023). *Inclusive language guide* (2nd ed.). https://www.apa.org/about/apa/equity-diversity-inclusion/language-guidelines

American Psychological Association. (2024). *Sexual orientation and gender diversity.* https://www.apa.org/topics/lgbtq

Anonymous. (2015). *Blood and visions: Womyn reconciling with being female.* Autonomous Womyn's Press.

Apostolou, M. (2019). Does fraternal birth order predict male homosexuality, bisexuality, and heterosexual orientation with same-sex attraction? Evidence from a Greek-speaking sample from Greece. *Archives of Sexual Behavior, 49*(2), 575–79. doi:10.1007/s10508-019-01466-3

Arístegui, I., Radusky, P. D., Zalazar, V., Lucas, M., & Sued, O. (2018). Resources to cope with stigma related to HIV status, gender identity, and sexual orientation in gay men and transgender women. *Journal of Health Psychology, 23*(2), 320–31. doi:10.1177/1359105317736782

Arli, D., Badejo, A., & Sutanto, N. (2020). Exploring the effect of intrinsic religiousness, extrinsic religiousness, and religious fundamentalism on people's attitude towards lesbians and gays in Indonesia. *Journal of Religion, Spirituality & Aging, 32*(2), 118–34. doi:10.1080/15528030.2019.1640830

Arseneau, J. R., Grzanka, P. R., Miles, J. R., & Fassinger, R. E. (2013). Development and initial validation of the sexual orientation beliefs scale (SOBS). *Journal of Counseling Psychology, 60*(3), 407–20. doi:10.1037/a0032799

Ascha, M., Sasson, D. C., Sood, R., Cornelius, J. W., Schauer, J. M., Runge, A., Muldoon, A. L., Gangopadhyay, N., Simons, L., Chen, D., Corcoran, J. F., & Jordan, S. W. (2022). Top surgery and chest dysphoria among transmasculine and nonbinary adolescents and young adults. *JAMA Pediatrics, 176*(11), 1115–22. doi:10.1001/jamapediatrics.2022.3424

Asexuals.net. (2022). *The history of asexuality.* https://www.asexuals.net/the -history-of-asexuality/

Atlantic. (2018, June 18). "I wanted to take my body off": Detransitioned [Video]. *Atlantic.* https://www.theatlantic.com/video/index/562988/detransitioned-film/

Bailey, J., Blanchard, R., Hsu, K., & Revelle, W. (2021). A map of desire: Multidimensional scaling of men's sexual interest in male and female children and adults. *Psychological Medicine, 51*(15), 2714–20. doi:10.1017/S0033291720001476

Bailey, J. M., Vasey, P. L., Diamond, L. M., Breedlove, S. M., Vilain, E., & Epprecht, M. (2016). Sexual orientation, controversy, and science. *Psychological Science in the Public Interest, 17*(2), 45–101. doi:10.1177/1529100617705148

Balenko, D. D., & Kondrashikhina, O. A. (2021). Psychological analysis of tolerance of representatives: Generation Y. *Modern Science, 2–3,* 418–24.

Ballard, J. (2021). *A queer dharma: Yoga and meditation for liberation.* North Atlantic.

Bauer, G. R., Scheim, A. I., Pyne, J., Travers., R., & Hammond, R. (2015). Intervenable factors associated with suicide risk in transgender persons: A respondent driven sampling study in Ontario, Canada. *BMC Public Health, 15,* 525. doi:10.1186/s12889-015-1867-2

Beagan, B. L., & Hattie, B. (2015). Religion, spirituality, and LGBTQ identity integration. *Journal of LGBT Issues in Counseling, 9*(2), 92–117. doi:10.1080/1553 8605.2015.1029204

Beard, K., Eames, C., & Withers, P. (2016). The role of self-compassion in the well -being of self-identifying gay men. *Journal of Gay & Lesbian Mental Health, 21*(1), 77–96. doi:10.1080/19359705.2016.1233163

Becker, M., & Hesse, V. (2020). Minipuberty: Why does it happen? *Hormone Research in Paediatrics, 93*(2), 76–84. doi:10.1159/000508329

Beckstead, A. L. (2012). Can we change sexual orientation? *Archives of Sexual Behavior, 41*(1), 121–34. doi:10.1007/s10508-012-9922-x

Benau, K. (2022). *Shame, pride, and relational trauma: Concepts and psychotherapy.* Routledge.

Benjamin, L. S. (n.d.). *SASB.* https://lornasmithbenjamin.com/sasb/

Benjamin, L. S. (2018). *Interpersonal reconstructive therapy for anger, anxiety and depression: It's about broken hearts, not broken brains.* American Psychological Association. doi:10.1037/0000090-000

Bereczkei, T., Gyuris, P., & Weisfeld, G. E. (2004). Sexual imprinting in human mate choice. *Proceedings of the Royal Society of London Series B: Biological Sciences, 271*(1544), 1129–34. doi:10.1098/rspb.2003.2672

Bickham, P. J., O'Keefe, S. L., Baker, E., Berhie, G., Kommor, M. J., & Harper-Dorton, K. V. (2007). Correlates of early overt and covert sexual behaviors in heterosexual women. *Archives of Sexual Behavior, 36*(5), 724–40. doi:10.1007/s10508-007-9220-1

Bigler, R. S., & Liben, L. S. (2006). A developmental intergroup theory of social stereotypes and prejudice. In R. V. Kail (Ed.), *Advances in child development and behavior* (pp. 39–89). Elsevier.

Blanchard, R. (2023). Studying fraternal birth order in homosexual women and bisexual men. *Archives of Sexual Behavior, 52*(7), 2973–78. doi:10.1007/s10508-022-02441-1

Blanchard, R., & Bogaert, A. F. (2004). Proportion of homosexual men who owe their sexual orientation to fraternal birth order: An estimate based on two national probability samples *American Journal of Human Biology, 16*, 151–57. doi:10.1002/ajhb.20006

Blume, A. W. (2020). *A new psychology based on community, equality, and care of the Earth: An Indigenous American perspective.* Praeger.

Bogaert, A. F. (2004). Asexuality: Prevalence and associated factors in a national probability sample. *Journal of Sex Research, 41*(3), 279–87. doi:10.1080/00224490409552235

Bogaert, A. F., & Skorska, M. N. (2020). A short review of biological research on the development of sexual orientation. *Hormones and Behavior, 119*, 104659. doi:10.1016/j.yhbeh.2019.104659

Bogaert, A. F., Skorska, M. N., Wang, C., Gabrie, J., MacNeil, A. J., Hoffarth, M. R., VanderLaan, D. P., Zucker, K. J., & Blanchard, R. (2018). Male homosexuality and maternal immune responsivity to the Y-linked protein NLGN4Y. *Proceedings of the National Academy of Sciences of the United States of America, 115*(2), 302–6. doi:10.1073/pnas.1705895114

Bonagura, A., Abrams, D., & Teller, J. (2022). Diagnostic differential between pedophilic-OCD and pedophilic disorder: An illustration with two vignettes. *Archives of Sexual Behavior, 51*(4), 2359–68. doi:10.1007/s10508-021-02273-5

Borgogna, N. C., & Aita, S. L. (2023). Stress testing the minority stress model: It's not just neuroticism. *Psychology of Sexual Orientation and Gender Diversity.* Advance online publication. doi:10.1037/sgd0000620

Bornstein, K. (2016). *Gender outlaw: On men, women and the rest of us.* Vintage.

Bouchard, K. N., Timmers, A. D., & Chivers, M. L. (2015). Gender-specificity of genital response and self-reported sexual arousal in women endorsing facets of bisexuality. *Journal of Bisexuality, 15*(2), 180–203. doi:10.1080/15299716.2015.1022924

Boucher, F. J. O., & Chinnah, T. I. (2020). Gender dysphoria: A review investigating the relationship between genetic influences and brain development. *Adolescent Health, Medicine and Therapeutics, 11*, 89–99. doi:10.2147/AHMT.S259168

Bourn, J. R., Frantell, K. A., & Miles, J. R. (2018). Internalized heterosexism, religious coping, and psychache in LGB young adults who identify as religious. *Psychology of Sexual Orientation and Gender Diversity, 5*(3), 303–12. doi:10.1037/sgd0000274

Bowleg, L., English, D., Del Rio-Gonzalez, A. M., Burkholder, G. J., Teti, M., & Tschann, J. M. (2016). Measuring the pros and cons of what it means to be a Black man: Development and validation of the Black Men's Experiences Scale (BMES). *Psychology of Men and Masculinity, 17*, 177–88. doi:10.1037/men0000026

Bozkurt, A., Bozkurt, O. H., & Sonmez, I. (2015). Birth order and sibling sex ratio in a population with high fertility: Are Turkish male to female transsexuals different? *Archives of Sexual Behavior, 44*(5), 1331–37. doi:10.1007/s10508-014-0425-9

Brach, T. (2019). *Radical compassion: Learning to love yourself and your world with the practice of RAIN*. Penguin.

Brady, S. (2008). The impact of sexual abuse on sexual identity formation in gay men. *Journal of Child Sexual Abuse, 17*(3–4), 359–76. doi:10.1080/10538710802329973

Brakefield, T. A., Mednick, S. A., Wilson, H. W., De Neve, J., Christakis, N. A., & Fowler, J. H. (2014). Same-sex sexual attraction does not spread in adolescent social networks. *Archives of Sexual Behavior, 43*(2), 335–44. doi:10.1007/s10508-013-0142-9

Breedlove, S. M. (2017). Prenatal influences on human sexual orientation: Expectations versus data. *Archives of Sexual Behavior, 46*(6), 1583–92. doi:10.1007/s10508-016-0904-2

Brewster, M. E., Moradi, B., DeBlaere, C., & Velez, B. L. (2013). Navigating the borderlands: The roles of minority stressors, bicultural self-efficacy, and cognitive flexibility in the mental health of bisexual individuals. *Journal of Counseling Psychology, 60*(4), 543–56. doi:10.1037/a0033224

Bridges, J. G., Lefevor, G. T., & Schow, R. L. (2019). Sexual satisfaction and mental health in mixed-orientation relationships: A Mormon sample of sexual minority partners. *Journal of Bisexuality, 19*(4), 515–38. doi:10.1080/15299716.2019.1669252

Brooks, V. (1981). *Minority stress and lesbian women*. Lexington.

brown, a. m. (2017). *Emergent strategy: Shaping change, changing worlds*. AK Press.

brown, a. m. (2021). *Holding change: The way of emergent strategy facilitation and mediation*. AK Press.

Brown-Beresford, E., & McLaren, S. (2021). The relationship between self-compassion, internalized heterosexism, and depressive symptoms among bisexual and lesbian women. *Journal of Bisexuality, 22*(1), 90–115. doi:10.1080/15299716.2021.2004483

Brownfield, J. M., Flores, M. J., Morgan, S. K., Allen, L. R., & Marszalek, J. M. (2018). Development and psychometric properties of the Evasive Attitudes of Sexual Orientation Scale (EASOS). *Psychology of Sexual Orientation and Gender Diversity, 5*(1), 44–56. doi:10.1037/sgd0000256

Bryan, C. J. (2022). *Rethinking suicide: Why prevention fails, and how we can do better*. Oxford University Press.

Buijs, L., Hekma, G., & Duyvendak, J. W. (2011). "As long as they keep away from me": The paradox of antigay violence in a gay-friendly country. *Sexualities, 14*(6), 632–52. doi:10.1177/1363460711422304

Burns, J. A., Beischel, W. J., & van Anders, S. M. (2022). Hormone therapy and trans sexuality: A review. *Psychology of Sexual Orientation and Gender Diversity*. Advance online publication. doi:10.1037/sgd0000588

Camp, J., Vitoratou, S., & Rimes, K. A. (2020). LGBQ+ self-acceptance and its relationship with minority stressors and mental health: A systematic literature review. *Archives of Sexual Behavior, 49*(7), 2353–73. doi:10.1007/s10508-020-01755-2

Camp, J., Vitoratou, S., & Rimes, K. A. (2022). The Self-Acceptance of Sexuality Inventory (SASI): Development and validation. *Psychology of Sexual Orientation and Gender Diversity, 9*(1), 92–109. doi:10.1037/sgd0000445

Campbell, C. K., Hammack, P. L., Gordon, A. R., & Lightfoot, M. A. (2022). "I was always trying to figure it out . . . on my own terms": Structural barriers, the internet, and sexual identity development among lesbian, gay, bisexual, and queer people of different generations. *Journal of Homosexuality, 70*, 2560–82. doi:10.1080/00918369.2022.2071136

Cantor, J. M., & Fedoroff, J. P. (2018). Can pedophiles change? Response to opening arguments and conclusions. *Current Sexual Health Reports, 10*(4), 213–20. doi:10.1007/s11930-018-0167-0

Cardona, N. D., Madigan, R. J., & Sauer-Zavala, S. (2022). How minority stress becomes traumatic invalidation: An emotion-focused conceptualization of minority stress in sexual and gender minority people. *Clinical Psychology: Science and Practice, 29*(2), 185–95. doi:10.1037/cps0000054

Cass, V. C. (1979). Homosexual identity formation: A theoretical model. *Journal of Homosexuality, 4*, 219–35. doi:10.1300/J082v04n03_01

Cerny, J. A., & Janssen, E. (2011). Patterns of sexual arousal in homosexual, bisexual, and heterosexual men. *Archives of Sexual Behavior, 40*(4), 687–97. doi:10.1007/s10508-011-9746-0

Cervini, E. (2020). *The deviant's war: The homosexual vs. the United States of America*. Farrar, Straus and Giroux.

Chan, K. K. S., & Leung, D. C. K. (2021). The impact of mindfulness on self-stigma and affective symptoms among sexual minorities. *Journal of Affective Disorders, 286*, 213–19. doi:10.1016/j.jad.2021.02.057

Chan, K. K. S., Yung, C. S. W., & Nie, G. M. (2020). Self-compassion buffers the negative psychological impact of stigma stress on sexual minorities. *Mindfulness, 11*(10), 2338–48. doi:10.1007/s12671-020-01451-1

Chivers, M. L., Rieger, G., Latty, E., & Bailey, J. M. (2004). A sex difference in the specificity of sexual arousal. *Psychological Science, 15*(11), 736–44. doi:10.1111/j.0956-7976.2004.00750.x

Chivers, M. L., Seto, M. C., & Blanchard, R. (2007). Gender and sexual orientation differences in sexual response to sexual activities versus gender of actors in sexual films. *Journal of Personality and Social Psychology, 93*(6), 1108–21. doi:10.1037/0022-3514.93.6.1108

Chivers, M. L., Seto, M. C., Lalumière, M. L., Laan, E., & Grimbos, T. (2010). Agreement of self-reported and genital measures of sexual arousal in men and women: A meta-analysis. *Archives of Sexual Behavior, 39*(1), 5–56. doi:10.1007/s10508-009-9556-9

Choi, A. Y., & Israel, T. (2016). Centralizing the psychology of sexual minority Asian and Pacific Islander Americans. *Psychology of Sexual Orientation and Gender Diversity, 3*(3), 345–56. doi:10.1037/sgd000018

Chudinova, N. A. (2018). Stigmatization of LGBT among students of Perm. *SGBN, 1*(2). https://cyberleninka.ru/article/n/stigmatizatsiya-lgbt-sredi-studenchestva-g-permi

Clair, M., Daniel, C., & Lamont, M. (2016). Destigmatization and health: Cultural constructions and the long-term reduction of stigma. *Social Science & Medicine, 165*, 223–32. doi:10.1016/j.socscimed.2016.03.021

Clark, A. N., & Zimmerman, C. (2022). Concordance between romantic orientations and sexual attitudes: Comparing allosexual and asexual adults. *Archives of Sexual Behavior, 51*(4), 2147–57. doi:10.1007/s10508-021-02194-3

Cole, C., & Harris, H. W. (2017). The lived experiences of people who identify as LGBT Christians: Considerations for social work helping. *Social Work & Christianity, 44*(1–2), 31–52.

Comas-Diaz, L., & Lian, C. T. H. (2023). *Connecting mindfulness to its cultural roots of Buddhism: A pathway for racial healing and justice.* A critical conversation at the APA's annual convention. Washington, DC.

Cramwinckel, F. M., van der Toorn, J., & Scheepers, D. T. (2018). Interventions to reduce blatant and subtle sexual orientation- and gender identity prejudice (SOGIP): Current knowledge and future directions. *Social Issues and Policy Review, 12*(1), 183–217. doi:10.1111/sipr.12044

Crews, D. A. (2012). *Exploring self-compassion with lesbian, gay and bisexual persons* [Unpublished doctoral dissertation]. University of Utah. https://collections.lib.utah.edu/details?id=195510&q=crews+2012+self-compassion

Dahl, A. L., Scott, R. K., & Peace, Z. (2015). Trials and triumph: Lesbian and gay young adults raised in a rural context. *Social Sciences, 4*(4), 925–39. doi:10.3390/socsci4040925

Day, J. K., Fish, J. N., Perez-Brumer, A., Hatzenbuehler, M. L., & Russell, S.T. (2017). Transgender youth substance use disparities: Results from a population-based sample. *Journal of Adolescent Health, 61*(6), 729–35. doi:10.1016/j.Jadohealth.2017.06.024

Dean, J. B., Stratton, S. P., & Yarhouse, M. A. (2021). The mediating role of self-acceptance in the psychological distress of sexual minority students on Christian college campuses. *Spirituality in Clinical Practice, 8*(2), 132–48. doi:10.1037/scp0000253

Dehlin, A. J., Galliher, R. V., Legerski, E., Harker, A., & Dehlin, J. P. (2019). Same and other-sex aversion and attraction as important correlates of quality and outcomes of Mormon mixed-orientation marriages. *Journal of GLBT Family Studies, 15*(1), 22–41. doi:10.1080/1550428X.2017.141672

Dehlin, J. P., Galliher, R. V., Bradshaw, W. S., & Crowell, K. A. (2015). Navigating sexual and religious identity conflict: A Mormon perspective. *Identity, 15*(1), 1–22. doi:10.1080/15283488.2014.989440

Del Giudice, M. (2014). Middle childhood: An evolutionary-developmental synthesis. *Child Development Perspectives, 8*(4), 193–200. doi:10.1111/cdep.12084

del Pino, H. E., Steers, W. N., Lee, M., McCuller, J., Hays, R. D., & Harawa, N. T. (2022). Measuring gender role conflict, internalized stigma, and racial and sexual identity in behaviorally bisexual Black men. *Archives of Sexual Behavior, 51*(2), 1019–30. doi:10.1007/s10508-021-01925-w

Deleted. (2021). *ExTrans people who have detransitioned or in the process of doing so, why?* [Online forum post]. Reddit. https://www.reddit.com/r/AskReddit/comments/swweab/extrans_people_who_have_detransitioned_or_in_the/

Diamond, L. M. (2003). What does sexual orientation orient? A biobehavioral model distinguishing romantic love and sexual desire. *Psychological Review, 110*(1), 173–92. doi:10.1037/0033-295X.110.1.173

Diamond, L. M. (2016). Sexual fluidity in male and females. *Current Sexual Health Reports, 8,* 249–56. doi:10.1007/s11930-016-0092-z

Diamond, L. M. (2021). The new genetic evidence on same-gender sexuality: Implications for sexual fluidity and multiple forms of sexual diversity. *Journal of Sex Research, 58*(7), 818–37. doi:10.1080/00224499.2021.1879721

Diamond, L. M., Dehlin, A. J., & Alley, J. (2021). Systemic inflammation as a driver of health disparities among sexually-diverse and gender-diverse individuals. *Psychoneuroendocrinology, 129,* Article 105215. doi:10.1016/j.psyneuen.2021.105215

Diamond, L. M., Dickenson, J. A., & Blair, K. L. (2017). Stability of sexual attractions across different timescales: The roles of bisexuality and gender. *Archives of Sexual Behavior, 46*(1), 193–204. doi:10.1007/s10508-016-0860-x

Diamond, L. M., Fagundes, C. P., & Butterworth, M. R. (2010). Intimate relationships across the life span. In M. E. Lamb, A. M. Freund & R. M. Lerner (Eds.), *The handbook of life-span development* (Vol. 2, pp. 379–433). John Wiley & Sons.

Diamond, L. M., & Rosky, C. J. (2017). Scrutinizing immutability: Research on sexual orientation and U.S. legal advocacy for sexual minorities. *Journal of Sex Research, 53*(4–5), 363–91. doi:10.1080/00224499.2016.1139665

Diamond, L. M., & Wallen, K. (2011). Sexual minority women's sexual motivation around the time of ovulation. *Archives of Sexual Behavior, 40*(2), 237–46. doi:10.1007/s10508-010-9631-2

Dozortseva, E. G., Dvoryanchikov, N. V., Demidova, L.Y., & Simonenkova, M. B. (2011). Features of gender-role identity in persons with non-traditional sexual orientation [Electronic resource]. *Psychology and Law, 1*(4). https://psyjournals.ru/journals/psylaw/archive/2011_n4/49306

Dyar, C., Feinstein, B. A., Stephens, J., Zimmerman, A. R., Newcomb, M. E., & Whitton, S. W. (2020). Nonmonosexual stress and dimensions of health: Within-group variation by sexual, gender, and racial/ethnic identities. *Psychology of Sexual Orientation and Gender Diversity, 7*(1), 12–25. doi:10.1037/sgd0000348

Ebsworth, M., & Lalumière, M. L. (2012). Viewing time as a measure of bisexual sexual interest. *Archives of Sexual Behavior, 41*(1), 161–72. doi:10.1007/s10508-012-9923-9

Ehrensaft, D. (2011). Boys will be girls, girls will be boys: Children affect parents as parents affect children in gender nonconformity. *Psychoanalytic Psychology, 28*(4), 528–48. doi:10.1037/a0023828

Ellis, L., & Blanchard, R. (2001). Birth order, sibling sex ratio, and maternal miscarriages in homosexual and heterosexual men and women. *Personality and Individual Differences, 30*(4), 543–52. doi:10.1016/S0191-8869(00)00051-9

English, D., Rendina, H. J., & Parsons, J. T. (2018). The effects of intersecting stigma: A longitudinal examination of minority stress, mental health, and substance use among Black, Latino, and multiracial gay and bisexual men. *Psychology of Violence, 8*(6), 669–79. doi:10.1037/vio0000218

Erzin, A. I., Antokhin, E. Y., & Semenova, T. S. (2017). Protective mechanisms and proactive coping strategies in homosexual adolescents. *Neurological Bulletin, 4,* 46–48.

Erzin, A I., & Semenova, T .S. (2017). Stigma as a factor of psychogenic depression in adolescents with homosexuality and bisexuality. *European Journal of Humanities and Social Sciences, 4,* 41–46. doi:10.25136/1339-3057.2017.4.25081

Erzin, A. I, Semenov, T. S., & Antokhin, E. Y. (2017). Personality traits and early maladaptive schemes as predictors of suicide risk among adolescent homosexuals. *Suicidology, 4*(29), 81–90.

Etengoff, C., & Rodriguez, E. M. (2021). Incorporating transformative intersectional psychology (tip) into our understanding of LGBTQ Muslims' lived experiences, challenges, and growth. *Journal of Homosexuality, 68,* 1075–82. doi:10.1 080/00918369.2021.1888582

Farr, R. H., Diamond, L. M., & Boker, S. M. (2014). Female same-sex sexuality from a dynamical systems perspective: Sexual desire, motivation, and behavior. *Archives of Sexual Behavior, 43*(8), 1477–90. doi:10.1007/s10508-014-0378-z

Fausto-Sterling, A. (2000). *Sexing the body: Gender politics and the construction of sexuality*. Basic Books.

Feinberg, L. (1996). *Transgender warriors*. Penguin.

Felipe, L. C., Garrett-Walker, J. J., & Montagno, M. (2022). Monoracial and multiracial LGBTQ+ people: Comparing internalized heterosexism, perceptions of racism, and connection to LGBTQ+ communities. *Psychology of Sexual Orientation and Gender Diversity, 9*(1), 1–11. doi:10.1037/sgd0000440

Flentje, A. (2020). AWARENESS: Development of a cognitive–behavioral intervention to address intersectional minority stress for sexual minority men living with HIV who use substances. *Psychotherapy, 57*(1), 35–49. doi:10.1037/pst0000243

Freund, K. W. (1974). Male homosexuality: An analysis of the pattern. In J. A. Loraine (Ed.), *Understanding homosexuality: Its biological and psychological bases*. American Elsevier.

Freund, K., & Blanchard, R. (1983). Is the distant relationship of fathers and homosexual sons related to the sons' erotic preference for male partners, or to the sons' atypical gender identity, or to both? *Journal of Homosexuality, 9,* 7–25. doi:10.1300/J082v09n01_02

Freund, K., & Blanchard, R. (1993). Erotic target location errors in male gender dysphorics, paedophiles, and fetishists. *British Journal of Psychiatry, 162,* 558–63. doi:10.1192/bjp.162.4.558

Freund, K., Langevin, R., Cibiri, S., & Zajac, Y. (1973). Heterosexual aversion in homosexual males. *British Journal of Psychiatry, 122*(567), 163–69. doi:10.1192/bjp.122.2.163

Freund, K., Langevin, R., & Zajac, Y. (1974). Heterosexual aversion in homosexual males: A second experiment. *British Journal of Psychiatry, 125,* 177–80. doi:10.1192/bjp.125.2.177

Frigerio, A., Ballerini, L., & Valdés Hernández, M. (2021). Structural, functional, and metabolic brain differences as a function of gender identity or sexual orientation: A systematic review of the human neuroimaging literature. *Archives of Sexual Behavior, 50*(8), 3329–52. doi:10.1007/s10508-021-02005-9

Fry, K. M., Grzanka, P. R., Miles, J. R., & DeVore, E. N. (2020). Is essentialism essential? Reducing homonegative prejudice by targeting diverse sexual orientation beliefs. *Archives of Sexual Behavior, 49*(5), 1725–39. doi:10.1007/s10508-020-01706-x

Gabdullina, E. (2023, August 30). Gender diversity does not attract Russians. *Kommersant, 159*, 5. https://www.kommersant.ru/doc/6185676

Gallup. (2022). *LGBT rights.* https://news.gallup.com/poll/1651/gay-lesbian-rights.aspx

Galupo, M. P., Ramirez, J. L., & Pulice-Farrow, L. (2017). "Regardless of their gender": Descriptions of sexual identity among bisexual, pansexual, and queer identified individuals. *Journal of Bisexuality, 17*(1), 108–24. doi:10.1080/15299716.z2016.1228491

Ganna, A., Verweij, K. J. H., Nivard, M. G., Maier, R., Wedow, R., Busch, A. S., Abdellaoui, A., Guo, S., Sathirapongsasuti, J. F., 23andMe Research Team, Lichtenstein, P., Lundström, S., Långström, N., Auton, A., Harris, K. M., Beecham, G. W., Martin, E. R., Sanders, A. R., Perry, . . . Zietsch, B. P. (2019). Large-scale GWAS reveals insights into the genetic architecture of same-sex sexual behavior. *Science, 365*(6456), eaat7693. doi:10.1126/science.aat7693

Garvey, J. C., Squire, D. D., Stachler, B., & Rankin, S. (2018). The impact of campus climate on queer-spectrum student academic success. *Journal of LGBT Youth, 15*(2), 89–105. doi:10.1080/19361653.2018.1429973

Germer, C. (2023). *Dr. Chris Germer: "We would never feel shame if we didn't wish to be loved"* [Video]. Awake Network. https://www.theawakenetwork.com/chris-germer-shame/

Gevlenko, D. V. (2018). *Homosexuality: Mask conflict. Youth of the third millennium* [Paper]. Forty-Second Regional Student Scientific and Practical Conference, Omsk State University.

Gibbs, J. J., & Goldbach, J. (2015). Religious conflict, sexual identity, and suicidal behaviors among LGBT young adults. *Archives of Suicide Research, 19*(4), 472–88. doi:10.1080/13811118.2015.1004476

Ginwright, S. A. (2022). *The four pivots: Reimagining justice, reimagining ourselves.* Penguin.

Giwa, S. (2022). *Racism and gay men of color: Living and coping with discrimination.* Rowman & Littlefield.

Goffman, E. (1963). *Stigma: Notes on the management of spoiled identity.* Simon & Schuster.

Gold, S. D., & Marx, B. P. (2007). Gay male sexual assault survivors: The relations among internalized homophobia, experiential avoidance, and psychological symptom severity. *Behaviour Research and Therapy, 45*(3), 549–62. doi:10.1016/j.brat.2006.05.006

Gómez Jiménez, F. R., Semenyna, S. W., & Vasey, P. L. (2020). The relationship between fraternal birth order and childhood sex-atypical behavior among the Istmo Zapotec muxes. *Developmental Psychobiology, 62*(6), 792–803. doi:10.1002/dev.21987

Grigoriou, J. A. (2014). Minority stress factors for same-sex attracted Mormon adults. *Psychology of Sexual Orientation and Gender Diversity, 1*(4), 471–79. doi:10.1037/sgd0000078

Gruia, D. C., Holmes, L., Raines, J., Slettevold, E., Watts-Overall, T. M., & Rieger, G. (2022). Stability and change in sexual orientation and genital arousal over time. *Journal of Sex Research, 60*(2), 294–304. doi:10.1080/00224499.2022.2 060927

Gulevich, O. A., Osin, E. N., Isaenko, N. A., & Brainis, L. M. (2018). Scrutinizing homophobia: A model of perception of homosexuals in Russia. *Journal of Homosexuality, 65*, 1838–66. doi:10.1080/00918369.2017.1391017

Hammack, P. L., Frost, M. D., Meyer, I. H., & Pletta, D. R. (2018). Gay men's health and identity: Social change and life course. *Archives of Sexual Behavior, 47*(1), 59–74. doi:10.1007/s10508-017-0990-9

Hanh, T. N. (2005). *Being peace.* Parallax.

Harper, G.W., Brodsky, A., & Bruce, D. (2012). What's good about being gay? Perspectives from youth. *Journal of LGBT Youth, 9*(1), 22–41. doi:10.1080/193 61653.2012.628230

Harris, H., & Yancey, G. I. (2021). The why and how of congregational discernment in LGBTQ+ inclusion: Models in the literature. *Religions, 12*(1), 14. doi:10.3390/rel12010014

Harris, H. W., Yancey, G. I., Cole, C., Cressy, V., Smith, N., Herridge, M., West, B., & Wills, L. (2021). Addressing LGBTQ+ inclusion: Challenges, faith, and resilience in the church and her people. *Social Work & Christianity, 48*(1), 75–105. doi:10.1080/15528030.2022.2038336

Harris, H., Yancey, G., Holmes, K., Jones, J., Goertzen, G., & Herridge, M. (2022). The role of older adults in congregational discernment: Lessons about LGBTQ+ inclusion. *Journal of Religion, Spirituality & Aging, 34*(4), 344–65. doi:10.1080 /15528030.2022.2038336

Hayes, S. C. (2022). Acceptance and defusion. *Cognitive and Behavioral Practice, 29*(3), 571–74. doi:10.1016/j.cbpra.2022.01.005

Hayes, S. C., & Strosahl, K. D. (Eds.). (2004). *A practical guide to acceptance and commitment therapy.* Springer.

Hayes, S. C., Strosahl, K. D., Bunting, K., Twohig, M., & Wilson, K. G. (2004). What is acceptance and commitment therapy? In S. C. Hayes & K. D. Strosahl (Eds.), *A practical guide to acceptance and commitment therapy* (pp. 1–30). Springer.

Helminen, E. C., Ducar, D. M., Scheer, J. R., Parke, K. L., Morton, M. L., & Felver, J. C. (2023). Self-compassion, minority stress, and mental health in sexual and gender minority populations: A meta-analysis and systematic review. *Clinical Psychology: Science and Practice, 30*(1), 26–39. doi:10.1037/cps0000104

Helminiak, D. A. (2004). The ethics of sex: A call to the gay community. *Pastoral Psychology, 52*(3), 259–67. doi:10.1023/B:PASP.0000010026.06675.02

Hendricks, M. L. (2022). Minority stress and change efforts. In D. C. Haldeman (Ed.), *The case against conversion "therapy": Evidence, ethics, and alternatives* (pp. 71–88). APA. doi:10.1037/0000266-004

Herek, G. M. (2018). *Facts about homosexuality and child molestation.* https:// lgbpsychology.org/html/facts_molestation.html

Herzog, J. I., & Schmahl, C. (2018). Adverse childhood experiences and the consequences on neurobiological, psychosocial, and somatic conditions across the lifespan. *Frontiers in Psychiatry, 9,* 420. doi:10.3389/fpsyt.2018.00420

Heyer, W. (2019, February 11). Hormones, surgery, regret: I was a transgender woman for 8 years—time I can't get back. *USA Today.* https://www.usatoday.com/story/opinion/voices/2019/02/11/transgender-debate-transitioning-sex-gender-column/1894076002/

Higa, D., Hoppe, M. J., Lindhorst, T., Mincer, S., Beadnell, B., Morrison, D. M., Wells, E. A., Todd, A., & Mountz, S. (2014). Negative and positive factors associated with the well-being of lesbian, gay, bisexual, transgender, queer, and questioning (LGBTQ) youth. *Youth & Society, 46*(5), 663–87. doi:10.1177/0044118X12449630

Hill, P. C., Smith, E., & Sandage, S. J. (2012). Religious and spiritual motivations in clinical practice. In J. D. Aten, K. A. O'Grady & E. L. Worthington (Eds.), *The psychology of religion and spirituality for clinicians* (pp. 69–99). Routledge.

Hill, W. (2015). *Spiritual friendship: Finding love in the church as a celibate gay Christian.* Brazos.

Ho, F., & Mussap, A. J. (2019). The Gender Identity Scale: Adapting the Gender Unicorn to measure gender identity. *Psychology of Sexual Orientation and Gender Diversity, 6*(2), 217–31. doi:10.1037/sgd0000322

Hoffarth, M. R., Hodson, G., & Molnar, D. S. (2018). When and why is religious attendance associated with antigay bias and gay rights opposition? A justification-suppression model approach. *Journal of Personality and Social Psychology, 115*(3), 526–63. doi:10.1037/pspp0000146

Holben, L. R. (1999). *What Christians think about homosexuality: Six representative viewpoints.* D&F Scott.

Hoskin, R. A. (2019). Femmephobia: The role of anti-femininity and gender policing in LGBTQ+ people's experiences of discrimination. *Sex Roles, 81,* 686–703. doi:10.1007/s11199-019-01021-3

Huber, C. (2003). *When you're falling, dive: Acceptance, freedom and possibility.* Keep It Simple Books.

Hudepohl, A. D., Parrott, D. J., & Zeichner, A. (2010). Heterosexual men's anger in response to male homosexuality: Effects of erotic and nonerotic depictions of male–male intimacy and sexual prejudice. *Journal of Homosexuality, 57,* 1022–38. doi:10.1080/00918369.2010.503511

Human Dignity Trust. (2024). *Map of countries that criminalise LGBT people.* https://www.humandignitytrust.org/lgbt-the-law/map-of-criminalisation/

Human Rights Watch. (2014). *World report 2014: Russia.* https://www.hrw.org/world-report/2014/country-chapters/russia

Human Rights Watch. (2018). *Russia: Events of 2017.* https://www.hrw.org/world-report/2018/country-chapters/russia

Huynh, K. D., & Lee, D. L. (2023). Emotion-focused coping strategies as mediators of the discrimination–mental health association among LGB POC. *Psychology of Sexual Orientation and Gender Diversity, 10*(3), 413–28. doi:10.1037/sgd0000562

Hyde, J. S., Bigler, R. S., Joel, D., Tate, C. C., & van Anders, S. M. (2019). The future of sex and gender in psychology: Five challenges to the gender binary. *American Psychologist, 74*(2), 171–3. doi:10.1037/amp0000307

Ilyin, A. N. (2020). Western tolerance: The rule of democracy or the onset of dehumanization? *Moscow University Bulletin, Series 18, Sociology and Political Science, 26*(3), 227–46. doi:10.24290/1029-3736-2020-26-3-227-246

Ilyushina, M., & Gelman, M. (2023, January 7). Moscow's war in Ukraine brought harsh tactics against gay Russians at home. *Washington Post*. https://www.washingtonpost.com/world/2023/01/07/russia-war-gay-persecution-homophobia

Intrusive Thoughts. (2017). *Living with sexual orientation OCD*. https://www.intrusivethoughts.org/ocd-symptoms/sexual-orientation-ocd/

Israel, E., & Strassberg, D. S. (2009). Viewing time as an objective measure of sexual interest in heterosexual men and women. *Archives of Sexual Behavior, 38*(4), 551–58. doi:10.1007/s10508-007-9246-4

Jewell, L. M., & Morrison, M. A. (2012). Making sense of homonegativity: Heterosexual men and women's understanding of their own prejudice and discrimination toward gay men. *Qualitative Research in Psychology, 9*(4), 351–70. doi:10.1080/14780887.2011.586098

Johns, M. M., Lowry, R., Haderxhanaj, L. T., Rasberry, C. N., Robin, L., Scales, L., Stone, D., & Suarez, N. A. (2020). Trends in violence victimization and suicide risk by sexual identity among high school students—Youth Risk Behavior Survey, United States, 2015–2019. *Morbidity and Mortality Weekly Report, 69*(Suppl-1), 19–27. doi:10.15585/mmwr.su6901a3

Johnson, H. J. (2016). Bisexuality, mental health, and media representation. *Journal of Bisexuality, 16*(3), 378–96. doi:10.1080/15299716.2016.1168335

Jones, J. M. (2023, February 22). U.S. LGBT identification steady at 7.2%. Gallup. https://news.gallup.com/poll/470708/lgbt-identification-steady.aspx

Jorgensen, S. C. J. (2023). Transition regret and detransition: Meanings and uncertainties. *Archives of Sexual Behavior, 52*, 2176–84. doi:10.1007/s10508-023-02626-2

Kalichman, S., Gore-Felton, C., Benotsch, E., Cage, M., & Rompa, D. (2004) Trauma symptoms, sexual behaviors and substance abuse: Correlates of childhood sexual abuse and HIV risk among men who have sex with men. *Journal of Child Sexual Abuse, 13*(1), 1–15. doi:10.1300/J070v13n01_01

Kashubeck-West, S., & Szymanski, D. M. (2008). Risky sexual behavior in gay and bisexual men: Internalized heterosexism, sensation seeking, and substance use. *Counseling Psychologist, 36*(4), 5614. doi:10.1177/0011000007309633

Katz, J. (1995). *Gay American history: Lesbians and gay men in the United States.* Thomas Crowell.

Katz-Wise, S. L., Reisner, S. L., Hughto, J. W., & Keo-Meier, C. L. (2016). Differences in sexual orientation diversity and sexual fluidity in attractions among gender minority adults in Massachusetts. *Journal of Sex Research, 53*(1), 74–84. doi:10.1080/00224499.2014.1003028

Kauffman, R. P., Guerra, C., Thompson, C. M., & Stark, A. (2022). Concordance for gender dysphoria in genetic female monozygotic (identical) triplets. *Archives of Sexual Behavior, 51*(7), 3647–51. doi:10.1007/s10508-022-02409-1

Kauth, M. R. (2022). The shame trap: Comment on "How minority stress becomes traumatic invalidation: An emotion-focused conceptualization of minority stress in sexual and gender minority people." *Clinical Psychology: Science and Practice, 29*(2), 203–4. doi:10.1037/cps0000061

Kays, J. L., Yarhouse, M. A., & Ripley, J. S. (2014). Relationship factors and quality among mixed-orientation couples. *Journal of Sex & Marital Therapy, 40*(6), 512–28. doi:10.1080/0092623X.2013.788107

Kiekens, W. J., la Roi, C., & Dijkstra, J. K. (2021). Sexual identity disparities in mental health among U.K. adults, U.S. adults, and U.S. adolescents: Examining heterogeneity by race/ethnicity. *Psychology of Sexual Orientation and Gender Diversity, 8*(4), 407–19. doi:10.1037/sgd0000432

Kingsbury, M., Hammond, N. G., Johnstone, F., & Colman, I. (2022). Suicidality among sexual minority and transgender adolescents: A nationally representative population-based study of youth in Canada. *Canadian Medical Association Journal, 194*(22) E767–E774. doi:10.1503/cmaj.212054

Kolodny, C., & Michelson, N. (2015, November 18). *Can a man enjoy sex with other men and still be straight?* https://podcasts.apple.com/us/podcast/can-a-man-enjoy-sex-with-other-men-and-still-be-straight/id962536224?i=1000357571903

Kon, I. S. (Ed.) (1989). *A history of classical sociology.* Progress.

Kozee, H. B., Tylka, T. L., & Bauerband, L. A. (2012). Measuring transgender individuals' comfort with gender identity and appearance: Development and validation of the Transgender Congruence Scale. *Psychology of Women Quarterly, 36,* 179–96. doi:10.1177/0361684312442161

Krolikowski, A. M., Rinella, M., & Radcliff, J. J. (2016). The influence of the expression of subtle and blatant sexual prejudice on personal prejudice and identification with the expresser. *Journal of Homosexuality, 63,* 228–49. doi:10.1080/00918369.2015.1083776

Kruglanski, A. W., & Webster, D. M. (1996). Motivated closing of the mind: "Seizing" and "freezing." *Psychological Review, 103,* 263–83. doi:10.1037/0033-295X.103.2.263

Kuhr, E. (2020, April 24). *1 in 5 Russians want gays and lesbians "eliminated," survey finds.* NBC News. https://www.nbcnews.com/feature/nbc-out/1-5-russians-want-gays-lesbians-eliminated-survey-finds-n1191851

Kumpasoğlu, G. B., Hasdemir, D., & Canel-Çınarbaş, D. (2020). Between two worlds: Turkish religious LGBTs relationships with Islam and coping strategies. *Psychology & Sexuality, 13*(2), 302–16. doi:10.1080/19419899.2020.1772354

Laliotis, D. (2021). *The dance of attachment: An EMDR relational approach* [Webinar]. https://emdrtherapy.com/emdr-trainings/master-emdr-training

Lamontagne, E., d'Elbée, M., Ross, M., Carroll, A., du Plessis, A., & Loures, L. (2018). A socioecological measurement of homophobia for all countries and its public health impact. *European Journal of Public Health, 28*(5), 967–72. doi:10.1093/eurpub/cky023

Landridge, D. (2007). Gay affirmative therapy: A theoretical framework and defence. *Journal of Gay & Lesbian Psychotherapy, 11*(1–2), 27–43. doi:10.1300/J236v11n01_03

Lassiter, J. M., O'Garro-Moore, J. K., Anwar, K., Smallwood, S. W., Burnett-Zeigler, I. E., Stepleman, L., Sizemore, K. M., Grov, C., & Rendina, H. J. (2022). Spirituality, self-compassion, and anxiety among sexual minority men: A longitudinal mediation analysis. *Anxiety, Stress & Coping, 36*(2), 229–40. doi:10.1080/10615806.2022.2033235

Lee, E. A., Ashai, S., Teran, M., & Shin, R. Q. (2023). Intersectional microaggressions, mental health outcomes, and the role of social support among Black

LGB adults. *Journal of Counseling Psychology, 70*(5), 464–76. doi:10.1037/cou0000684

Leedy, G., & Connolly, C. (2007). Out in the Cowboy State. *Journal of Gay & Lesbian Social Services, 19*(1), 17–34. doi.org/10.1300/J041v19n01_02

Lefevor, G. T., Boyd-Rogers, C. C., Sprague, B. M., & Janis, R. A. (2019). Health disparities between genderqueer, transgender, and cisgender individuals: An extension of minority stress theory. *Journal of Counseling Psychology, 66*(4), 385–95. doi:10.1037/cou0000339

Lefevor, G. T., Davis, E. B., Paiz, J. Y, & Smack, A. C. P. (2021). The relationship between religiousness and health among sexual minorities: A meta-analysis. *Psychological Bulletin, 147*(7), 647–66. doi:10.1037/bul0000321

Lefevor, G. T., Etengoff, C., Davis, E. B., Skidmore, S. J., Rodriguez, E. M., McGraw, J. S., & Rostowsky, S. S. (2023). Religion/spirituality, stress, and resilience among sexual and gender minorities: The religious/spiritual stress and resilience model. *Perspectives on Psychological Science, 18*(6), 1537–61. doi:10.1177/17456916231179137

Lefevor, G. T., Sorrell, S. A., Kappers, G., Plunk, A., Schow, R. L., Rosik, C. H., & Beckstead, A. L. (2020). Same-sex attracted, not LGBQ: The implications of sexual identity labelling on religiosity, sexuality, and health among Mormons. *Journal of Homosexuality, 67*, 940–64. doi:10.1080/00918369.2018.1564006

LeVay, S. (2016). *Gay, straight, and the reason why: The science of sexual orientation* (2nd ed.). Oxford University Press.

Li, G., Sham, W. W. L., & Wong, W. I. (2022). Are romantic orientation and sexual orientation different? Comparisons using explicit and implicit measurements. *Current Psychology, 42*, 24288–24301. doi:10.1007/s12144-022-03380-9

Li, G., & Wong, W. I. (2018). Single-sex schooling: Friendships, dating, and sexual orientation. *Archives of Sexual Behavior, 47*(4), 1025–39. doi:10.1007/s10508-018-1187-6

Linehan, M. M. (1993). *Cognitive-behavioral treatment of borderline personality disorder*. Guilford.

Lippa, R. A. (2012). Effects of sex and sexual orientation on self-reported attraction and viewing times to images of men and women: Testing for category specificity. *Archives of Sexual Behavior, 41*(1), 149–60. doi:10.1007/s10508-011-9898-y

Lippa, R. A. (2016). Biological influences on masculinity. In Y. J. Wong & S. R. Wester (Eds.), *APA handbook of men and masculinities* (pp. 187–209). APA. doi:10.1037/14594-009

Lisitsa, E. (2023). *Turning against bids: A relationship killer*. https://www.gottman.com/blog/turning-against-bids-the-ultimate-relationship-killer/

Litt, B. (2016. November 8). *From eye to "I": Transforming attachment and identity with EMDR therapy* [Workshop]. Salt Lake City, Utah.

Little, A. C., Penton-Voak, I. S., Burt, D., & Perrett, D. I. (2002). Evolution and individual differences in the perception of attractiveness: How cyclic hormonal changes and self-perceived attractiveness influence female preferences for male faces. In G. Rhodes & L. A. Zebrowitz (Eds.), *Facial attractiveness: Evolutionary, cognitive, and social perspectives* (pp. 59–90). Ablex.

Littman L. (2021). Individuals treated for gender dysphoria with medical and/or surgical transition who subsequently detransitioned: A survey of 100 detransitioners. *Archives of Sexual Behavior, 50*(8), 3353–69. doi:10.1007/s10508-021-02163-w

Lloyd, S., & Operario, D. (2012). HIV risk among men who have sex with men who have experienced childhood sexual abuse: Systematic review and meta-analysis. *AIDS Education & Prevention, 24*(3), 228–41. doi:10.1521/aeap.2012.24.3.228

Louis, C., & Browne, T. (2023, April 22). *Black lives, in mind: Braiding the threads—young, black, and queer* [Webinar]. Connecticut Society for Psychoanalytic Psychology.

Luxmoore, J. (2022, November 4). Russian orthodox church backs anti-LGBT legislation. *Church Times.* https://www.churchtimes.co.uk/articles/2022/4-november/news/world/russian-orthodox-church-backs-anti-lgbt-legislation

MacDougall, H., Henning-Smith, C., Sarkin, C., & Gonzales, G. (2022, June). Self-rated health among gay, lesbian, bisexual adults: Rural/urban differences. *University of Minnesota Rural Health Research Center Policy Brief.* https://rhrc.umn.edu/wp-content/uploads/2022/06/UMN_Self-rated-health-1.pdf

Mackinnon, A. (2022, October 7). LGBTQ Russians were Putin's first target in his war on the West. *Foreign Policy.* https://foreignpolicy.com/2022/10/07/lgbtq-russia-ukraine-war-west/

Mahaffey, A. L., Bryan, A. D., Ito, T. A., & Hutchison, K. E. (2011). In search of the defensive function of sexual prejudice: Exploring antigay bias through shorter and longer lead startle eye blink. *Journal of Applied Social Psychology, 41*(1), 27–44. doi:10.1111/j.1559-1816.2010.00700.x

Mahon, C. P., Pachankis, J. E., Kiernan, G., & Gallagher, P. (2021). Risk and protective factors for social anxiety among sexual minority persons. *Archives of Sexual Behavior, 50*(3), 1015–32. doi:10.1007/s10508-020-01845-1

Mallory, A. B., & Russell, S. T. (2021). Intersections of racial discrimination and LGB victimization for mental health: A prospective study of sexual minority youth of color. *Journal of Youth and Adolescence, 50*(7), 1353–68. doi:10.1007/s10964-021-01443-x

Malty, J., & Day, L. (1998). Amending a measure of the Quest religious orientation: Applicability of the scale's use among religious and non-religious persons. *Personality and Individual Differences, 25*(3), 517–22. doi:10.1016/S0191-8869(98)00078-6

Manley, M. H., Diamond, L. M., & van Anders, S. M. (2015). Polyamory, monoamory, and sexual fluidity: A longitudinal study of identity and sexual trajectories. *Psychology of Sexual Orientation and Gender Diversity, 2*(2), 168–80. doi:10.1037/sgd0000098

Manning, J. T., Fink, B., & Trivers, R. (2023). Digit ratio (2D:4D; Right-Left 2D:4D) and multiple phenotypes for same-sex attraction: The BBC Internet Study revisited. *Archives of Sexual Behavior.* Advance online publication. doi:10.1007/s10508-023-02703-6

Matos, M., Carvalho, S. A., Cunha, M., Galhardo, A., & Sepodes, C. (2017). Psychological flexibility and self-compassion in gay and heterosexual men: How they relate to childhood memories, shame, and depressive symptoms. *Journal of LGBT Issues in Counseling, 11*(2), 88–105. doi:10.1080/15538605.2017.1310007

Mayfield, W. (2001). The development of an internalized homonegativity inventory for gay men. *Journal of Homosexuality, 41*, 53–76. doi:10.1300/J082v41n02_04

McFarland, S. G. (1989). Religious orientations and the targets of discrimination. *Journal for the Scientific Study of Religion, 28*(3), 324–36. doi:10.2307/1386743

McKay, S., Skues, J. L., & Williams, B. J. (2018). With risk may come reward: Sensation seeking supports resilience through effective coping. *Personality and Individual Differences, 121*, 100–105. doi:10.1016/j.paid.2017.09.030

McNeil, J., Ellis, S. J., & Eccles, F. J. R. (2017). Suicide in trans populations: A systematic review of prevalence and correlates. *Psychology of Sexual Orientation and Gender Diversity, 4*(3), 341–53. doi:10.1037/sgd0000235

Melkov, S. V. (2017a). *Features of self-awareness of men with stigmatized sexual identity.* Moscow Pedagogical State University.

Melkov, S. (2017b). Reading the idea of L. S. Vygotsky about growing into culture in the context of the problems of modern times. *Personality Development, 1*, 76–93.

MENA Rights Group. (2023, September 5). *Lebanon: Attack on freedoms targets LGBTI people.* MENA Rights Group. https://menarights.org/en/articles/lebanon-attack-freedoms-targets-lgbti-people

Mereish, E. H., & Poteat, V. P. (2015). A relational model of sexual minority mental and physical health: The negative effects of shame on relationships, loneliness, and health. *Journal of Counseling Psychology, 62*(3), 425–37. doi:10.1037/cou0000088

Metz, S. (2022, April 3). *Mormon leader reaffirms faith's stance on same-sex marriage.* ABC News. https://abcnews.go.com/US/wireStory/mormon-leader-reaffirms-faiths-stance-sex-marriage-83852258

Meyer, I. H. (2016). The elusive promise of LGBT equality. *American Journal of Public Health, 106*(8), 1356–58. doi:10.2105/AJPH.2016.303221

Michli, S., & El Jamil, F. (2022). Internalized homonegativity and the challenges of having same-sex desires in the Lebanese context: A study examining risk and protective factors. *Journal of Homosexuality, 69*, 75–100. doi:10.1080/00918369.2020.1809893

Mittleman, J. (2023). Stable and shifting sexualities among American high school students, 2015 to 2021. *Socius, 9*. doi:10.1177/23780231231196012

Money, J. (1986). *Lovemaps: Clinical concepts of sexual/erotic health and pathology, paraphilia, and gender transposition of childhood, adolescence, and maturity.* Irvington.

Moradi, B., & Grzanka, P. R. (2017). Using intersectionality responsibly: Toward critical epistemology, structural analysis, and social justice activism. *Journal of Counseling Psychology, 64*(5), 500–13. doi:10.1037/cou0000203

Morandini, J. S., Menzies, R. E., Moreton, S. G., & Dar-Nimrod, I. (2022). Do beliefs about sexual orientation predict sexual identity labeling among sexual minorities? *Archives of Sexual Behavior, 52*(3), 1239–54. doi:10.1007/s10508-022-02465-7

Morandini, J. S., Veldre, A., Holcombe, A. O., Hsu, K., Lykins, A., Bailey, J. M., & Dar-Nimrod, I. (2019). Visual attention to sexual stimuli in mostly heterosexuals. *Archives of Sexual Behavior, 48*(5), 1371–85. doi:10.1007/s10508-019-1419-4

Morrison, M. A., & Morrison, T. G. (2002). Development and validation of a scale measuring modern prejudice toward gay men and lesbian women. *Journal of Homosexuality, 43*, 15–37. doi:10.1300/j082v43n02_02

Morrison, M. A., & Morrison, T. G. (2011). Sexual orientation bias toward gay men and lesbian women: Modern homonegative attitudes and their association with discriminatory behavioral intentions. *Journal of Applied Social Psychology, 41*(11), 2573–99. doi:10.1111/j.1559-1816.2011.00838.x

Morrison, T. G., Kiss, M. J., Bishop, C., & Morrison, M. A. (2019). "We're disgusted with queers, not fearful of them": The interrelationships among disgust, gay men's sexual behavior, and homonegativity. *Journal of Homosexuality, 66*, 1014–33. doi:10.1080/00918369.2018.1490576

Movement Advancement Project. (2019, November). *Where we call home: Transgender people in rural America.* https://www.lgbtmap.org/file/Rural-Trans -Report-Nov2019.pdf

Nathanson, D. L. (1997). Affect theory and the compass of shame. In M. R. Lansky & A. P. Morrison (Eds.), *The widening scope of shame* (pp. 339–354). Analytic Press.

Neely, M. E., Schallert, D. L., Mohammed, S. S., Roberts, R. M., & Chen, Y.-J. (2009). Self-kindness when facing stress: The role of self-compassion, goal regulation, and support in college students' well-being. *Motivation and Emotion, 33*, 88–97. doi:10.1007/s11031-008-9119-8

Neff, K. (2023). *Self-compassion guided practices and exercises.* https://self -compassion.org/category/exercises/#

Neff, K. D. (2003). Self-compassion: An alternative conceptualization of a healthy attitude toward oneself. *Self and Identity, 2*(2), 85–101. doi:10.1080/15298860309032

Neff, K. D., Kirkpatrick, K. L., & Rude, S. B. (2017). Self-compassion and adaptive psychological functioning. *Journal of Research in Personality, 41*(1), 139–54. doi:10.1016/j.jrp.2006.03.004

Nguyen, D., Brazelton, G., Renn, K., & Woodford, M. (2018). Exploring the availability and influence of LGBTQ+ student services resources on student success at community colleges: A mixed methods analysis. *Community College Journal of Research and Practice, 42*(11), 1–14. doi:10.1080/10668926.2018.1444522

Nicholson, A. A., Siegel, M., Wolf, J., Narikuzhy, S., Roth, S. L., Hatchard, T., Lanius, R. A., Schneider, M., Lloyd, C. S., McKinnon, M. C., Heber, A., Smith, P., & Lueger-Schuster, B. (2022). A systematic review of the neural correlates of sexual minority stress: Towards an intersectional minority mosaic framework with implications for a future research agenda. *European Journal of Psychotraumatology, 13*(1), Article 2002572. doi:10.1080/20008198.2021.2002572

Norris, A. L., Marcus, D. K., & Green, B. A. (2015). Homosexuality as a discrete class. *Psychological Science, 26*(12), 1843–53. doi:10.1177/0956797615598617

O'Handley, B. M., Blair, K. K., & Hoskin, R. A. (2017). What do two men kissing and a bucket of maggots have in common? Heterosexual men's indistinguishable salivary α-amylase responses to photos of two men kissing and disgusting images. *Psychology & Sexuality, 8*(3), 173–88. doi:10.1080/19419899.2017.1328459

O'Kane, K. M. K., Milani, S., Chivers, M. L., & Dawson, S. J. (2022). Gynephilic men's and androphilic women's visual attention patterns: The effects of gender and sexual activity cues. *Journal of Sex Research, 60*(6), 880–89. doi:10.1080/0 0224499.2022.2033675

Okun, T. (2023). *One right way along with perfectionism, paternalism, objectivity, and qualified.* White Supremacy Culture. https://www.whitesupremacyculture.info/one-right-way.html

Ozerina, A. A., & Rodionov, G. A. (2020). *Features of emotional intelligence in young people with different types of sexual orientation* [Paper]. International Scientific and Practical Conference, Moscow State Regional University.

Pachankis, J. E., & Bränström, R. (2018). Hidden from happiness: Structural stigma, sexual orientation concealment, and life satisfaction across 28 countries. *Journal of Consulting Clinical Psychology, 86*(5), 403–15. doi:10.1037/ccp0000299

Pachankis, J. E., & Bränström, R. (2019). How many sexual minorities are hidden? Projecting the size of the global closet with implications for policy and public health. *PLOS One, 14*(6), e0218084. doi:10.1371/journal.pone.0218084

Pachankis, J. E., Clark, K. A., Klein, D. N., & Dougherty, L. R. (2021). Early timing and determinants of the sexual orientation disparity in internalizing psychopathology: A prospective cohort study from ages 3 to 15. *Journal of Youth and Adolescence, 3*, 1–3. doi:10.1007/s10964-021-01532-x

Pachankis, J. E., & Safren, S. A. (Eds.). (2019). *Handbook of evidence-based mental health practice with sexual and gender minorities.* Oxford University Press.

Pachankis, J. E., Soulliard, Z. A., Morris, F., & Seager van Dyk, I. (2023). A model for adapting evidence-based interventions to be LGBQ-affirmative: Putting minority stress principles and case conceptualization into clinical research and practice. *Cognitive and Behavioral Practice, 30*(1), 1–17. doi:10.1016/j.cbpra.2021.11.005

Pantalone, D. W., Iwamasa, G. Y., & Martell, C. R. (2019). Affirmative cognitive-behavioral therapy with culturally diverse populations. In K. S. Dobson & D. J. Dozois (Eds.), *Handbook of cognitive-behavioral therapies* (4th ed., pp. 464–87). Guilford.

Patel, S. (2019). "Brown girls can't be gay": Racism experienced by queer South Asian women in the Toronto LGBTQ community. *Journal of Lesbian Studies, 23*(3), 410–23. doi:10.1080/10894160.2019.1585174

Paz Galupo, M., Taylor, S. M., & Cole, D. (2019). "I am double the bi": Positive aspects of being both bisexual and biracial. *Journal of Bisexuality, 19*(2), 1–17. doi:10.1080/15299716.2019.1619066

Penzel, F. (2007). *How do I know I'm not really gay/straight?* International OCD Foundation. https://iocdf.org/expert-opinions/homosexual-obsessions/

Perez-Brumer, A., Silva-Santisteban, A., Salazar, X., Vilela, J., & Reisner, S. L. (2020). In search of "my true self": Transmasculine gender identity processes, stigma, and mental health in Peru. In N. Nakamura & C. H. Logie (Eds.), *LGBTQ mental health: International perspectives and experiences* (pp. 13–27). APA. doi:10.1037/0000159-002

Perkins, T. (2022, May 17). *Donation email for Family Research Council.*

Pew Research Center. (2015, May 12). *America's changing religious landscape.* http://www.pewforum.org/2015/05/12/americas-changing-religious-landscape/

Pfaus, J. G., Kippin, T. E., Coria-Avila, G. A., Gelez, H., Afonso, V. M., Ismail, N., & Parada, M. (2012). Who, what, where, when (and maybe even why)? How the experience of sexual reward connects sexual desire, preference, and performance. *Archives of Sexual Behavior, 41*(1), 31–62. doi:10.1007/s10508-012-9935-5

Pique Resilience Project. (n.d.). *Pique Resilience Project.* https://www.piquerespro ject.com

Pitt, R., N. (2010). "Still looking for my Jonathan": Gay Black men's management of religious and sexual identity conflicts. *Journal of Homosexuality, 57,* 39–53. doi:10.1080/00918360903285566

Pittinsky, T. L., Rosenthal, S. A., & Montoya, R. M. (2011). Liking is not the opposite of disliking: The functional separability of positive and negative attitudes toward minority groups. *Cultural Diversity and Ethnic Minority Psychology, 17*(2), 134–43. doi:10.1037/a0023806

Qian, M., Wong, W. I., Nabbijohn, A. N., Wang, Y., MacMullin, L. N., James, H. J., Fu, G., Zuo, B., & VanderLaan, D. P. (2023). Children's implicit gender–toy association development varies across cultures. *Developmental Psychology, 59*(12), 2287–95. doi:10.1037/dev0001590

Raes, F., Pommier, E., Neff, K. D., & Van Fucht, D. (2011). Construction and factorial validation of a short form of the self-compassion scale. *Clinical Psychology & Psychotherapy, 18,* 250–55. doi:10.1002/cpp.702

Rahman, Q., Xu, Y., Lippa, R. A., & Vasey, P. L. (2020). Prevalence of sexual orientation across 28 nations and its association with gender equality, economic development, and individualism. *Archives of Sexual Behavior, 49*(2), 595–96. doi:10.1007/s10508-019-01590-0

Raines, J., Holmes, L., Watts-Overall, T. M., Slettevold, E., Gruia, D. C., Orbell, S., & Rieger, G. (2021). Patterns of genital sexual arousal in transgender men. *Psychological Science, 32*(4), 485–95. doi:10.1177/0956797620971654

Ramirez, J. L., & Galupo, M. P. (2019). Multiple minority stress: The role of proximal and distal stress on mental health outcomes among lesbian, gay, and bisexual people of color. *Journal of Gay & Lesbian Mental Health, 23*(2), 145–67. doi:10.1080/19359705.2019.1568946

Rawls, J. (1971). *A theory of justice.* Harvard University.

Ray, T. N., & Parkhill, M. R. (2020). Examining disgust and emotion regulation difficulties as components of aggression toward perceived gay men. *Psychology of Violence, 10*(4), 462–71. doi:10.1037/vio0000265

Raymond, M., Turek, D., Durand, V., Nila, S., Suryobroto, B., Vadez, J., Barthes, J., Apostolou, M., & Crochet, P-A. (2022). Increased birth rank of homosexual males: Disentangling the older brother effect and sexual antagonism hypothesis. *Peer Community Journal, 3,* e22. doi:10.1101/2022.02.22.481477

Recorder, E. E. L., Johnson, T. W., & Wassersug, R. J. (2020). Castration for pleasure: Exploring extreme castration ideations in fiction. *Archives of Sexual Behavior, 51*(4), 2337–51. doi:10.1007/s10508-022-02295-7

Repko, A., & Aleksandrova, O. V. (2020). *Features of gender identity of men with homosexual orientation* [Paper]. International Scientific Conference of Young Scientists, St. Petersburg State University.

Reyes, M., Davis, R. D., David, A. J., Rosario, C. J., Dizon, A., Fernandez, J. L., & Viquiera, M. A. (2017). Stigma burden as a predictor of suicidal behavior among lesbians and gays in the Philippines. *Suicidology Online, 8,* 1–10. http://www.suicidology-online.com/pdf/SOL-2017-8-26.pdf

Riddle Scale. (2022, May 6). In *Wikipedia.* https://en.wikipedia.org/wiki/Riddle_scale

Rieger, G., Rosenthal, A. M., Cash, B. M., Linsenmeier, J. A. W., Bailey, J. M., & Savin-Williams, R. C. (2013). Male bisexual arousal: A matter of curiosity? *Biological Psychology, 94*(3), 479–89. doi:10.1016/j.biopsycho.2013.09.007

Rikel, A. M. (2020). Social representations about homosexuality among different generations of modern Russians. *Vestnik Moskovskogo Universiteta. Seriya 14. Psikhologiya* [Moscow University Psychology Bulletin], *4*, 110–34.

Rodriguez, E. M., & Ouellette, S. C. (2000). Gay and lesbian Christians: Homosexual and religious identity integration in the members and participants of a gay-positive church. *Journal for the Scientific Study of Religion, 39*(3), 333–47. doi:10.1111/0021-8294.00028

Rodriguez, M. A., Xu, W., Wang, X., & Liu, X. (2015). Self-acceptance mediates the relationship between mindfulness and perceived stress. *Psychological Reports, 116*(2), 513–22. doi:10.2466/07.PR0.116k19w4

Roisman, G. I., Clausell, E., Holland, A., Fortuna, K., & Elieff, C. (2008). Adult romantic relationships as contexts of human development: A multimethod comparison of same-sex couples with opposite-sex dating, engaged, and married dyads. *Developmental Psychology, 44*(1), 91–101. doi:10.1037/0012-1649.44.1.91

Rooks, J., & Han, C. (2021, December 14). *The psychological needs that make people adopt attitudes and make choices—and that drive the extreme positions that often divide society.* Maine Public Radio. https://www.mainepublic.org/show/maine-calling/2021-12-14/the-psychological-needs-that-make-people-adopt-attitudes-and-make-choices-and-that-drive-the-extreme-positions-that-often-divide-society

Rosario, M., & Schrimshaw, E. W. (2008). Predicting different patterns of sexual identity development over time among lesbian, gay, and bisexual youths: A cluster analytic approach. *American Journal of Community Psychology, 42*(3–4), 266–82. doi:10.1007/s10464-008-9207-7

Roselli, C. E. (2018). Neurobiology of gender identity and sexual orientation. *Journal of Neuroendocrinology, 30*(7), e12562. doi:10.1111/jne.12562

Rosenkrantz, D. E., Black, W. W., Abreu, R. L., Aleshire, M. E., & Fallin-Bennett, K. (2017). Health and health care of rural sexual and gender minorities: A systematic review. *Stigma and Health, 2*(3), 229–43. doi:10.1037/sah0000055

Rosenkrantz, D. E., Rostosky, S. S., Riggle, E. D. B., & Cook, J. R. (2016). The positive aspects of intersecting religious/spiritual and LGBTQ identities. *Spirituality in Clinical Practice, 3*(2), 127–38. doi:10.1037/scp0000095

Rosik, C. H., Lefevor, G. T., McGraw, J. S., & Beckstead, A. L. (2022). Is conservative religiousness inherently associated with poorer health for sexual minorities? *Journal of Religion and Health, 61*, 3055–75. doi:10.1007/s10943-021-01289-4

Rullo, J. E. (2012). *Bisexuality: Beyond the prevailing assumptions about male and female sexual orientation* [Unpublished doctoral dissertation]. University of Utah.

Rullo, J. E., Strassberg, D. S., & Miner, M. H. (2015). Gender-specificity in sexual interest in bisexual men and women. *Archives of Sexual Behavior, 44*(5), 1449–57. doi:10.1007/s10508-014-0415-y

Russell, G. M. (2023, May 17). *Guest post: Hanging posters up for a better community.* Out Boulder Country. https://www.outboulder.org/blog/guest-post-hanging-posters-up-for-a-better-community

Russell, G. M., & Bohan, J. S. (2006). The case of internalized homophobia: Theory and/as practice. *Theory & Psychology, 16*(3), 343–66. doi:10.1177/0959354306064283

Russian Public Opinion Research Center. (2021, July 21). *Same-sex marriage: Taboo or new norm?*

Ryan, W. S., Legate, N., Weinstein, N., & Rahman, Q. (2017). Autonomy support fosters lesbian, gay, and bisexual identity disclosure and wellness, especially for those with internalized homophobia. *Journal of Social Issues, 73*(2), 289–306. doi:10.1111/josi.12217

Sadr, M., Khorashad, B. S., Talaei, A., Fazeli, N., & Hönekopp, J. (2020). 2D:4D Suggests a role of prenatal testosterone in gender dysphoria. *Archives of Sexual Behavior, 49*(2), 421–32. doi:10.1007/s10508-020-01630-0

Safron, A., & Hoffmann, H. (2017). What does sexual responsiveness to one's nonpreferred sex mean? *Archives of Sexual Behavior, 46*(5), 1199–1202. doi:10.1007/s10508-017-0954-0

Safron, A., & Klimaj, V. (2022). Learned but not chosen: A reward competition feedback model for the origins of sexual preferences and orientations. In D. P. VanderLaan & W. I. Wong (Eds.), *Gender and sexuality development: Focus on sexuality research* (pp. 443–90). doi:10.1007/978-3-030-84273-4_16

Salvati, M., Chiorri, C., & Baiocco, R. (2019). The relationships of dispositional mindfulness with sexual prejudice and internalized sexual stigma among heterosexual and gay/bisexual men. *Mindfulness, 10*, 2375–84. doi:10.1007/s12671-019-01215-6

Santtila, P., Högbacka, A.-L., Jern, P., Johansson, A., Varjonen, M., Witting, K., von der Pahlen, B., & Sandnabba, N. K. (2009). Testing Miller's theory of alleles preventing androgenization as an evolutionary explanation for the genetic predisposition for male. *Evolution and Human Behavior, 30*(1), 58–65. doi:10.1016/j.evolhumbehav.2008.08.004

Saraff, S., Singh, T., Kaur, H., & Biswal, R. (2022). Stigma and health of Indian LGBT population: A systematic review. *Stigma and Health, 7*(2), 178–95. doi:10.1037/sah0000361

Sarno, E. L., Newcomb, M. E., & Mustanski, B. (2020). Rumination longitudinally mediates the association of minority stress and depression in sexual and gender minority individuals. *Journal of Abnormal Psychology, 129*(4), 355–63. doi:10.1037/abn0000508

Sassenberg, K., Winter, K., Becker, D., Ditrich, L., Scholl, A., & Moskowitz, G. B. (2022). Flexibility mindsets: Reducing biases that result from spontaneous processing. *European Review of Social Psychology, 33*(1), 171–213. doi:10.1080/10463283.2021.1959124

Savin-Williams, R. C. (2016). Sexual orientation: Categories or continuum? Commentary on Bailey et al. (2016). *Psychological Science in the Public Interest, 17*(2), 37–44. doi:10.1177/1529100616637618

Savin-Williams, R. C. (2021). *Bi: Bisexual, pansexual, fluid, and nonbinary youth.* New York University Press.

Schnarrs, P. W., Stone, A. L., Bond, M. A., Salcido, R., Jr., Dorri, A. A., & Nemeroff, C. B. (2022). Development and psychometric properties of the sexual and gender minority adverse childhood experiences (SGM-ACEs): Effect on sexual and gender minority adult mental health. *Child Abuse & Neglect, 127*, 1–17. doi:10.1016/j.chiabu.2022.105570

Schudson, Z. C., Dibble, E. R., & van Anders, S. M. (2017). Gender/sex and sexual diversity via sexual configurations theory: Insights from a qualitative study with gender and sexual minorities. *Psychology of Sexual Orientation and Gender Diversity, 4*(4), 422–37. doi:10.1037/sgd0000241

Schudson, Z. C., & van Anders, S. M. (2021). Gender/sex diversity beliefs: Scale construction, validation, and links to prejudice. *Group Processes & Intergroup Relations, 25*(4), 1011–36. doi:10.1177/1368430220987595

Scicchitano, D. (2021). The "real" Chechen man: Conceptions of religion, nature, and gender and the persecution of sexual minorities in postwar Chechnya. *Journal of Homosexuality, 68*, 1545–62. doi:10.1080/00918369.2019.1701336

Scourfield, J., Roen, K., & McDermott, L. (2008). Lesbian, gay, bisexual and transgender young people's experiences of distress: Resilience, ambivalence and self-destructive behaviour. *Health & Social Care in the Community, 16*(3), 329–36. doi:10.1111/j.1365-2524.2008.00769.x

Semenova, T. S., Babin, S. M., Ivashinenko, D. M., & Podsadnyj, S. A. (2019). Psychological well-being and premorbid personality traits in adolescents with homosexual and bisexual orientation. *Bulletin of Psychotherapy, 69*, 97–106.

Semon, T. L., Hsu, K. J., Rosenthal, A., & Bailey, J. M. (2017). Bisexual phenomena among gay-identified men. *Archives of Sexual Behavior, 46*(1), 237–45. doi:10.1007/s10508-016-0849-5

Set, Z., & Ergin, Ö. (2020). The investigation of the mediator effect of sexism and defense style in the relationship between homophobia and aggression. *Nöropsikiyatri Arşivi, 57*(2), 113–19. doi:10.29399/npa.24743

Seto, M. C. (2017). The puzzle of male chronophilias. *Archives of Sexual Behavior, 46*(1), 3–22. doi:10.1007/s10508-016-0799-y

Severson, N., Munoz-Laboy, M., & Kaufman, R. (2014). "At times, I feel like I'm sinning": The paradoxical role of non-lesbian, gay, bisexual and transgender-affirming religion in the lives of behaviorally-bisexual Latino men. *Culture, Health, & Sexuality, 16*(2), 136–48. doi:10.1080/13691058.2013.843722

Shaekhov, Z. D. (2021). Psychological well-being the context of gender and sexual identity. *Natsional'nyy psikhologicheskiy zhurnal, 3*(43), 31–42.

Shaekhov, Z. D., & Malysheva, N. G. (2021). Impact of belief in a competitive world and internalized homophobia on psychological well-being. *Vestnik Moskovskogo Universiteta. Seriya 14. Psikhologiya* [Moscow University Psychology Bulletin], *1*, 265–88. doi:10.11621/vsp.2021.01.11

Shapiro, F. (2017). *Eye movement desensitization and reprocessing (EMDR) therapy: Basic principles, protocols, and procedures* (3rd ed.). Guildford.

Sherman, A. D. F., Poteat, T. C., Budhathoki, C., Kelly, U., Clark, K. D., & Campbell, J. C. (2020). Association of depression and post-traumatic stress with polyvictimization and emotional transgender and gender diverse community connection among Black and Latinx transgender women. *LGBT Health, 7*(7), 358–66. doi:10.1089/lgbt.2019.0336

Siegel, D. (2014). *Mindfulness as integration.* https://drdansiegel.com/mindfulness-as-integration/

Simon, K. A., Vázquez, C. P., Bruun, S. T., & Farr, R. H. (2020). Retrospective feelings of difference based on gender and sexuality among emerging adults. *Psychology of Sexual Orientation and Gender Diversity, 7*(1), 26–39. doi:10.1037/sgd0000349

Simon, W., & Gagnon, J. H. (1986). Sexual scripts: Permanence and change. *Archives of Sexual Behavior, 15*(2), 97–120. doi:10.1007/BFC1542219

Singh, A. A. (2019). *The racial healing handbook: Practical activities to help you challenge privilege, confront system racism, and engage in collective healing.* New Harbinger.

Singh, A. A., Cokley, R. K., & Gorritz, F. B. (2022). Using the APA guidelines for psychological practice to develop trans-affirming counseling for trans and gender nonconforming clients. In D. C. Haldeman (Ed.), *The case against conversion "therapy": Evidence, ethics, and alternatives* (pp. 147–67). APA. doi:10.1037/0000266-008

Singh, A. A., Meng, S. E., & Hansen, A. W. (2014). "I am my own gender": Resilience strategies of trans youth. *Journal of Counseling & Development, 92,* 208–18. doi:10.1002/j.1556-6676.2014.00150.x

Singh, R. S., & O'Brien, W. H. (2019). The impact of work stress on sexual minority employees: Could psychological flexibility be a helpful solution? *Stress and Health, 36*(1), 59–74. doi:10.1002/smi.2913

Skerven, K., Whicker, D., & LeMaire, K. (2019). Applying dialectical behaviour therapy to structural and internalized stigma with LGBTQ clients. *Cognitive Behaviour Therapist, 12,* E9. doi:10.1017/S1754470X18000235

Skidmore, S. J., Lefevor, G. T., Golightly, R. M., & Larsen, E. R. (2022). Religious sexual minorities, belongingness, and suicide risk: Does it matter where belongingness comes from? *Psychology of Religion and Spirituality, 15*(3), 356–66. doi:10.1037/rel0000470

Skidmore, S. J., Lefevor, G. T., Larsen, E. R., Golightly, R. M., & Abreu, R. L. (2022). "We are scared of being kicked out of our religion!": Common challenges and benefits for sexual minority Latter-day Saints. *Psychology of Sexual Orientation and Gender Diversity, 10*(4), 663–74. doi:10.1037/sgd0000571

Skorska, M. N., & Bogaert, A. F. (2017). Prenatal androgens in men's sexual orientation: Evidence for a more nuanced role? *Archives of Sexual Behavior, 46*(6), 1621–24. doi:10.1007/s10508-017-1000-y

Slettevold, E., Holmes, L., Gruia, D., Nyssen, C. P., Watts-Overall, T. M., & Rieger, G. (2019). Bisexual men with bisexual and monosexual genital arousal patterns. *Biological Psychology, 148,* 107763. doi:10.1016/j.biopsycho.2019.107763

Solomon, S. E., Rothblum, E. D., & Balsam, K. F. (2005). Money, housework, sex, and conflict: Same-sex couples in civil unions, those not in civil unions, and heterosexual married siblings. *Sex Roles, 52*(9), 561–75. doi:10.1007/s11199-005-3725-7

Stanisławski, K. (2019). The Coping Circumplex Model: An integrative model of the structure of coping with stress. *Frontiers in Psychology, 10,* Article 694. doi:10.3389/fpsyg.2019.00694

Statista. (2023). *Attitudes toward LGBT persons in Russia 2021.* https://www.statista.com/statistics/1030193/russia-attitudes-toward-lgbt-persons/

Stief, M. C., Rieger, G., & Savin-Williams, R. C. (2014). Bisexuality is associated with elevated sexual sensation seeking, sexual curiosity, and sexual excitability. *Personality and Individual Differences, 66,* 193–98. doi:10.1016/j.paid.2014.03.035

Stiksma, M. (2021). *Understanding the campus expression climate: Fall 2020*. Heterodox Academy. https://heterodoxacademy.org/wp-content/uploads/2021/03/Campus-Expression-Survey-Report-2020.pdf

Storms, M. D. (1980). Theories of sexual orientation. *Journal of Personality and Social Psychology, 38*(5), 783–92. doi:10.1037/0022-3514.38.5.783

Strizzi, J., Fernández-Agis, I., Patrón-Carreño, T., & Alarcón-Rodríguez, R. (2016). Positive aspects of being lesbian, gay or bisexual in Spain: An exploratory study. *Journal of Psychology & Psychotherapy, 6*(2), 1–8. doi:10.4172/2161-0487.1000257

Strkalj, G., & Pather, N. (2021). Beyond the sex binary: Toward the inclusive anatomical sciences education. *Anatomical Sciences Education, 14*(4), 513–18. doi:10.1002/ase.2002

Struve, J., Fradkin, H., & Beckstead, A. L. (2018). Beyond the gay/straight binary: Gender and/or sexually diverse male survivors. In R. Gartner (Ed.), *Understanding the sexual betrayal of boys and men: The trauma of sexual abuse* (pp. 284–310). Routledge.

Sumerau, J. E., Grollman, E. A., & Cragun, R. T. (2018). "Oh my God, I sound like a horrible person": Generic processes in the conditional acceptance of sexual and gender diversity. *Symbolic Interaction, 41*(1), 62–82. doi:10.1002/symb.326

Sweet, H. B., & Reigeluth, C. (2018). *Educating the public about gender issues: Solutions for the future* [Roundtable]. National Multicultural Conference Summit, Denver, Colorado.

Swift-Gallant, A., Aung, T., Rosenfield, K., Dawood, K., & Puts, D. (2023). Organizational effects of gonadal hormones on human sexual orientation. *Adaptive Human Behavior and Physiology, 9*, 344–70. doi:10.1007/s40750-023-00226-x

Swift-Gallant, A., Coome, L. A., Aitken, M., Monks, D. A., & VanderLaan, D. P. (2019). Evidence for distinct biodevelopmental influences on male sexual orientation. *PNAS, 116*(26), 12787–92. doi:10.1073/pnas.1809920116

Swift-Gallant, A., Coome, L. A., Monks, D. A., & VanderLaan, D. P. (2017). Handedness is a biomarker of variation in anal sex role behavior and recalled childhood gender nonconformity among gay men. *PLOS One 12*(2), e0170241. doi:10.1371/journal.pone.0170241

Tan, P. P. (2005). The importance of spirituality among gay and lesbian individuals. *Journal of Homosexuality, 49*, 135–44. doi:10.1300/J082v49n02_08

Tan, S., & Weisbart, C. (2021). Asian-Canadian trans youth: Identity development in a hetero-cis-normative White world. *Psychology of Sexual Orientation and Gender Diversity, 9*(4), 488–99. doi:10.1037/sgd0000512

Tassone, D., Dawson, S. J., & Chivers, M. L. (2019). The impact of homonegativity on gynephilic men's visual attention toward non-preferred sexual targets. *Personality and Individual Differences, 149*, 261–72. doi:10.1016/j.paid.2019.05.062

Tate, C. C., Youssef, C. P., & Bettergarcia, J. N. (2014). Integrating the study of transgender spectrum and cisgender experiences of self-categorization from a personality perspective. *Review of General Psychology, 18*(4), 302–12. doi:10.1037/gpr0000019

Temnikova, O. A., & Averina, E. A. (2016). Society's attitude towards supporters of the LGBT community. *Scientific Community of Students of the XXI Century, Social Sciences, 6*(42), 39–44.

Thomas, K. (2022, April 6). I was allowed to transition at 18 without question—but I regretted it. *Telegraph*. https://www.telegraph.co.uk/news/2022/04/06/allowed -transition-18-without-question-regretted/

Tierney, D., Spengler, E. S., Schuch, E., & Grzanka, P. R. (2021). Sexual orientation beliefs and identity development: A person-centered analysis among sexual minorities. *Journal of Sex Research, 58*(5), 625–37. doi:10.1080/00224499.202 1.1878344

Truszczynski, N., Singh, A. A., & Hansen, N. (2022). The discrimination experiences and coping responses of non-binary and trans people. *Journal of Homosexuality, 69*, 741–55. doi:10.1080/00918369.2020.1855028

Tucker, R. P., Testa, R. J., Reger, M. A., Simpson, T. L., Shipherd, J. C., & Lehavot, K. (2019). Current and military-specific gender minority stress factors and their relationship with suicide ideation in transgender veterans. *Suicide and Life-Threatening Behavior, 49*(1), 155–66. doi:10.1111/sltb.12432

Turkheimer, E. (2000). Three laws of behavior genetics and what they mean. *Current Directions in Psychological Science, 9*(5), 160–64. doi:10.1111/1467 -8721.00084

van Anders, S. M. (2015). Beyond sexual orientation: Integrating gender/sex and diverse sexualities via sexual configurations theory. *Archives of Sexual Behavior, 44*(5), 1177–1213. doi:10.1007/s10508-015-0490-8

Van Assche, J., Swart, H., Schmid, K., Dhont, K., Al Ramiah, A., Christ, O., Kauff, M., Rothmann, S., Savelkoul, M., Tausch, N., Wölfer, R., Zahreddine, S., Saleem, M., & Hewstone, M. (2023). Intergroup contact is reliably associated with reduced prejudice, even in the face of group threat and discrimination. *American Psychologist, 78*(6), 761–74. doi:10.1037/amp0001144

Vandello, J. A., Wilkerson, M., Bosson, J. K., Wiernik, B. M., & Kosakowska-Berezecka, N. (2023). Precarious manhood and men's physical health around the world. *Psychology of Men & Masculinities, 24*(1), 1–15. doi:10.1037/men 0000407

van der Star, A., Pachankis, J. E., & Bränström, R. (2021). Country-level structural stigma, school-based and adulthood victimization, and life satisfaction among sexual minority adults: A life course approach. *Journal of Youth Adolescence, 50*, 189–201. doi:10.1007/s10964-020-01340-9

VanderLaan, D. P., Skorska, M. N., Peragine, D. E., & Coome, L. A. (2022). Carving the biodevelopment of same-sex sexual orientation at its joints. *Archives of Sexual Behavior, 52*, 2939–62. doi:10.1007/s10508-022-02360-1

Velez, B. L., Polihronakis, C. J., Watson, L. B., & Cox, R., Jr. (2019). Heterosexism, racism, and the mental health of sexual minority people of color. *Counseling Psychologist, 47*(1), 129–59. doi:10.1177/0011000019828309

Vigna, A. J., Poehlmann-Tynan, J., & Koenig, B. W. (2018). Does self-compassion covary with minority stress? Examining group differences at the intersection of marginalized identities. *Self and Identity, 17*(6), 687–709. doi:10.1080/1529886 8.2018.1457566

Vincke, J., & Bolton, R. (1994). Social support, depression, and self-acceptance among gay men. *Human Relations, 47*(9), 1049–62. doi:10.1177/001872679404700902

Walsh, J. P. (2020). Social media and moral panics: Assessing the effects of technological change on societal reaction. *International Journal of Cultural Studies, 23*(6), 840–59. doi:10.1177/1367877920912257

Wibowo, E., Bertin, E., Johnson, T. W., Kavanagh, A., & Wassersug, R. J. (2023). Diagnosis and medical care of male individuals who seek ablation of their genitalia without a desire for feminization. *Archives of Sexual Behavior, 52*(3), 859–64. doi:10.1007/s10508-023-02586-7

Wibowo, E., Wong, S., Wassersug, R. J., & Johnson, T. W. (2023). Choosing castration: A thematic analysis of the perceived pros and cons of genital injuries and ablation by men who voluntarily sought castration. *Archives of Sexual Behavior, 52*(3), 1183–94. doi:10.1007/s10508-022-02434-0

Williams, M. T. (2008). Homosexuality anxiety: A misunderstood form of OCD. In L. V. Sebeki (Ed.), *Leading-edge health education issues* (pp. 195–205). Nova.

Williams, M. T., & Farris, S. G. (2011). Sexual orientation obsessions in obsessive–compulsive disorder: Prevalence and correlates. *Psychiatry Research, 187*(1–2), 156–59. doi:10.1016/j.psychres.2010.10.019

Williams, M. T., Wetterneck, C., Tellawi, G., & Duque, G. (2015). Domains of distress among people with sexual orientation obsessions. *Archives of Sexual Behavior, 44*(3), 783–89. doi:10.1007/s10508-014-0421-0

Wright, S. C., Aron, A., McLaughlin-Volpe, T., & Ropp, S. A. (1997). The extended contact effect: Knowledge of cross-group friendships and prejudice. *Journal of Personality and Social Psychology, 73*(1), 73–90. doi:10.1037/0022 -3514.73.1.73

Wu, Q., Ji, Y., Lin, X., Yang, H., & Chi, P. (2021). Gender congruence and mental health problems among Chinese transgender and gender non-conforming individuals: A process model involving rumination and stigma consciousness. *Journal of Clinical Psychology, 78*(4), 622–36. doi:10.1002/jclp.23248

Xu, Y., Norton, S., & Rahman, Q. (2021). Childhood gender nonconformity and the stability of self-reported sexual orientation from adolescence to young adulthood in a birth cohort. *Developmental Psychology, 57*(4), 557–69. doi:10.1037/ dev0001164

Yadavaia, J. E., & Hayes, S. C. (2012). Acceptance and commitment therapy for self-stigma around sexual orientation: A multiple baseline evaluation. *Cognitive and Behavioral Practice, 19*(4), 545–59. doi:10.1016/j.cbpra.2011.09.002

Yadegarfard, M., Meinhold-Bergmann, M. E., & Ho, R. (2014) Family rejection, social isolation, and loneliness as predictors of negative health outcomes (depression, suicidal ideation, and sexual risk behavior) among Thai male-to-female transgender adolescents. *Journal of LGBT Youth, 11*(4), 347–63. doi:10.1080/1 9361653.2014.910483

Yarhouse, M. A., & Carr, T. L. (2011). The exemplar project: Finding what makes a church exemplary in its ministry to persons who experience same-sex attraction or who struggle with sexual identity concerns. *Edification, 4*(2), 32–40.

Yarhouse, M. A., Dean, J. B., Stratton, S. P., & Lastoria, M. (2018). *Listening to sexual minorities: A study of faith and sexual identity on Christian college campuses.* IVP Academic.

Yarhouse, M. A., Stratton, S. P., & Dean, J. B. (2023). Stewarding diverse sexual and gender identities. In P. Glanzer & A. Smith (Eds.), *Stewarding our bodies: A vision for Christian student development.* Abilene Christian University Press.

Yarhouse, M. A., & Zaporozhets, O. (2019). *Costly obedience: What we can learn from the celibate gay Christian community.* Zondervan.

Ybarra, M. L., Mitchell, K. J., Kosciw, J. G., & Korchmaros, J. D. (2015). Understanding linkages between bullying and suicidal ideation in a national sample of LGB and heterosexual youth in the United States. *Prevention Science, 16*(3), 451–62. doi:10.1007/s11121-014-0510-2

Yule, M. A., Brotto, L. A., & Gorzalka, B. B. (2017). Sexual fantasy and masturbation among asexual individuals: An in-depth exploration. *Archives of Sexual Behavior, 46*, 311–28. doi:10.1007/s10508-016-0870-8

Yurcaba, J. (2022, August, 12). *After "Don't Say Gay" bill passed, anti-LGBTQ "grooming" rhetoric surged 400% online.* NBC News. https://www.nbcnews.com/nbc-out/out-news/-dont-say-gay-bill-passed-lgbtq-online-hate-surged-400-rcna42617

Zamani, G. E. M., & Choudhuri, D. D. (2016). Tracing LGBTQ community college students' experiences. *New Directions for Community Colleges, 2016*(174), 47–63. doi:10.1002/cc.2016.2016.issue-174

Zayka, A. S., & Lebedeva, E. I. (2020). *Features of the socio-psychological adaptation of LGB adolescents* [Paper]. International Scientific Conference of Young Scientists, St. Petersburg State University.

Zentner, M., & Von Aufsess, C. (2022). Is being gender nonconforming distressing? It depends where you live: Gender equality across 15 nations predicts how much gender nonconformity is related to self-esteem. *Psychological Medicine, 52*(10), 1857–65. doi:10.1017/S0033291720003645

Zhang J. (2022). Femme/butch/androgyne identity and preferences for femininity across face, voice, and personality traits in Chinese lesbian and bisexual women. *Archives of Sexual Behavior, 51*(7), 3485–95. doi:10.1007/s10508-022-02334-3

Zietsch, B. P., Sidari, M. J., Abdellaoui, A., Maier, R., Långström, N., Guo, S., Beecham, G. W., Martin, E. R., Sanders, A. R., & Verweij, K. J. H. (2021). Genomic evidence consistent with antagonistic pleiotropy may help explain the evolutionary maintenance of same-sex sexual behaviour in humans. *Nature Human Behaviour, 5*(9), 1251–58. doi:10.1038/s41562-021-01168-8

Zueva, D. Y., & Kazaryan, M. Y. (2020). *Features of childhood experiences in men with same-sex attraction as predictors of violations in their psychological well-being.* https://fulltext.kurskmed.com/fulltext/Electron_publications_KSMU/conference/2020/CD-2139.pdf

Index

About the Contributors

Each coeditor and coauthor listed in their bios what they considered their primary social labels, locations, and characteristics of how they personally experience the world. This is to inform you and other readers about our potential biases, expertise, privileges, and disadvantages on the subject. We also hope it dismantles some stereotypes.

Editors

A. Lee Beckstead (he/him), PhD, is white-Peruvian, gay, cisgender, currently nondisabled, and spiritual; was excommunicated from the Church of Jesus Christ of Latter-day Saints; and has been in a primary relationship with a man since 1997. He has been a psychologist in private practice since 2003 in Salt Lake City, Utah. He conducted a qualitative study from 1998 to 2001 on 50 individuals who tried to change their sexual orientation through psychotherapy. Half reported benefits, half reported harms, and many reported mixed results. Since 2005, he has co-facilitated weekend retreats for male survivors of sexual abuse (MenHealing.org). He served on the 2009 American Psychological Association task force making recommendations for those seeking therapy to change their sexual orientation. In 2012, he initiated the LGBTQ-affirmative Psychotherapist Guild of Utah to file ethical complaints against Utah clinicians providing sexual orientation change efforts (SOCE). In 2013, he shifted focus and organized a workshop to foster dialogue and understanding with these individuals. Since then, he's been meeting twice per month with therapists and educators holding differing views on sexual orientation, gender, and religion (ReconciliationAndGrowth.org). He testified as an expert witness in a 2015 New Jersey legal case against a Jewish organization accused of consumer fraud due to offering SOCE. From 2016, he's been part of a diverse research team studying the health and satisfaction of individuals who are single and celibate or noncelibate or in a same-gender/queer or mixed-orientation relationship

(4OptionsSurvey.com). He is also the lead coeditor of the LGBTQIA+ Peacemaking Book Project.

Jacks Cheng (tā [他]/he/they), PhD, EdM, is a queer migrant of Taiwanese heritage to Canada and the United States. Tā works as a supervising psychologist at NYC Health + Hospitals/Jacobi and assistant professor of psychiatry and behavioral sciences at Albert Einstein College of Medicine. Tā is also the 2023 chair of the Committee on Early Career Psychologists of the American Psychological Association. Tā received a doctorate in counselling psychology from Indiana University and is passionate about cultural-affirmative and anti-colonialist approaches in research and practice, with a particular interest in empowering sexual and gender diverse, migrant, and people of color communities in oppressive spaces.

Sulaimon Giwa (he/him/his), PhD, is associate professor and interim dean of social work at Memorial University of Newfoundland and Labrador in Canada. Sulaimon is a scholar-activist who self-identifies as Black, Muslim, and gay. His intersectional identity adds depth to his contributions in the field of LGBTQ+ studies, demonstrating his unwavering commitment to fostering inclusive discourse from diverse perspectives. Through his academic and community pursuits, Sulaimon demonstrates his astute understanding of the intricacies surrounding identity and representation within the LGBTQ+ community, promoting crucial conversations on equity and social justice. He authored the 2022 book *Racism and Gay Men of Color: Living and Coping with Discrimination.*

Mark A. Yarhouse, PsyD, is a clinical psychologist who specializes in conflicts tied to religious identity and sexual and gender identity. He assists people who are navigating the complex relationship between their sexual or gender identity and Christian faith. He is the Dr. Arthur P. and Mrs. Jean May Rech Chair in Psychology at Wheaton College, where he runs the Sexual and Gender Identity (SGI) Institute. He is an award-winning teacher and researcher and is the past recipient of the Gary Collins Award for Excellence in Christian Counseling. He was a past participant with the Ethics and Public Policy Center think tank in Washington, DC, and he was named senior fellow with the Council of Christian Colleges and Universities to conduct a study of students navigating sexual identity concerns at Christian colleges and universities. He has been a consultant to the National Institute of Corrections to address issues facing sexual minorities in corrections, and he was part of a consensus panel from the American Psychological Association on sexual orientation and gender identity change efforts that convened to provide input to the Substance Abuse and Mental Health Services Administration (SAMHSA) in Washington, DC. He is currently the chair of the task force on LGBT issues for Division 36 (Psychology of Religion and Spirituality) of the American Psychological Association. He was also invited to write the featured white paper on sexual identity for the Christ on Campus Initiative, edited by Don A. Carson for the Gospel Coalition. He has published over 80 peer-reviewed journal articles and book chapters and is author or coauthor of several books, including *Understanding Sexual Identity: A Resource for Youth Ministers* and *Understanding Gender Dysphoria: Navigating Transgender Issues in a Changing Culture*. His most recent books are *Sexual Identity and Faith* and *Costly Obedience: Listening to and Learning from Celibate Gay Christians*.

Iva Žegura (she/her) graduated from and specialized in clinical psychology at the Department of Psychology, Faculty of Philosophy, in Zagreb and is currently pursuing doctoral studies at Sigmund Freud University Vienna, Austria. She is a licensed clinical psychologist and is educated in gestalt integrative therapy, cybernetic psychotherapy, and sexual therapy. She works at the University Psychiatric Hospital Vrapče in Zagreb, and collaborates with several national universities and departments of psychology. She introduced the concept of affirmative and sensitive LGBTAIQ+ mental health practice in Croatia and the region. The Section for Psychology of Sexuality and Psychology of Gender of the Croatian Psychological Association was established on her initiative in 2007. In 2015, she facilitated the implementation of legalization and health care for trans people based on SOC WPATH within the Croatian health-care system. She is a member of the national list of experts for transgender health care at the Croatian Ministry of Health. She is the president of the Section for Clinical Psychology and Section for Psychology and Human Rights, and vice president of the Section for Psychology of Sexuality and Psychology of Gender. From 2021, she has been a member of the board of directors of the European Professional Association for Transgender Health (EPATH) and now she is president-elect. She collaborates with the Global Education Institute of WPATH and APA IPsy Net. She is a member of several national, European, and international professional associations. In 2022, she received the APA Division 52 International Psychology Global Citizen Psychologist Citation Award for exceptional volunteer professional engagement and contribution to increasing visibility and strengthening the availability of psychological scientific and practical knowledge both in local and international community related to LGBTQ+ mental health. In 2024, she received the highest professional award in Croatia "Ramiro Bujas" from the Croatian Psychological Association for exceptional achievements in the social affirmation of psychology.

Authors

R.A.[1] is an Arab woman and MSc psychology student currently residing in Cyprus. She has worked in numerous nonprofit and nongovernmental organizations advocating for minority groups. She is currently pursuing a career in social psychology research with a special interest in the Arab LGBTQIA+ community residing in the Middle East.

Jenna Brownfield (she/her), PhD, is a licensed psychologist in private practice in Minneapolis, Minnesota. She earned her doctorate in counseling psychology from the University of Missouri–Kansas City. She is a White, bi/queer, cis woman with a midwestern United States upbringing.

Pichit Buspavanich (he/him), MD, is a clinical psychiatrist and psychotherapist from Berlin, currently working with a focus on affective disorders as well as gender incongruence.

Nate Cannon, BA, MFA, CDP, is a nationally recognized speaker, consultant, and author who trains and educates consumers and professionals through his experiences as a transgender man living well in recovery with both mental health diagnoses and a neurological disability. He has over 10 years of experience working with dementia, law, mental health, and chemical dependency. To learn more about his work, visit NateCannon.org.

Marty A. Cooper (he/him), PhD, is a White/Native American cisgender gay male. He is an associate professor at State University of New York (SUNY) College at Old Westbury in the graduate Mental Health Counseling Program. Dr. Cooper is a candidate and fellow of New York University's Postdoctoral Program in Psychoanalysis and Psychotherapy. He is a licensed psychologist, a licensed mental health counselor, and a nationally certified counselor with regional and international experience. His research focuses on the intersections of multiple minority statuses with specific emphasis on sexual orientation and gender identity. Additional research interests include ageism and Indigenous populations. Dr. Cooper also has a private practice in New York City. He is a volunteer psychologist with the New York City Medical Reserve Corp, the Post-Emergency Canvassing Operations, HealthRight International, and Physicians for Human Rights.

Edward (Ward) B. Davis, PsyD, is a clinical psychologist, professor of psychology, and director of clinical training in the Wheaton Clinical Psychology

---

[1] This coauthor chose to use their initials instead of their full name for safety reasons.

Doctoral Program (Illinois). He identifies as a White, cisgender, heterosexually married, Christian man who is religiously traditional but sociopolitically liberal. Dr. Davis has over 100 publications and 100 professional presentations, mostly focusing on positive psychology and the psychology of religion and spirituality. Most of Dr. Davis's publications, presentations, and research grants have focused on these areas, including the recently published *Handbook of Positive Psychology, Religion, and Spirituality*. Dr. Davis also serves on the editorial boards of three journals: *Psychology of Religion and Spirituality* (associate editor), *Spirituality in Clinical Practice* (consulting editor), and *Journal of Psychology and Theology* (editorial board). During his career, Dr. Davis has received several awards, including Wheaton College's Senior Scholarship Achievement Award, Biola University's Sorenson Outstanding Faculty Award, and the Margaret Gorman Early Career Award from the American Psychological Association's Division 36 (Society for the Psychology of Religion and Spirituality).

Janet B. Dean is a professor of pastoral counseling at Asbury Theological Seminary in Wilmore, Kentucky, as well as a licensed clinical psychologist and an ordained elder in the Church of the Nazarene. She and her research partners have completed multiple national studies regarding the experiences of sexual and gender minorities at traditionally religious postsecondary educational institutions. In addition to their various publications in this area, including the book *Listening to Sexual Minorities: A Study of Faith and Sexual Identity on Christian College Campuses*, Dr. Dean has presented before the American Psychological Association, the Christian Association for Psychological Studies, state associations in counseling and psychology, and other professional organizations. She also serves on the Task Force on LGBT Issues of APA's Division 36, the Society for the Psychology of Religion and Spirituality. Dr. Dean regularly consults with religious colleges and universities as well as churches and religious groups wanting to provide better ministerial care for sexual and gender minorities.

Jeannie DiClementi (she/her/hers), PsyD, is a White, cisgender, lesbian, wife, mother, grandmother, great-grandmother, licensed psychologist, community activist, and boat rocker. She has worked in academia for nearly 30 years and is in the process of retiring from Purdue University Fort Wayne. She has worked as a clinician with LGBTQIA+ clients since the mid-1980s and with HIV+ clients during the peak years of the HIV pandemic. In her current university faculty position, she created the campus Safe Zone training, the LGBTQIA+ Resource Center, the LGBTQIA+ Task Force, and mental health education and suicide prevention programming. She mentors LGBTQIA+ graduate students for the American Psychological Association's Graduate Student Association.

She provides consultation and training on clinical work with LGBTQIA+ clients for Northeast Indiana mental health centers, including clinical psychology internship programs.

Weston V. Donaldson (he/him), PhD, ABPP, is a board-certified clinical geropsychologist working at the Milwaukee VA Medical Center, living on the traditional homeland of the Potowatomi, Ho-Chunk, and Menominee tribes, known as Wisconsin. Weston is a White, Euro-American, currently nondisabled, cisgender gay man. He has had particular interest in aging issues, specifically LGBTQ+ aging, since graduate school, and this has been a focus of his research and writing activity since that time, with a focus on long-term care and aging services settings. Through his work in various health-care settings (skilled nursing, inpatient rehab, outpatient primary care), he has witnessed many LGBTQIA+ people moving through the challenges that can arise with aging. His hope is that through continued advocacy, training, and experience, providers and care locations can become safer for and more affirmative of older LGBTQIA+ people.

Samuel Eshleman Latimer, PsyD, is a licensed clinical psychologist who specializes in conflict management at the Cincinnati Center for Dialectical Behavior Therapy. He also serves as a postdoctoral research assistant at Xavier University and leads a local discussion group that values viewpoint diversity, called "Braving Controversy." Samuel grew up attracted to the same gender, with periods of gender dysphoria. Samuel currently identifies his gender as male and his sexual orientation as fluid. Samuel has given talks on conflict management, gender, sexuality, and other social psychology topics in clinical and academic settings. He is passionate about science and spirituality.

Alejandro Gepp-Torres (he/él), MD, is a child and adolescent psychiatrist and gender, sex, and relationship diversity therapist from Valparaíso, Chile. He studied medicine at Universidad de Valparaíso. After that, he enrolled in the Child and Adolescent Psychiatry Program at the same university. At the same time, he worked with adolescents with substance abuse disorders. After graduating, he started working at Hospital Carlos van Buren, taking charge of the Gender Identity Program, and teaching consultation psychiatry and developmental psychology. Eventually, he became the chief of the Mental Health Unit in the same hospital. He also works with a foundation called Diversalud, where a group of medical professionals who work with gender diversity do activism to give access to affirming care to people across the country. He was raised in a Catholic family and identifies as a proud and happy gay man.

Debra Harley (she/her), PhD, CRC, LPC, is a licensed professional counselor and professor in Lexington, Kentucky. She is an African American cisgender woman with a southern United States upbringing. She is a Provost's Distinguished Service Professor at the University of Kentucky and graduate faculty in the Counselor Education Program in the Department of Early Childhood, Special Education, and Counselor Education and coordinator of the counselor education doctoral program. One of her research areas is cultural diversity and the influence of intersectionality in people's lives, especially of marginalization, disability, race, age, sexual identity, and rurality. She has published over 90 refereed articles, 85 book chapters, and five books that include *Disability Studies for Human Services: An Interdisciplinary and Intersectionality Approach*, *Cultural Diversity in Mental Health and Disability Counseling for Marginalized Groups*, *Disability and Vocational Rehabilitation in Rural Settings*, *Handbook of LGBT Elders*, *Contemporary Mental Health Issues among African Americas*, and *Disability and Vocational Rehabilitation in Rural Settings*.

Helen Harris, EdD, is a licensed clinical social worker, retired associate professor emerita, researcher, and author who is grateful for God's love for all of creation and is committed to communicating honor and respect for and in each person. Her pronouns are she/her/hers, and her deep desire is to be experienced as an ally. Dr. Harris has worked in crisis management, residential childcare; foster care and adoption; medical social work, including hospital, home health, and hospice; and loss and grief counseling and therapy with children, adolescents, and adults. Dr. Harris is the senior coeditor of the developing Routledge Resources Online: Death, Dying, and Bereavement. She has written and published in the areas of field education, integration of faith and practice, loss and grief, and congregational discernment and LGBTQ+ inclusion. She is the recipient of the 2022 Diana R. Garland Legacy Award. Dr. Harris continues to teach adjunctively and stays active in her church and with volunteer work. Her primary source of joy is family, including her husband, two adult children, and three precious grandchildren.

Heather Hoffmann, PhD, is a middle-age White (mostly) heterosexual cis woman with no religious affiliation who is interested in the factors that contribute to sexual arousal. She has examined the role of conditioning processes in sexual arousal as well as olfactory sexual arousal contagion (i.e., whether we can perceive sexual arousal from body odor). She is an experimental psychologist who performs laboratory and field conditioning studies using psychophysiological and subjective measures. She teaches a range of courses (e.g., Human Sexuality, Introduction to Neuroscience, Behavioral Pharmacology, Behavioral Neuroscience, Conditioning and Learning, Research Methods and Statistics,

Pleasures of the Brain, Gay and Lesbian Identities) to undergraduates at a liberal arts college in the midwestern United States. She is a former president of the International Academy of Sex Research.

Jay Tekulvē Jackson-Vann, LMFT, is a licensed marriage and family therapist in private practice in Utah and via telehealth in Georgia, Nevada, Michigan, Colorado, and Florida. He describes himself as a queer person of faith who focuses on his individual and individualized relationship with God rather than identifying as a member of a religious organization, although he does maintain some level of activity in the Church of Jesus Christ of Latter-day Saints.

Jeanna Jacobsen (they/them) is a queer, White, culturally Mormon, genderqueer female who holds a MSW and PhD in social work and a MS in instructional design and technology. For over 20 years, they have practiced clinical social work with an emphasis on suicide prevention and trauma-informed care. Their clinical work has focused on supporting the queer community and helping individuals heal from trauma. Dr. Jacobsen has taught in undergraduate and graduate social work programs since 2009. Their scholarship has focused on intersecting identities, specifically related to sexuality, gender, and spirituality. As a feminist qualitative research methodologist, they support students whose research utilize critical theories. Recent research and publications/presentations have focused on teaching diversity and difference in the social work classroom.

Tyler Lefevor, PhD, identifies as a White cisgender, gay/queer Mormon man. He is an associate professor of psychology at Utah State University. His work focuses primarily on understanding how and when religiousness relates to health for sexual and gender minorities. In addition, he maintains a small private therapy practice focused on helping sexual and gender minorities to thrive, particularly those raised in conservative religious traditions.

S. Candice Metzler (she/her/they/them), PhD, LCSW, is White, trans, intersex, queer, and relatively nondisabled and comes from a western United States upbringing. They are a clinical therapist in private practice in Salt Lake City, Utah, with more than a decade of experience providing mental health treatment and support to LGBTQI+ individuals and families. Candice has spent much of her adult life working to address critical issues through public education, organizing, consultation, and activism. Candice has been involved in community organizing and public education for more than 25 years. She served as the executive director of Transgender Education Advocates of Utah between 2015 and 2022. Candice has also served on numerous boards, including the

LQBTQ+ Therapist Guild of Utah, Equality Utah, and as the chair of Transgender Education Advocates of Utah from 2010 to 2015. Candice has more than a decade of experience providing consultation and education to government and private business leaders, including her work as a volunteer trainer with the U.S. Department of Justice providing training to local and regional law enforcement. She continues to serve as a contributing member of the Reconciliation and Growth Project. Candice loves teaching and worked as an adjunct instructor at the University of Utah between 2015 and 2020. She has also guest lectured on numerous college and university campuses throughout Utah since 2005.

Sara Mishly (she/her), MA, is a clinical psychologist, licensed in more than one Arab country, and is currently practicing in the Arab world. She has lived in different Arab countries and has a passion for enhancing mental health services in the Arab world. She has devoted most of her career to working with and writing about the mental health and psychosocial experiences of Arab LGBTQIA+ individuals residing in the Middle East.

Elizabeth Morgan (she/her), PhD, is the associate vice president for academic affairs and associate professor of psychology at Springfield College in Massachusetts. She is a White feminist ally and activist for the LGBTQIA+ community. Her research primarily focuses on sexuality and sexual identity development in emerging adulthood with consideration of social and cultural forces that help shape the construction of identity. She is the current executive director of the Society for the Study of Emerging Adulthood and a past president of the organization, as well as a past president of the International Society for Research on Identity. She coedited a book in the Oxford University Press series on Emerging Adulthood titled *Sexuality in Emerging Adulthood*, and her article "Contemporary Issues in Sexual Orientation and Identity Development in Emerging Adulthood" is one of the most read articles from the journal *Emerging Adulthood*. She also manages the LGBTQIA+ Safe Zone workshops on her college campus and is a founding board member of the Longmeadow Pride Alliance.

Annelise Parkes Murphy (she/her/hers), CMHC, is a clinical mental health counselor in private practice who works specifically with queer individuals who have experienced clinically defined trauma from religious association. She is White, cisgender, and polyamorous and was raised in the Church of Jesus Christ of Latter-day Saints faith, although she no longer believes in the religion of her youth. She presently holds the position of clinical director at Ginger Zen Therapy in South Jordan, Utah. She graduated with distinction from the University of Utah, where she earned a Bachelor of Science in psychology, with a notable 3.9 GPA. Building on her commitment to mental health, Annelise pursued advanced studies at Bradley University, achieving a Master of Arts in counseling with a specialization in clinical mental health counseling and an impressive 4.0 GPA. Annelise's professional journey encompasses valuable roles as a CMHC intern at the Utah Pride Center and subsequently as an ACMHC at Corner Canyon Counseling and Psychological Services. Her expertise is evident in her role as a religious trauma group facilitator and curriculum creator, and she actively engages with esteemed organizations such as Chi Sigma Iota, the American Counseling Association, WPATH World Professional Association of Transgender Health, Utah Mental Health Counselors Association, and the Reclamation Collective. Annelise is also a published researcher, serving as the head researcher and author of "A Prospective Investigation of the Decision to Open Up a Romantic Relationship," featured in the journal *Social Psychological and Personality Science*. With unwavering dedication to mental health advocacy and a wealth of experience, Annelise Parkes Murphy continues to make a significant impact in the field of clinical counseling.

Matthew Nielson, PhD, professionally, is a developmental psychologist who studies gender identity development across the life span. He is particularly interested in how gender norms are socialized, what happens when people don't want to conform to gender norms, and what happens when they do. His work has been published in developmental, gender, and sexuality journals. Personally, he is a White cisgender man, and he generally identifies as gay. He was raised in the Church of Jesus Christ of Latter-day Saints (Mormon) but no longer practices this religion.

Jeff Paulez (he/him), PhD, identifies as a White cisgender gay/queer spiritual man who was raised Evangelical Christian. He is a licensed psychologist in private practice at Wander Haven Psychology, an online accessible practice centering the queer/LGBTQ+ community for individual and relationship healing. His dissertation focused on the intersection of queer sexuality, religion, and spirituality. Dr. Paulez previously served as the trauma psychologist at Colorado State University, where he facilitated individual and group healing spaces. He continues to provide trauma-informed therapy, training, and advocacy and integrates liberation-focused practices in his work.

Eduardo Peres (he/they), MD, from a personal background, is a genderqueer pansexual mixed-race Latino, an immigrant, atheist, and happily married for the past 11 years (and counting) in a nonmonogamous agreement. From a professional background, he is a Brazilian medical doctor, trained in psychosexual therapy with an advanced specialist training in Gender, Sex and Relationship

Diversity (GSD) Affirmative Therapy. He currently lives in London, where he is working as a sexual health and HIV specialty doctor. He has professional experience working with gender and sexual health within community-based services, through an affirmative, intersectional, and holistic approach. He has also been involved in lecturing to younger health-care professionals, mainly medical and nursing students, about LGBTQIA+ health and social determinants of health. He is currently involved in several projects raising awareness about vulnerable minoritized communities, mainly focusing on the intersection between GSD, migration health, and a Latin American identity. He believes that intersectional and affirmative approaches are necessary to improve health outcomes and overall well-being and that changes focusing on equity and inclusivity are an important element toward achieving them.

Kristina Pham is a feminist, Jewish woman and a psychology instructor at Casper College in Wyoming, where she has been a faculty member since fall 2020. She is the proud mother of a radical feminist lesbian daughter and a transgender daughter who, like their mother, are determined to bring change and acceptance for all members of the LGBTQIA+ community. Kristina completed her master's degree in general psychology at Grand Canyon University. She is currently completing research for her dissertation in educational leadership with a specialization in humane education at Antioch University. Kristina frequently speaks on LGBTQIA+ issues, from the importance of pronouns to helping therapists create inclusive practices. Kristina also regularly speaks on innovative classroom practices and was awarded an adjunct-of-the-year award from Maricopa Community Colleges for her curriculum development in 2018.

Neo Samas is a Congolese American trans man who is a serial entrepreneur and a published author under the name Neo L. Sandja. He migrated from the Democratic Republic of the Congo to the United States in 2004 to pursue his education in mass communication. He began his social transition in 2010 and his medical transition in December 2011. In 2012, he created FTM Fitness World, a company dedicated to empowering trans men through mental, emotional, and physical fitness. In 2014, the company hosted a three-day annual conference along with the first historical bodybuilding competition for trans men. This organization is known today as the International Association of Trans Bodybuilders and Powerlifters. In 2016, Neo published his first book, *Right Mind Wrong Body: The Ultimate Trans Guide to Being Complete and Living a Fulfilled Life*. In his book, he shares his experience as an African trans man and the lessons he has learned throughout his life from a physical, mental, emotional, and spiritual perspective. Neo is also a business consultant, public speaker, life coach, and a certified neurolinguistic programming practitioner through the Association for Integrative Psychology. He has used his skills along with his passion for emotional intelligence to empower people in all the roles that he plays on a daily basis. As a soul who is always transcending societal barriers, Neo calls himself an alignment catalyst and an energy guide who helps people find the Healer, Divine Creator, and Problem Solver within themselves.

Katina Sawyer, PhD, is an associate professor of management and organizations in the Eller College of Management at the University of Arizona. She is a White, heterosexual, and cisgender woman. Before coming to Eller, she worked as an assistant professor of management at the George Washington University and as an assistant professor of psychology in human resource development at Villanova University. She earned a dual PhD in psychology (industrial organizational) and women's studies from Pennsylvania State University in 2012 and a BA in psychology from Villanova University in 2006. Her research focuses on diversity, equity, and inclusion in organizations, positive organizational scholarship, and employee well-being. She has received research grants from the National Science Foundation and the Society for Human Resource Management, as well as various early-career research awards. She has also received both national and university-wide early-career teaching awards. Finally, in alignment with her focus on practical impact, she was awarded the Presidential Scientist-Practitioner Distinction from the Society for Industrial and Organizational Psychology in 2019.

Stephen P. Stratton, PhD, is professor of counseling and pastoral care and a licensed psychologist (Kentucky). He is a White, European American, straight, cisgender, and nondisabled man who counts the intersection of sexuality, gender, and religion/spirituality among Christian college students as a primary and passionate focus. He is a fellow with the Sexual and Gender Identity Institute and coauthor of the book *Listening to Sexual Minorities: A Study of Faith and Sexual Identity on Christian College Campuses*. Dr. Stratton holds membership in both counseling and psychology professional guilds, and he regularly presents at the state, national, and international conferences of these organizations. He is an at-large member of the board of directors for the Christian Association for Psychological Studies (CAPS). He is a past president for the Kentucky division of the Association for Spiritual, Ethical, and Religious Values in Counseling. He is also a representative for Division 36 (Psychology of Religion and Spirituality) to the Task Force on Sexual and Gender Identity, which meets at the American Psychological Association.

Alex Toft was formerly a research fellow, most recently working at Nottingham Trent University in the School of Social Sciences. His research focused on sexuality, gender, disability, spirituality, and identity. During his academic career, he published widely in journals such as *Sexualities, Sociological Research Online*, and the *Journal of Bisexuality*. However, the world of academia with its obsession on making huge amounts of money became a stifling and unpleasant place to work. Nowadays you will find him tending green spaces and caring for plants.

Lauren Wadsworth is a board-certified clinical psychologist who owns multiple clinics/practices in the Western New York area. She identifies as White, European American, nondisabled, cisgender, and queer. She is founder and director of Genesee Valley Psychology, clinical senior instructor in psychiatry at the University of Rochester Medical Center, and diversity, equity, and inclusion senior advisor at McLean Hospital/Harvard Medical School. She is also a cofounder of Twin Star Intersectional Diversity Trainers and author of *Did That Just Happen?! Beyond "Diversity": Creating Sustainable and Inclusive Organizations*, a groundbreaking book on fostering diversity and inclusion in the workplace.

www.ingramcontent.com/pod-product-compliance
Lightning Source LLC
Chambersburg PA
CBHW031136270326
41929CB00011B/1646